# The Sociology of Terrorism

This is the first terrorism textbook based on sociological research. It adopts an innovative framework that draws together historical and modern and local and global processes for a range of individuals, groups and societies. Individual behaviour and dispositions are embedded within these broader relationships and activities, allowing a more holistic account of terrorism to emerge. In addition, the shifting forms of identification and interwoven attitudes to political violence are discussed in order to explain the emergence, continuation and end of 'terrorist' careers.

The book draws on examples from across the discursive spectrum, including religious, 'red' and 'black' racialist, nationalist and trans-national. It also spans territories as diverse as Chechnya, Germany, Italy, Japan, Northern Ireland, Pakistan, Palestine, Saudi Arabia, South America, the UK and the US.

**Stephen Vertigans** is Professor of Sociology in the School of Applied Social Studies, Robert Gordon University, Scotland. He has published widely on terrorism and related militant groups, with recent books including *Militant Islam: A Sociology of Characteristics, Causes and Consequences* (2009) and *Terrorism and Societies* (2008).

# The Sociology of Terrorism

Peoples, places and processes

**Stephen Vertigans**

Routledge
Taylor & Francis Group

LONDON AND NEW YORK

First published 2011
by Routledge
2 Park Square, Milton Park, Abingdon, Oxon, OX14 4RN

Simultaneously published in the USA and Canada
by Routledge
711 Third Avenue, New York, NY 10017

*Routledge is an imprint of the Taylor & Francis Group, an informa business*

© 2011 Stephen Vertigans

*British Library Cataloguing-in-Publication Data*
A catalogue record for this book is available from the British Library

*Library of Congress Cataloging in Publication Data*
Vertigans, Stephen.
The sociology of terrorism : peoples, places and processes / by Stephen
Vertigans.
p. cm.
Includes bibliographical references.
1. Terrorism--Social aspects. 2. Terrorism--Psychological aspects. I. Title.
HV6431.V469 2011
303.6'25--dc22
2010052907

ISBN: 978-0-415-57265-1 hbk
ISBN: 978-0-415-57266-8 pbk
ISBN: 978-0-203-85581-2 ebk

Typeset in Times
by Taylor & Francis Books

MIX
Paper from
responsible sources
FSC
www.fsc.org   FSC® C018575    Printed and bound in Great Britain by MPG Printgroup

# Contents

# Acknowledgements

There are a number of people who have been instrumental in the development of this book who I would like to thank.

At Routledge the support and encouragement from Gerhard Boomgaarden and Jennifer Dodd has been both considered and considerate. It has been a pleasure working with them. The ideas within this book have evolved over time and I am grateful to all those who have contributed to the process whether at conferences or university seminars. Stephen Mennell, Phil Sutton, Chris Thorpe, Megan Todd, Val Vertigans and Cas Wouters have provided illuminating comments on some, or all, of the contents and I am extremely grateful for their efforts. As ever both mistakes and royalties are mine. Finally throughout my time at the Robert Gordon University I have been encouraged and supported by Joyce Lishman. Her constructive management will be sorely missed.

# Introduction

## The absent friend: Sociology, missing from action

Today terrorism and counter-terrorism are amongst the most divisive issues facing many contemporary societies. Perhaps unsurprisingly the interrelated topics have become a burgeoning area of academic study. Post September 2001 there was an impressive and rapid increase in the publication of books and papers that has to some extent been maintained. Based upon the quantity of publications it could be anticipated that levels of knowledge and understanding about the subject matter have been significantly enhanced. To some extent this is true.[1] Important contributions have been made within political science, international relations, security studies, psychology and to a lesser extent economics. Typologies, power, economic exclusion, political (non) participation, defence and individual factors have become embedded within perceptions about the causes and consequences of terrorism. Yet stereotypes continue to pervade popular perceptions that feed upon, and are fed by, sensationalised media images and self-serving political portrayals. That these impressions often connect with prevailing opinion about other ethnic groups or religions, including, most notably at present, Islam, is considered evidence to support reinforced and inflated demonisation of associated groups and individuals. In the case of groups associated with al-Qa'ida, as Milton-Edwards (2006) commented, religion becomes the explanation, and the multitude of factors which contribute to people becoming violent in the name of Islam are neglected.

By comparison, little or no attention has been allocated to understanding the origins of these impressions and the ways in which they may interact with subsequent experiences within processes that result in the formulation of terror groups. Instead clichés dominate which fail to acknowledge that terrorists originate from across the world, in different societies that often have a history of political violence, with a multitude of socio-economic experiences, varying levels of qualifications and resources and include male and female attackers of different ages. There are a number of reasons why such caricatures continue to pervade. One of the main factors I shall argue in this book is that although sociology has the concepts and theoretical tools to enhance deep rooted levels of knowledge and understanding, the discipline's contributions are severely restricted. Hence, this needs to be addressed.

Sociological insights should be positioned within studies of terrorism to help push the boundaries beyond the media friendly images of pantomime villains, Hollywood styled attacks and heart wrenching victims.

Therefore this book seeks to contribute towards the implementation of sociological perspectives into terrorism. I should stress at this point that this is not an exhaustive exploration of either sociology or terrorism. The sociological novice will not be hugely disadvantaged because concepts and theories are explained and only applied in a manner that is designed to help to understand the processes in and out of terrorism. Nor is this the book for detailed examination of sociological contributions. Instead I intend to restrict sociology to the spheres in which sociological thinking can help enhance insights that are currently lacking. Hence sociology and terrorism become interwoven but in a discrete manner that will not deter readers from other disciplines or with broader interests. Indeed, this is not even an exclusively sociological approach. My primary aim is to examine the social processes and to do so will require the incorporation of contributions from psychology, political science, anthropology and economics to name but a few relevant disciplines. Although the book is explicitly underpinned by sociological ways of thinking, disciplinary rivalries and jealousies will be put aside, if only temporarily, when contributions from other disciplines compliment and supplement. Similarly I am not assuming that readers will have a detailed grasp of terrorism, and the glossary is designed to provide sufficient information about groups in order to make the sociological applications meaningful. Although it is not necessary to be interested in sociology in order to hopefully find this book of value, it probably is necessary to be interested in terrorism. If you are not now may be a good place to stop reading.

## Introductory posturing

Within studies of terrorism, social science would seem to be ideally positioned to confront the stereotypes. Sageman (2007) observes that social scientific methods such as statistics, sampling theory, survey techniques and data analysis provide the key to unlocking the mysteries surrounding terrorism. Yet most of the experts tend to come from the fields of journalism and intelligence analysis and lack training in social scientific procedures. However as Silke (2006: 36) argues in his analysis of suicide and terrorism, social science 'has not prepared society to view either suicides or terrorists as rational, reasonable, relatively ordinary individuals. They are instead portrayed as bizarre, sick and crazy.' Hence despite the multitude of publications, political interventions and media interest, understanding processes of terrorism remains confused, is frequently sensationalised, overly generalised and less than illuminating. Terrorists remain fundamentally flawed, abnormal characters whose actions can be attributed to individual problems rather than systemic faults. A more thorough review of research contributions is included in the following chapter.

By comparison, sociological contributions largely replicate the standard criticism of the discipline, namely an over-concentration upon social strains and social structures. Causes of terrorism are frequently identified in a 'top down' approach that incorporates poverty, education and religious institutions, stalled social mobility, relative deprivation, generational divides and cultural templates that tend to be based upon stereotypical portrayals of religions. These factors can often be located within the 'roots' of terrorism, but they all fail to connect with difference, individual experiences and decisions while sharing an inclination towards determinism. As Raufer (2005: x) remarks with respect to terrorism and the 'Latin world' but which can easily be extended across the world, 'we had some expectations of sociology but ... our disappointment could be said to be inversely proportionate to our hopes.' Insights into underlying social processes behind the formation and closure of terror groups, recruitment, retention and disengagement of members are also less noticeable. Almost inevitably, individual transformations and ontological security are ignored, presumably on the grounds that they do not fit neatly within the parameters established by dominant perspectives of sociology. The individual is located within analysis only as the recipient of the social pressures that bear down upon her/him. Furthermore, although social scientific studies more generally identify several factors within causes of terrorism, interactions between them are much less apparent. Somewhat immodestly this book seeks to contribute towards addressing the sociological neglect.

The originality and intended appeal of this book is therefore based upon a sociological framework for terrorism that is designed to draw together historical and modern social processes for a range of individuals, groups and societies. This approach aims to illuminate shifting individual and collective identification and interwoven attitudes to violence that can help explain the careers of terrorists from beginning to end. By embedding individual activities and relations within broader social, cultural and political processes I aim to contribute to a more holistic approach to terrorism. To help in the formulation of this approach and the commencement of what it actually means, the following review of the chapters is slightly more detailed than is perhaps conventional.

## Review of the book

The book can be loosely divided into two main sections and loosely by different stages of processes within terrorism, namely history, wider social makeup (habitus), joining, staying, acting and leaving.

Hitherto, accounts of terrorism tend to examine the behaviour in chronological isolation. Contemporary causes and effects have been identified but rarely embedded within historical processes. This is in some ways understandable. Initial spurts of terror activity are usually, at least at first glance, new forms of collective action for the activists and the victims of those actions. By adopting violent tactics, groups are overturning social constraints. Both the terror groups and their members will therefore have different processes of justification, legitimisation and individual and collective identification. Their behaviour can be considered, not always correctly, to be a breach of the past and preceding ways of confrontation and thinking. Nevertheless, without a grasp of longer term activities and relations, it is very difficult to explain why terrorism happens at particular junctures and in certain places. For example, explanations that outline the significance of relative deprivation or political exclusion almost invariably fail to explain why these variables become instrumental within a distinct period when they have been noticeable for generations. In other words it is pertinent to ask, why did these forms of collective identification and terrorism emerge at that particular time and not at an earlier stage when the 'causes' were also prominent? Equally, these chronological restrictions cannot explain what it is about the peoples and cultures that result in political violence in comparison with other societies that experience similar 'causes' but with very different outcomes. In the first part of the book, historical and contemporary processes and experiences will be entwined because only through this interconnection can the timeliness of terrorism and variable reactions between and within societies be understood.

The remaining chapters explore the social processes associated with recruitment, retention and disengagement/leaving within terrorist careers. Emotions and rationalities are embedded within these processes and are consequently explored throughout. Inevitably there are overlaps between and within these chapters. I have tried to provide continuums, charting pathways through terrorism. The chapters are designed to try to replicate processes in and out of terrorism. Yet often these routes are convoluted, confused and blurred. Individual levels of commitment can shift across the spectrum of radicalism, ranging from intenseness to disinterest, from anger to mild irritation and back again. Moreover, joining and remaining in groups and committing acts of political violence do not follow a step by step guide. Individuals join, become immersed within the group and then commit the actions. Hence actions follow group dynamics in the ordering; but this is not inevitable in reality. Therefore, there may not be the clear symmetry that may on occasion be the impression the book's structure unintentionally provides. Moreover the approach adopted means that there is overlap between chapters; history influences 'make-up' or habitus, this disposition informs groups and actions, and so on. Similarly social dynamics impact upon people deciding to join, remaining in and leaving groups. Inevitably this means that some of the relations and activities are described in greater depth where it is considered most relevant, but which will also apply to other seemingly discrete stages and interactions. On occasion I may fail to strike the right balance between the different components and continuums. I have tried to cross reference but there will be some instances where the issues and dynamics are addressed more fully in a later chapter. The only solution to this, I am afraid, is to read the whole book.

The starting point for the book faithfully follows the template for so many books about terrorism, with Chapter One providing a (very brief) discussion about terminology used. This leads into a more substantive analysis of social scientific explanations. From these accounts I draw out the concepts and contributions that assist, complement and supplement my sociological approach. The chapter concludes by elaborating upon the sociological framework that I propose, namely the people, places and the significance of social processes.

To begin positioning the sociological approach in Chapter Two, I argue it is essential to explore preceding processes and activities in order to comprehend contemporary terror behaviour. Locating related ideas and forms of behaviour within a longer term perspective throws light upon their deep rooted nature and helps us to understand subsequently how and why they can interact with the contemporary. Through drawing upon the past, it is possible to elucidate the significance of previous attitudes to political violence, the extent to which those beliefs have been retained within elements of collective consciousness, and changes in social solidarities and constraints. Together they can help to explain the shift in individual restraints and adaptation of terrorism through the normalising of violence.

This then leads into the third chapter which applies the concept of habitus in the form of socially constructed 'make-up' or 'second nature' to terrorism. Building upon the historical explorations, the chapter describes dispositions, reflexes and behaviour acquired through social relations and activities, embedded both within the legacy of characteristics across generations and individual histories. Nevertheless, this does not imply that terrorism is simply history repeating itself. Innovative shifts in habitus both accompany and underlie social changes. In environments where terror groups form and operate, these innovations in disposition accord with broader changes and concomitant shifts between individual and social restraints and resultant displacement of forms of conduct. Within this interwoven relationship individuals become terrorists as both a product of their, and preceding generations, norms, values and experiences and the production of new forms of discourse and behaviour that challenge the dominant constraint mechanisms. Both longer term individual and social developments and the accompanying processes are explored. These enable both reproduction and transformation towards political violence to be embedded within contemporary social relations and activities.

To help illuminate the interconnection of history and modern terrorism, examples are extracted from societies that have experienced high profile terror groups with different discourses during the last 40 years. Particular attention is placed upon Germany and Italy (Left and Right Wing), Japan (Left Wing and religious), Northern Ireland (nationalism), Pakistan (religious), Saudi Arabia (religious), Sri Lanka (nationalism), United States (Left and Right Wing) and Colombia (various). Therefore Chapters Two and Three trace the history of movements and the framing of contemporary triggers alongside historical grievances which, as Gupta (2008) points out, are hugely significant in the success or otherwise of groups. The past does not disappear from historical memories; on the contrary it is re-energised. Furthermore concomitant

historical socio-cultural processes that enable people to overcome contemporary social and individual constraints upon the use of public violence
when committing acts of terrorism are also explored.

Contrary to popular perceptions, in Chapter Four I suggest that joining
terror groups is rarely single track and/or the outcome of top-down manip-
ulators. Instead routes into terror groups are multifarious, with recruitment a
multitude of frequently gradual processes, agents and motivations. That
existing social networks are instrumental in individuals joining or forming
groups (della Porta 1995, Sageman 2004, 2008) is arguably the one general
commonality; a similarity shared with religious and social movements
(Dawson 2010, Diani 1995, McAdam 1986, Melucci 1989). Social capital is
integral within networks and group dynamics. By comparison, virtual
groups that form through the Internet, again contrary to prevailing opinion,
are not prominent, not least because as Chapter Five establishes, only people
who are trusted, usually with informal references, are recruited. This places
considerable onus upon group relations and the extent to which individuals
are already connected through existing peer, familial and educational networks (Atran 2004, Sageman 2004, 2008, Silke 2003, Vertigans 2008). Such
affective and expressive relations are also integral to individual decision-
making in joining or being part of the formation of groups. Differences within
stage-based decision-making is further emphasised by the distinctions that are
noticeable between individuals who collectively form groups and subsequent
generations who join after the 'previous generation' of members chose to
become politically violent.

Despite the acknowledgement of the personal and social characteristics
within religious and social movements, such recognition has not been trans-
ferred into studies of terrorism. Instead studies struggle to recognise that
terror groups operate at multiple levels that offer positive inducements and
appeal across emotions and logical reasoning. Examinations of the processes
and stages into religious and social movements such as models of conversion,
networks of faith and social networks of activists are also utilised where
aspects, if not all the explanations, prove illuminating. To sum up, this chapter
seeks to identify social relationships, emotional experiences and processes of
rationalisation that result in people joining, and being recruited by, terror
groups.

Group dynamics and processes of delineation are instrumental in the next
stage of terror careers, namely the retention of terror members. Chapter Five
concentrates upon the emotional and rational reasons why people remain
terrorists and the symbolism, routines and relationships within group habitus
and fields that are integral to these decisions. Elias and Scotson's (2008)
examination of demarcation between the 'outsiders' and the 'established'
opposition through processes of group identification and concomitant stigmatisation is adapted. In order to further illuminate processes within group
protection and continuation, Georg Simmel's (1906, 1965b, 1999) work and
related studies on secrecy and trust are also incorporated. It is argued that

secrecy and trust reinforce both group identity and loyalties based around shared forms of habitus, capital and associated rules, rituals and codes that hinder disengagement. For groups to operate effectively and clandestinely and for individuals to share information, cooperate, interact, manage risks and uncertainties, trust must be an integral component of members' relationships and solidarity. In other words, without trust terror groups would disintegrate. Complete reciprocal knowledge is unobtainable, so to avoid decomposition or being incapable of formation, mutually based relationships are required through trusting individuals in areas of uncertainty. Clearly there are mechanisms that can be introduced to minimise the risk, but they must still incorporate an element of trust. There are grounds to suggest that just like 'normal' people terrorists are more inclined to trust people with whom they share layers of disposition. In essence, relationships must be sufficiently robust for individuals to be considered trustworthy. The nature of the relationship can therefore result in greater willingness to trust other (potential) terrorists. Inversely, breaches of trust contribute to decisions to leave groups while a lack of secrecy makes groups vulnerable to infiltration and arrest.

Implicit within the analysis of individual and group behaviour is the rejection of the popular belief that political violence is the outcome of individual innate aggression. Instead, in Chapter Six I argue that behaviour and entwined norms and values are learnt through social interaction and the extent to which they are exposed to violence and experiences which are considered to legitimise attacks. Through experiences, learnt discourse and spiralling emotions, people's levels of restraint shift and they adopt violent actions. The reasons why this only applies to a small minority are investigated. Some attention is also placed upon strategic reasons behind group decisions to adopt violence as a tactic and how these interconnect with individual and collective feelings. When combined they contribute to heightened emotions and responsibility becomes shared and therefore diminished. Nevertheless, despite the emphasis upon shifting levels of constraint, successful groups must also be able to restrain the use of violence and hence control emotions.

By examining the engagement of people within attacks, consideration will be given to the one frequently obvious categorisation that can be applied to some groups, namely that their members are disproportionately male. For example, terrorists associated with the far right, 'al-Qa'ida' and loyalists, and to a lesser extent, republicans in Northern Ireland, have been predominantly men. The reasons for this gender imbalance will be explored, drawing upon both historical material established in Chapter Two and contemporary gender relations and processes of identification. Conversely the engagement of women within terror groups in Chechnya, the Palestinian territories and Sri Lanka and within the 'red' urban groups of the 1970s will be explored. Within these groups, women's experiences contributed to processes of radicalisation alongside opportunities to participate within existing relationships. Such opportunities are often lacking for females in other societies.

Disengagement as the final phase in the terror career is examined in Chapter Seven. Terrorists, like other classifications of people, have a shifting identification that is interwoven with social relationships, collective loyalties and levels of trust. Consequently membership of social and political groups is always fluid, contingent upon the nature of relationships and experiences within and beyond the group that can result in collective reinforcement or redefinitions, allegiances and commitment changing through arrest, failure, different loyalties, frustration, disillusionment etc. For individuals to consciously remove themselves from the group requires shifting individual and collective boundaries of identification that can be influenced by feelings such as disgust, anger, disillusionment, fatigue or the appeal of life outside the group, the possibility of mainstream reintegration or minimised sentence. Again it is possible to note the interweaving of emotive and rational reasoning within these later stages in the terror career. Crucially as Bjørgo and Horgan (2009) explain, gaining greater knowledge and understanding about these end processes within terrorism would enhance government attempts to force or encourage terrorists and groups to end their armed struggle.

The book concludes by drawing together historical and contemporary social processes and activities which help to enhance levels of understanding about the interaction between individual and group experiences and broader social influences that result in terrorists' careers. The final chapter finishes with a discussion about possible implications of the research for policy makers, the study of terrorism generally and sociological contributions in particular.

In summary, I am not aiming to provide a definitive exploration of either sociological approaches to terrorism or processes of terrorism. Nor do I provide an extensive critical review of either field. Instead I only draw upon contributions that can help illuminate the processes of terrorism. Nor do I engage in the denigration of terror ideologies, motives or actions. Obviously this does not mean that I am intending to convert, propagate, disseminate or glamorise terrorism. For any counter-terrorist or government jurisprudent who may be reading, I stress this in the firmest terms. Instead, I am aiming to gain insights into the processes through which groups form, people join, stay, leave and groups disband. I have no intention of proffering opinion on which groups are correct, where ideologies are mistaken, tactics flawed and actions immoral. By avoiding what are largely subjective judgements I intend to adopt a more detached approach. Such an undertaking may well make the task of the potential book reviewer easier. To further assist in their attempts at classification I should point out that to date I have been described by other reviewers, who may conceivably have had particular attachments of their own, as an apologist for Islam, a Zionist, a Bushite, an anti-capitalist and anti-imperialist. I appreciate that I have yet to inadvertently represent numerous groups and ideologies and seek to address this neglect within this and subsequent publications.

# 1 A sociological approach to terrorism
## People, places and processes

### Definitions

There is seemingly a convention for books about terrorism to include a lengthy, often turgid, discussion concerning definitions of 'terrorism' and 'terrorist.' I am not one to challenge customs but cannot really engender much enthusiasm for the debate because ultimately I do not possess the linguistic ability, conflict resolution techniques or patience to provide universally acceptable definitions. This leads to what Brannan, Esler and Strindberg (2001: 11) described as a 'perverse situation where a great number of scholars are studying a phenomenon, the essence of which they have (by now) simply agreed to disagree about.' The concept is hugely controversial and definitions are sensitive to location, periods of history, power, shifting perceptions of morality, international relations, military hardware and how these interact with the person, institution, government or international agency who is defining.[1] I will try to restrict this discussion specifically to the reasoning behind the inclusion of my definitions while pointing the reader, who has thus far managed to avoid the semantics of terrorism, to Schmid's (1984) seminal study and most decent textbooks.

Using the word 'terrorist' is even more value laden, immediately bringing forth the image of the caricature with shifty eyes, evil expressions and physical deformities. When taken into consideration alongside the definition of terrorism, there is a danger that I am simply reinforcing the over concentration upon the acts of terror and their emotive outcomes, rather than the processes within and beyond that are the primary aim of this book. Hence, I have serious misgivings about definitions, but obviously have to apply terms that are understandable and which enable the reader to appreciate what and who is being discussed. New terms would not eradicate all the problems because I would still be establishing parameters that would imply certain values and impressions. Therefore, lacking the imagination to develop different terms that will be universally both meaningful and acceptable, I am sticking with terrorism and terrorists. I was tempted to include quotation marks to indicate my unease with the words but the sections quickly became typographically cluttered. Consequently, alongside aesthetics, my caveat is the reiteration that the terms are social constructions that are formulated within long-term processes. As such, I intend to apply the detached stance and am describing terrorism as it is conceived; I am not seeking to pass moral, political or ethical judgement.

For the purposes of this book I am defining terrorism as 'the targeted and intentional use of violence for political purposes through actions that can range in intended impact from intimidation to loss of life'. Examples from pro-life, animal liberation, eco terror or narco terror groups are not included because they do not adopt violence in order to assume political power and this is one of the main criteria for incorporation within this book. Nor am I including individual terrorists such as the American Unabomber, Theodore Kaczynski. Government and irregular combatants such as guerrillas could be included but are not in this book on the grounds of expediency. In essence I want to concentrate upon 'terrorism from below' and groups that are predominantly associated with this form of political violence before possibly extending the focus outwards and upwards in subsequent publications. Although this definition replicates the tendency to concentrate upon the act and describe the tactic, this book is very much about exploring the processes that contribute to attacks and the end of the act. The 'terrorist' is 'someone who actively and deliberately engages in activities that contribute towards acts of terrorism.' This includes individuals whose roles range from bomb maker to maker of accompanying bombast. To reiterate, these definitions are flawed and are not designed to attain the unattainable within studies of terrorism, namely universal agreement and thereby eternal acclaim. My ambition is rather modest, merely to inform the reader that this is what and who I think I am talking about.

## Social scientific review of terrorism

One convention that I am more enthusiastic about for this book is a critical review of academic explanations for terrorism and individual participation. Such a review helps to introduce ideas, events and experiences that will be accommodated across the remainder of the book. Critical analysis also enables me to distance myself at the onset from some of the less 'helpful' contributions. This chapter concludes with an attempt to intertwine the divisive concepts of emotions and rationality which crosscut many of the following contributions.

Popular explanations such as brainwashing, cultural factors, frustration-aggression, identity crisis, mental illness, narcissism, political exclusion and oppression, rational choice, poverty and relative deprivation all feature prominently within studies of terrorism. These accounts provide differing degrees of illumination although some share the tendency noted amongst research into cults and sects that 'the public, media, policy-makers and even academics accept irrationality as an explanation for behaviour that is new, strange, and (apparently or actually) dangerous' (Iannacone 2004). By selecting pertinent emotive and rational aspects, this chapter is designed to overcome such partiality and to provide the basis for understanding contemporary factors behind the emergence of terror groups.

Psychological contributions within academic disciplines have been considerable. Psychologists such as Bandura (2004), Bjørgo (2005), Crenshaw (1981, 1992, 1998), Horgan (2005, 2009), Reich (1998), Silke (2003) and Taylor and Quayle (1994)[2] have illuminated individual factors that contribute to political violence. Nevertheless, academic enquiry continues into what is psychologically wrong with individuals and/or the social agencies that they are exposed to. The mental well-being of suicide bombers, in particular, has been the subject of considerable speculation. For instance, Juergensmeyer (2003) associates Islamic suicide bombers with sexual repression, the symbolism of the explosion and the sexual attractions of 72 virgins following martyrdom. The Palestinian bombers according to Volkan (2001) have disturbed personal identities and are targeted by recruiters who are looking out for individuals with these profiles. Salib (2003) and Rosenberger (2003) argue that these bombers may be suffering from shared or paranoid delusions. For Lachkar (2002) they have a borderline personality disorder, dominated by shame. Piven (2002: 128) exemplifies the broader perception when declaring, 'I have termed [terror behaviour] psychotic because such a dearth of empathy and such malignant rage, alongside such distorted paranoid displacements constitute a massive deformation and reality testing.' If these vulnerable individuals did not have enough to worry about then they need to concern themselves about their reported susceptibility to brainwashing by unscrupulous leaders, religious teachers, militant families and on-line groomers. Parallels can be drawn with prevailing opinion regarding recruitment processes into cults (Barker 1984, Dawson 2006, 2010). Other morally 'distasteful' individuals such as perpetrators of domestic violence are also explained through reference to flawed victim and aggressor psychologies. Just like terrorism studies, the emphasis is upon sick individuals rather than social processes; yet as Price (2005) explains this is often unfounded.

With an extensive array of publications depicting terrorists as mentally flawed, it could be expected that there is considerable supporting evidence. There is not. On the contrary, McCauley (2002) concludes that the majority of studies committed to psychological evaluations of terrorism found little support for psychological disorders. Similarly the 'brainwashing' argument also lacks credible evidence. Arguing that particular terrorists went to a madrassa, met a certain ideologue or were born into an infamous fascistic family does not explain why they and not other students, peers and family members joined nor why some individuals subsequently leave. In fact, studies have shown that many terrorists originated outwith brainwashing centres. Sageman's (2008) exploration of *jihadists* is illustrative in documenting how the vast majority grew up within secular environments.[3] Socialisation is hugely important (and Chapter Five elaborates upon this), introducing individuals to ideas, behaviour and people and contributing to shifting levels of restraint and collective identification. Yet socialisation is fundamentally different from brainwashing.

The question then arises, why does the impression of the weak, manipulated or 'crazy' terrorist continue to resonate within academic and public spheres despite the lack of evidence? McCauley (2002) helps to answer this when explaining how in some ways it is easier to understand terrorism if terrorists are considered to be psychologically abnormal, devoid of moral feeling and empathy. This places the blame upon the individual (or devious recruiters in instances of brainwashing) rather than social processes, and means that the actions can be dismissed as the outcomes of the irrational, rather than considering the possibility that the actions and accompanying rhetoric may have some validity. Just as with accounts of recruitment into cults, there is a tendency to draw upon these types of explanation for behaviour that challenges the prevailing opinion. Within psychology there are indicators of mental illness, low self-esteem, authoritarianism[4] and vulnerability within some terrorists which increase vulnerability to the appeal of charismatic leaders, discourse and group dynamics.

Despite the inapplicability of these characteristics to explain general processes of terrorism, there are examples when psychological weaknesses are instrumental in people becoming terrorists. And although mental illness is not as widespread within new recruits as it is portrayed, Horgan (2005: 6) points to 'the processes whereby members become brutalized and more committed as a *result* of membership and increased psychological commitment to the group.' Accordingly, engagement within terror groups can be hugely stressful, heavily laden with risk. Individuals are required to overcome ontological insecurities as they confront internalised taboos over killing and the threat of being killed. In other words the mental well-being of members may deteriorate during the terrorists' careers; an observation which becomes more noticeable when members disengage. Of greater relevance is the emphasis placed within psychology on feelings such as anger, revenge and humiliation which I argue below need to be incorporated within a sociological approach.

Although there is a long-standing tendency[5] to associate terrorism with mental instability and illness psychologists, such as those listed earlier, have generally been at the critical forefront of challenges to popular perceptions. Having initially been sidetracked by the pursuit of a terrorist personality, the realisation that such a personality does not exist has freed some psychologists to produce some of the most groundbreaking and influential studies. These have been instrumental in highlighting unexceptional qualities of terrorists or, as Crenshaw (1981: 390) mentioned, 'the outstanding common characteristic of terrorists is their normality' and the considered rationality of their approach. Terrorists need to reflect, delay gratification, control emotion, restrain behaviour and often undertake largely mundane activities (Crenshaw 1981, 1998); characteristics that do not accord with prevailing popular opinion. Perhaps unsurprisingly terrorists also tend to consider themselves to be normal.[6] At a pragmatic level there is considerable support for such claims. Groups could not operate effectively if members were dysfunctional; their behaviour would be inconsistent, unreliable and such individuals would be likely to arouse suspicion and threaten security, secrecy and hinder operations. Some of the aspects identified within these studies, in particular, social learning, affective ties, group dynamics and collective identification, are explored throughout this book and consequently are not explicitly explored in this chapter. At this juncture Taylor and Horgan's (2006: 586) critical analysis of the field is of particularly pertinent relevance. They argue that terrorism has been 'characterised as a psychological state of some kind disconnected from context and history; this necessarily leads to a focused attempt to identify unique and/or personal qualities.' Examples of these are discussed below. Instead of focusing upon terrorism as a state, Taylor and Horgan (ibid.) propose that involvement should be considered as a 'process variable such as the changing context that the individual operates in, and also the relationships between events and the individual as they affect behaviour.' In so doing, they position psychological factors within the complex relationship between political context, organisational framework and the individual. When expounding upon the approach to be developed within this book I argue that social processes are integral to understanding terrorism.

Individual events and experiences are often put forward to explain the motivation of terrorists. This is a perspective that is promoted not least by terrorists and their families. Thus they will point to particular salient events or policies, the death of a friend, the arrest of a family member, the destruction of property, witnessed killing of a child, the rising threat of a rival group or army, national hypocrisy and international injustice. In turn these incidents are responsible for a variety of emotions including resentment, anger and indignation which fuels a desire for revenge or retaliation. There is often an element of self-serving about these accounts. If groups are to justify the nature of their activities to themselves and to attract broader support they are portrayed as defensive, reacting to threats and challenges, defending the community, symbols, culture or religion from attack. Sageman (2008) also points out that even if the (former) terrorists are completely honest with researchers they are inclined to consider their activities positively and make associations with altruistic motivations. Moreover their interpretations and understanding of the actions will change over time, influenced by multiple factors including the outcome of attacks and ultimate success or otherwise of the group. This is not to say that these accounts are inherently flawed. Crenshaw (1998: 227) comments that although these recollections 'may be self-serving, that does not mean that they are not also, in some significant way, revealing.' And of course, individual accounts cannot be assumed to be representative of other members and still leave unanswered the generic questions, namely why is it that only a relatively few people are sufficiently inspired to join or form groups from the masses who have shared the reported experiences?

Emphasis upon individual factors is particularly noticeable within studies of female engagement. Conversely, women terrorists are often invisible within academic explorations. When their roles are acknowledged, personal or domestic issues are introduced within sociologically tinged studies in order to differentiate motivations behind the involvement of women compared to men. Victor (2004) for instance, considers that Palestinian female suicide bombers have been more reluctant to join groups and tend to do so for personal reasons. These include episodes of loss and imprisonment of family members and friends, humiliation, shame and dishonour. Similar feelings have also been expressed by men. Yet within nationalist struggles in Chechnya, the Palestinian territories and Sri Lanka, it is often only female terrorists who are widely reported to have experienced, and be motivated by, personal trauma (Nacos 2005, Speckhard 2008, Speckhard and Ahkmedova 2006).[7] Male involvement is associated with religious and nationalist factors. Certainly women have been influenced by personal motivations but these are often accommodated alongside discursive reasoning (Cunningham 2003, Jacques and Taylor 2008). Moreover, although influential studies such as Sageman (2004) explain that many people join groups through their own initiative which recruiters respond to, this acknowledgement has yet to cross the gender divide. The previously prevailing perception of individuals becoming terrorists through coercion and exploitation is often now concentrated upon females who are reported to be more inclined to be manipulated by (male) recruiters (McKay 2005, Ness 2005, Victor 2004); an observation which hints at unscrupulous terrorist leaders and female weakness and vulnerability.[8] Yet studies of female terrorists such as the 'Black Widows' in Chechnya indicate that many women are self-starters and only formally become involved within the wider movement when requesting resources and training with which to undertake attacks (Speckhard 2008, Speckhard and Akhmedova 2006).

The more widespread sociological neglect of female violence and tendency to over-concentrate upon male violence has contributed to the invisibility of females and reliance upon stereotypes within academic studies. Hence academics are ill prepared to explain incidents and patterns such as female perpetrated acts of domestic violence (Kelly 1991). As Gentry (2004) and Sjoberg and Gentry (2007, 2008) comment, the portrayals of female terrorists reflect the public narratives of women who commit acts of violence more generally. Speckhard (2008: 1029) argues that amongst Western audiences 'there is a great deal of denial about the violent and militant capability of women. … Likewise there tends to be a denial that women can be and are often as violent as men.' Consequently 'it seems there are only a very limited number of instances in which society can understand a woman being violent' (MacDonald 1991: xvii). The instances include fighting off a sexual attacker, mothers defending her children and some sporting activities (Whaley-Eager 2008). Beyond these instances, 'women's violence falls outside of these ideal-typical understandings of what it means to be a woman' that emphasise nurturing, sensitivity and domesticity (Sjoberg and Gentry 2007: 2). The act of violence therefore is for Keitner (2002) a 'double transgression' both against the law and gender stereotypes. This has meant that if women are not associated with violence then there are limited conceptual frameworks that can be applied to help understand the behaviour, and the impact of female terror attacks upon the intended audience is considerably greater than the equivalent acts by men.

When female terrorists do become prominent[9] the distance between their behaviour and normative expectations is often explained in two principle ways which rely upon clichés and exaggerate the psychological traits identified above. The first is through reference to individual defects; their mental weakness, vulnerability and experiences of being traumatised because they have been raped by rival groups[10] or through the death of family members of friends.[11] The second, which builds upon the weaknesses, is because violence is inherently 'male,' women who commit acts of political violence must be acting like men,[12] and as such are reported as having high levels of testosterone and/or are lesbians,[13] are being manipulated by men or only become involved through their romantic commitment or infatuation with male lovers.[14] In other words, women are considered to only become involved if they are psychologically or sexually deviant, men want them to participate and women are powerless to prevent their engagement in violence. Yet numerous studies have shown that women, with no identified forms of mental illness, have proactively joined a variety of discursive and nationalist groups. Despite this, media and academic narrative remains rooted in the old clichés that also incorporate women's physical characteristics which are often the defining features within reports and not their discursive consciousness.[15] In one indicative example raised by Nacos (2005: 438), ETA's Idoia Lopez Riano, who was charged with 23 assassinations, was described by *The Times* in London as having 'the looks of a Mediterranean film star' and 'is one of the few women who manages to look good even in a police shot.' Sexualised images tend to diminish the member's credibility and influence, further reinforcing the distinction between male and female members. Conversely the constructed sexuality of female leaders such as the Weather Underground's Bernardine Dohrn is applied by Taylor (2000: 300) to explain how control was maintained over male members by 'keeping her blouse unbuttoned and breasts exposed during strategy meetings.' Dohrn's leadership and those of equivalent females in similar groups is interwoven with physical characteristics and sexuality. Hence the Japanese Red Army's Fusako Shigenobu is described as 'lustful' and 'sexually promiscuous'[16] and Ulrike Meinhof and Gudrun Esslin from the German Red Army Faction are the 'bandit queen' and 'blond bombshell.' For Nacos (2005) the appearance of men only tends to be reported with regard to a particular facet such as hair colour or physical build which connects into their actions or police investigations. One suspects that Osama bin Laden's spaniel-like brown eyes would have gained considerably more attention had he been a she. Inevitably there is not one universal form of reportage. Important distinctions can exist in the ways in which female terrorists are reported in the Western and Arab media. Perhaps surprisingly in light of the (Western) impression of Western gender equality against a patriarchal Middle East, it is the Arab press that has tended to focus more upon female motivations, commitment and ideological struggle, with less attention placed upon gender stereotypes and biographical problems.[17]

In essence it can easily be argued that the weaknesses of attempts to understand general processes of terrorism are magnified when applied to women. Arguably the greater distance between idealised feminine behaviour and female terrorists compared with idealised masculinity and male terrorists, reinforced by media portrayals that either sexualise or demonise the women, has resulted in female behaviour being more incomprehensible and more offensive to normative expectations. Studies of women with some notable exceptions tend to be more emotive and less detached and lag behind the emerging insights into male counterparts. Cunningham's (2003) summary of the portrayals of women's engagement is apt; namely their involvement is considered not to arise through conscious participation but to stem from personal reasons. Females are therefore reluctant terrorists except, I would add, for those women who are considered to be like men. With female terrorists believed to comprise between 20 and 30 per cent of all terror groups[18] and their membership of militant groups increasing 'regionally, logistically and ideologically,' extending from nationalistic and Left-Wing groups with whom they have been more associated to the Far Right in America where their involvement is becoming increasingly noticeable (Cunningham 2003: 171), it is crucially important that these weaknesses are acknowledged and addressed. Hence, there would have to be a shift away from the inflexible association between violence and men that contributes to popular narratives that deny women conscious and deliberate participation towards a more detached approach to female violence more generally.

Sociological influences are more overtly prominent within the repositioning of absolute poverty as a primary cause of terrorism and this has become intertwined with international politics. Gupta (2008) explains that there is nothing unique about the role of poverty attaining prominence. On the contrary, in the 4th century BCE Aristotle blamed poverty for acts of political violence. Over 2,300 years later and in the post September 2001 environment, blame was reapportioned to poverty. Indeed there was a 'war on poverty' alongside its bigger and frankly much better known sibling, 'war on terror.' President G.W. Bush's (2002) speech was indicative of numerous international statements of this period in which he declared that 'We fight against poverty because hope is an answer to terror.' At the time of writing neither war could be declared to have been won. Without wishing to confront the failings of the terror side of the War family,[19] or that dashed hopes can be instrumental within radicalisation or even the implication that poverty is only being fought in order to safeguard American security, it is important to consider the extent to which people living in absolute poverty become terrorists.

Some support can be found within particular cells, for example the Casablanca bombers in 2003 (Alonso and Rey 2007), although it would be more accurate to classify the form of poverty as being 'relative' (discussed below). Moreover reported financial rewards to the families of suicide bombers could be another factor (relatively) poor individuals take into consideration when deliberating possibilities in Iraq, Pakistan and Palestinian territories (Beg and Bokhari 2009, von Hippel 2002). Nevertheless there is little evidence to suggest that money alone motivates suicide bombers. Overall, terrorists tend to originate from the middle classes. As I explain in Chapter Four, the absolute poor have little inclination towards terrorism, not least because they are more interested in finding water, food, shelter, money and employment. This argument also assumes that terror groups have an open-door policy; these bands of desperadoes will allow anyone to join. For reasons of security, efficiency and effectiveness terror groups have a recruitment policy. The poor are excluded on the same grounds that they are poor; namely they lack appropriate education, communications skills, IT aptitude and social networks.

Certainly groups such as the 'red' urban groups of the 1970s claimed to represent the poor within an empathetic policy that hinted at vicarious poverty. Generally though the links lacked credibility and there was little support for these white middle class groups from the white and black working classes they claimed to represent. Nationalist groups will often refer to poverty but this is within the wider framed injustice of repression and the denial of the nation. Religious groups such as those associated with al-Qa'ida, whose inner core have been very middle class, and the Aum Supreme Truth, with those involved in violence largely very well educated, have only infrequently sought to utilise poverty in order to mobilise support. An argument could be made for the impact of poverty in the radicalisation of West European Muslims but this would not be absolute and as I explain elsewhere is crosscut by numerous other factors.[20]

A number of proposed terror causes cannot be neatly classified according to academic discipline. Two such examples which tend to be discussed together are relative deprivation and the frustration-aggression hypothesis (Davies 1969, Dollard *et al.* 1939, Friedland 1992, Gurr 1970 and Heitmeyer 2005) and narcissism-aggression (Pearlstein 1991) which stems from Freudian emphasis upon a lack of empathy. Terrorists are considered to experience relative deprivation through unemployment,[21] poor education, marginalisation, discrimination, or as Elias (1996) outlines, blocked social mobility which tends to be monopolised by older generations, and inter-generational conflict, especially during extended periods of peace. In essence people believe that the 'system' does not provide them with something that they consider themselves to be entitled to and their goals and aspirations are unfulfilled. The frustration of these people leads to political violence against the perceived source of the frustration such as institutions or government officials. When these experiences interact with ideologies inciting violence people are more likely to become terrorists. As I explained above there are examples for absolute poverty that can be drawn upon. And there is some support to link radicalisation with some regions which are undergoing rapid transformation and concomitant dislocation, alienation and anomie. Nevertheless, the people suffering the most are rarely identified within terror groups for some of the reasons identified above.

If we were to apply the underlying rationale behind the frustration-aggression thesis to gender, at first glance it could be anticipated that females would be more frustrated by relative deprivation, systemic restrictions and thus more inclined towards political violence. Yet since Dollard *et al.*'s (1939) influential study, proponents of the thesis have argued that on the contrary women are less likely to react aggressively. Dollard argues that from childhood boys learn that aggression is an appropriate, often necessary, reaction to frustration while girls are taught to restrain violent responses. Certainly different values and expectations exist within and between societies over gender behaviour and use of violence. In this regard the attempt to explain gender difference severely undermines the thesis. If the frustrations of women are controllable through social controls, then the universal applicability of the frustration-aggression model is hugely problematic. Moreover the overriding implication is that male violence can be traced to different forms of socialisation that allows, even encourages, aggressive responses. In other words frustration and aggression are not the causes but the effects.

Within the broader accounts of 'irrational terrorism,' where political violence does not appear comprehensible against normative behaviour, people can be considered to have little to live for and are thus fatalistic. The Palestinian suicide bombers are perhaps the best examples. Alternatively they can be described as nihilistic, perpetuating terror acts in order to gain notoriety or to live forever within local folklore and possibly heaven. Again this can be applied to the Palestinian territories and the tendency for 'martyrs' to be celebrated within communities with their images emblazoned on posters and cards throughout neighbourhoods.[22] And of course the martyr may also be considering the possibility of salvation; hence even within one location and possibly just one attack, by applying Durkheim's suicide typology we can suggest that individuals are motivated by a combination of fatalism, altruism and egoism (Sutton and Vertigans 2005).

Situations in which individuals find themselves facing severe financial hardships with little or no prospect of improvement can be influenced by feelings of fatalism and the prospect of martyrdom. Alonso and Rey (2007) suggest that through suicide bombings the perpetrators become 'winners.' Why this should happen and not other alternative outlets for frustration such as withdrawal, depression, self harm or escapism is not explained. Nor can this account for the incidences of terrorists who have not experienced relative deprivation or the millions, if not billions, of people who do not turn to political violence. By extending this argument it could be argued that terrorism would be more likely to occur during recessions when greater numbers of people experience relative poverty. Although there do appear to be correlations between the surge of the Far Right in places like the United States (Crothers 2002, Freilich and Pridemore 2005, Van Dyke and Soule 2002) and former East Germany and economic downturns, the evidence is far from overwhelming. For instance, although there may be a correlation in American downturns in agriculture and manufacturing and Far Right support, there has also been growth in places such as New Mexico amongst those who were not economically deprived (Tapia 2000). Nor is Far Right support restricted to the working classes, exemplified by Dobratz and Shanks-Meile's (2000) study which discovered that around a third of their respondents belonged to the middle class. Finally many terrorists do not experience these forms of frustration. Across various groups ranging from most of the al-Qa'ida hardcore to Meinhof and Mahler in the German Red Army Faction and Palestinian groups, members and supporters originate from across the socio-economic spectrum (Krueger and Malecková 2003).

There are also pragmatic issues involved with terror groups that have been drawn from social movement studies (McAdam *et al.* 2001, Tarrow 1996, Tilly 1978). One of the most significant is the political opportunity structures which tend to countenance the association of terrorism as a form of expression by the politically alienated when other forms are denied.[23] Experiences in the United States, West Germany, Spain, Italy, India, Pakistan, Sri Lanka and Colombia to name but a few are indicative of the fact that democracy is not a panacea for terrorism. Instead, like other forms of protest groups, terrorism frequently formulates when individuals are able to organise and express grievances either through formal channels or by illicit activities. In some instances there is a trajectory of protest. Across a range of case studies terrorism has arisen in the wake of the perceived failures of non violent tactics.[24] Conversely, as I detail in the following chapters, terrorism also arises in locations where governments encourage sympathetic shifts in discursive consciousness such as Right Wing in the United States and Islamic in Saudi Arabia and Pakistan. In these settings the gap narrows between normative and radical ideas and behaviour. To further confuse possibilities, groups can also emerge after governments have made concessions or fail to deliver promised reforms or policies. Dashed hopes feature within the recollections of both Left-Wing and Right-Wing groups, religious and secular.

Resources within the group are also crucially important. Just as with social movements, resources have to be available and coordinated into collective goals and actions. Accordingly, both religious and secular ideologies (discussed below) and group leadership qualities, social networks, supporters and financial sources affect the likelihood of people becoming members and are discussed in Chapter Four. Therefore as Atran (2004) outlines with regard to suicide activities, terror groups recruit more highly educated members in part because they have experience of postponing immediate rewards in the present for longer-term (possibly eternal) benefits in the future.

Within the analysis it is also important to incorporate the pull factors of the ideology alongside the push elements. Hence, discourses can rationalise situations and appeal to individuals through their explanatory framework and incorporation of material, psychological, political, social and cultural facets. They are, as Melucci (1990: 6) observed, 'one of the main tools which can be used to guarantee integration.' The appeal of group ideas will be heavily influenced by the extent to which they interconnect with peoples' emotional experiences and rational evaluation and intentions. For example, attempts at scapegoating and stigmatisation are likely to be more successful if individuals have had limited or bad experiences of the West, government brutality, immigrants, Jews, capitalism and so on. Equally the surrounding ideological problems such as capitalism and Western imperialism and solutions such as communism, national independence and religious empires are more likely to be acknowledged by people who can interpret personal, virtual, social or political experiences within the group's frames of reference. In essence explanations have to have greater accord if they are to be legitimised and ultimately justify the shift to violence against de-legitimised regimes (Vertigans 2008, 2009). After internalisation, as Smelser (2007) explains, ideology can become part of individual motivation framed within a system of meaning which helps to formulate and impose 'us' and 'them' demarcations. Again this is noticeable within secular ideologies such as communism (against capitalism and government and business sponsors) and religions (against godless regimes, related institutions and promoters). Of course emphasis upon the ideological pulling power is restricted and fails to provide a broader explanation for why exactly particular policies appeal in certain locations and to restricted groups and individuals. In other words, a composite level of understanding requires insights both into the interconnection between discourse and individual. Moreover, as I shall argue in subsequent chapters, the impression of ideology initiating motivation and hence the image of the terrorist as an ideologue may be overstated. Certainly there is evidence to suggest that discursive consciousness follows for many participants after group allegiance.

The following chapters establish that many of the above top-down and bottom-up, push and pull factors are for some individuals, but crucially not all, contributing triggering factors or events. Similarly identified root causes such as poverty, stalled social mobility, humiliation and oppression can be instrumental in the radicalisation towards terrorism but again these 'causes' in isolation fail to explain why they lead to terrorism for some people and not many others. Crucially, few studies explore the interactions between them. Sociology can, and should, be capable of providing the framework to incorporate these multiple facets.

## A sociological approach

The huge increase in books about terrorism may indicate a saturated market. However, as I argue above, sociological contributions are limited. Certainly there have been some exceptional contributions; not least della Porta's (1992, 1995) comparative study of 'red' West German and Italian groups, Tilly's (1978) work on political opportunity structures which facilitate independent organisation and collective action and Bruce's (1992) exploration of loyalists in Northern Ireland. More recently Smelser (2007) and Gupta (2008) have both adopted sociological stances if not always explicitly. Smelser draws upon social and psychological ways of thinking to help illuminate aspects of terrorism and counter-terrorism. He does not though adopt the processual approach and consequently terrorists' careers within key historical and contemporary processes and experiences are not embedded. Such an approach, particularly with respect to contemporary developments, is more noticeable within Gupta's (2008) life cycle approach. By comparison to Gupta's approach I am incorporating a broader selection of groups, placing greater emphasis on the roles of history, emotions and group dynamics and these are embedded within a more explicitly sociological framework. Alongside the explicitly sociological studies have been contributions 'on the cusp' such as Hoffman (2006), Stern (2003) and Wilkinson (1974, 1981, 2003). However, these studies have tended to concentrate upon issues within terrorism and have not applied particular sociological concepts and perspectives in order to illuminate the processes through terrorism.

I am not entirely sure why sociology has not become a serious contributor within terrorism studies since the field first became prominent in the 1970s. There are three possible explanations for the early neglect. First, terrorism was considered to be political and therefore the domain of political science. Second, as Malešević (2010: 194) argues with respect to war and violence more generally, 'the hegemony of "anti-militarist" social theory in the second half of the twentieth century ... has "cleansed" sociology of the study of warfare by simultaneously ignoring its prolific, diverse and imaginative "bellicose" tradition and by reinterpreting the classics in strictly "pacifist" terms.' In essence the distaste for war and devastation post 1945 contributed to the slippage of political violence from sociological enquiry and emergence of other concepts that were considered to be more appropriate for the new era such as social stratification, urbanisation, deviance, gender inequality, education, rationalisation and secularisation. The association of intellectual bellicose ideas and theories, often mistakenly under the rubric of social Darwinism, with Nazism led to social theory being sanitised of its militarist heritage and replaced by 'pacifist' themes (Malešević 2010).[25] Third, groups that aroused interest at that time were Left-Wing groups of Western Europe, America and Japan and the Palestinian and (Northern) Irish nationalists. These groups attracted considerable support on campuses and promulgated ideas that were not dissimilar to the views of many sociologists. Consequently it is certainly possible that sociologists were willing to leave terrorism to political science because they were reluctant to respond through the application of the discipline's critical tools upon groups whose ideas they supported, if not necessarily their methods. In other words sociologists may have felt unable to be critically detached. Obviously within sociological study complete detachment is impossible; sociologists can never be completely detached from the people, institutions or movements under investigation. Nevertheless this should not prevent exploration. Providing the interconnections between knowledge and object are acknowledged this can be tested against criterion that Norbert Elias called 'reality-congruence.' Terms and evidence that are used, tested and refined become more congruent with reality. Sociologists have the epistemological tools with which to create sufficient distance between themselves and their subjects in order to avoid inappropriately opinionated and involved explanations without recourse to positivism or empiricism.

Sociological ambiguities, misgivings and neglect have continued. Conversely the surge of religious and Far Right groups delivered discourses that were distinct from those of sociologists. Indeed, instead of empathy these ideas were so different they caused disdain and often revulsion. Within the distaste over religious groups it is possible to locate the continuing pervasive influence of the secularisation thesis. Sociologists still tend to disregard resurgent religions as an outpost in the doomed struggles of irrational victims against modernisation; and because the discourses are religious, they should be left to the sociologists of religion. However, this sub-discipline is more interested in non-violent ideas and behaviour. Hence religious terrorists become fragments lost in the increasingly demarcated and jumbled sociological mosaic. Fascist groups are disregarded with even greater haste, their members are viewed as beyond contempt and academic study. There is no ambiguity about why Far Right groups are disliked within sociology, but there is for some of the religious groups. For instance, terror groups associated with religion can be Muslim, Sikh, Hindu and Jewish. In other words they belong to groups that are ethnic minorities in the West. Sociologists can be reluctant to approach subjects that depict minorities negatively, and their confusion becomes magnified when the groups are critical of the West. Although they may not agree with the sentiments to the same extent as with the discourse of the 1970s groups, many sociologists would find it difficult to critically analyse actions that are committed against American aggression and Western imperialism. Moreover, lacking in-depth knowledge about the groups, their discourse and their followers has meant that when sociologists venture into the field they can lack awareness of the nuances or even knowledge of the spectrum across the broader movement, resulting in a generic cultural template. The tendency to associate religion with terrorism, thereby incorporating the vast majority of passive Muslims, is indicative of this.

My final observation is that according to the classical sociological demarcations of class and race, the poor, uneducated and ethnic minorities could be expected to be at the forefront of terrorism. Yet from the nineteenth-century anarchists onwards this has rarely been the case, while the relevance of gender has infrequently been acknowledged within terror groups. In this regard it could be argued that the post-war sociological concepts have been ill-suited for the task of examining terrorism and the complex, fluid interactions which cannot be rooted within working-class, racial or ethnic cultures and structural impositions. There has been no subsequent urgency to incorporate more contemporaneous and flexible frameworks that can accommodate the vicissitudes within and between groups and members and interweaving social processes and historical residues.

Clearly the overarching aim for the book is the development of a socio-logical approach to terrorism. Nevertheless, it is not proposed that this should replicate some of the hermeneutic weaknesses within other disciplines' studies. On the contrary, to enhance levels of understanding about terrorism requires the significance of the past – of economic and cultural influences, political repression and inclusion, individual decision-making and identification – to be grasped. Therefore, this book seeks to draw upon some illuminating eco-nomic, historical, political and psychological explorations of terrorism but within a resolutely sociological framework. By utilising sociological concepts and ways of thinking, it is intended to provide a more holistic exploration of this form of political violence, drawing together the past and present, inclu-sion and exclusion and local and global. This is to be achieved through the interweaving of individual, group and societal dynamics that provide the emotional and rational basis for contemporary decisions and actions which are prominent throughout the terrorists' and terror groups' 'careers.' Socio-logical contributions can therefore help to understand how terror groups emerge, people join, retain membership, behaviour is transformed, violent acts are committed and participants leave in locations that have a history of political violence and where habitus has retained residues of political violence. Ultimately it is hoped that this sociological approach will better inform knowledge and understanding about historical and contemporaneous envir-onments and group dynamics that enable individual and social transitions into and out of political violence. All these different phases and elements are interconnected by social processes which seamlessly interconnect individual and social figurations.

## People and places

Although there are important gaps in knowledge and understanding it is important that I do not overstate the weaknesses. There are numerous excel-lent studies of specific terror groups and societies. Information about the emergence and actions of different groups is widely available. In this book the intention is to concentrate upon a range of groups from a selection of poli-tical and geographical positions. Groups to be studied include Western 'red' urban groups, the American 'Far Right,' republicans and loyalists in North-ern Ireland, Sri Lankan, Chechen and Palestinian religio-nationalists, reli-gious national and trans-national militants from Pakistan, Saudi Arabia and England (all Islamic) and Japan (Aum Supreme Truth). Reference will also be made to some of the relatively restricted literature concerning groups in South America. The analysis is supplemented by a multitude of auto/biographies, websites, court transcripts, government reports, media articles and other rele-vant studies and established within long-term social processes. Arguably, one of the benefits of a sociological approach is that, as Hamm (2007) suggests, related methods of investigation do not necessarily rely on direct access to terrorists, certainly by comparison with psychologists, and publicly available information can be utilised. Such accounts are critically applied. Moreover the exploration of individuals is not undertaken in isolation because their actions, emotions and rationale are always embedded within broader and longer-term social relations and processes. In so doing I am intending to overcome one of the criticisms Weinberg and Eubank (1987) raised about studies of Italian terrorists and which can be applied across regions, namely that there is a tendency to concentrate on short-term fluctuations that occurred around the time of attacks.

In addition to specific studies of regions and groups, concepts and ways of thinking will be adopted from studies that have applied terms from other areas of academic expertise, especially crime (Hamm 2007, Taylor and Horgan 2006), social movements (della Porta 1995, Koopmans 1993, Tarrow 1989) and cults (Dawson 2006, 2010, Lofland and Stark 1965, Robbins 1988). Aspects within terrorism can also be illuminated through findings from activists' careers in and out of non-violent movements, in particular social and religious. By emphasising commonalities between violent and non-violent groups, I aim to locate the normality within the 'abnormal.' This is in part because the resonance of identified abnormal characteristics of people who join terror groups is lagging behind those associated with social and, to a much lesser extent, religious movements. Terror groups continue to be demarcated as separate cells with little or no connection to broader movements. To this end it may well be that the 'cells' do not accord with the 'progressive' association that many of those studying social movements seem to use when deciding what does and does not fit within the parameters. Right-Wing participants within movements are an obvious example, whose overarching objective appears to result in their exclusion from social movement studies even though their activities, resources, organisation and mobilisation accords with definitions of what a social movement is. Thus stereotypical impressions of terrorists have much in common with conceptions of earlier generations of these other movement's members. The connection between collective action and social disintegration that continues to influence views of causes and roots of terrorism, was made in social movement studies 50 years ago by Kornhauser (1959). Although the perspective has continued to resonate to varying degrees it was quickly challenged (della Porta 1990, 1995, Oberschall 1993, Tilly 1978). Instead of members belonging to lowly positions with insecure, weak levels of aggregation during the surge of movements in the 1960s it was discovered that recruits stemmed largely from the middle classes who were integrated within a number of social networks with high levels of education. Della Porta (ibid.), Oberschall (ibid.), Sutton and Vertigans (2006) and Tilly (ibid.), amongst others, have identified that political violence is an extreme manifestation of the protest repertoire within these movements. This observation repositions terrorism within the broader movements, acknowledging both commonalities within the movement and the collective nature of the terror group activities.

Within studies of cults, Dawson (2006) and Iannacone (2004) point out that the popular conception is that recruits are a combination of maladjusted, marginal losers and young naïve idealists who are duped by older members. These conceptions stem in part from the belief that membership of cults is a form of deviancy which can only be explained through reference to the preceding marginal existence of the 'deviants' and/or their psychological flaws and cognitive limitations. Moreover, scant knowledge of the poor and underprivileged socio-economic backgrounds of recruits to late nineteenth-century and early twentieth-century Christian sectarian groups such as the Jehovah's Witnesses, Mormons and Pentecostalists was applied to the new religious movements that emerged from the 1960s onwards (Dawson 2010). Frequently such accounts for the appeal of cults are underpinned by the 'relative deprivation' theory which was first applied to social movements. Although the concept has been severely criticised and challenged by resource-mobilisation theory, new social movement theory and rational choice theory amongst others, Dawson (2006) argues that its influence continues within studies of religious movements. Thus, despite the lack of evidence and the variable levels of deprivation and achievement within cults, seminal studies such as Glock (1964) and Gurr (1970) remain prominent.

Perceptions of terrorists tend to follow the above stereotypes of cult members. Yet as Bakker (2006) remarks, in his study of *jihadis* in Europe, those involved seem to live 'normal' lives that are similar to other members of the communities in which they reside. Most work or study, some are married, have children or live with parents or friends. This is by no means universal, for instance Sageman's (2004) research discovered that most of those involved within 'Islamic' terror networks were full-time *jihadis*. There are, however, other conceived characteristics which differ. Within studies of both new social and religious movements the membership of both males and females has been acknowledged. This is less noticeable within terrorism where there has been a tendency to identify the behaviour with young single males. To some degree men are over represented within terror groups. Their age is, however, less easily categorised and could be considered to be only 'young' in the eyes of the middle aged researcher. Sageman's (2004) study of transnational *jihadis* discovered the average age of those joining was 26 years and most of his sample were married and had children.[26] Bakker's (2006) research upon *jihadis* in Europe and which drew upon Sageman's findings, found people were involved from different ages ranging from 16 to 59, the averages within particular terror networks stretched from 20.5 to 34 years and the overall average for the individuals studied was 27.3.[27] Nor does the age profile remain static within groups. In the West German 'red' groups, for instance, Neuberger and Valentini (1996) refer to the first generation becoming active when aged around 22–23 while the second generation were around 28–30 years old.

By comparison, studies of the age profile of female terrorists have been less rigorous. Pape's (2005) study identified that women were likely to be in their mid twenties and above while Skaine's (2006) sample ranged from nineteen to twenty-nine. MacDonald's (1991) research also discovered a similar age range. Based upon limited information, it would be premature to draw any definitive conclusions for these gender variations. There have been high profile cases reported of the involvement of older women, including most notoriously the 'suicide granny' or 'HAMAS hag'[28] in the Palestinian territories. However, if there are significant gender differences in the age profile this may well be indicative of shifting perceptions of women within the respective societies and internalised restraints. In essence, it is more acceptable for younger women to become involved in terror groups but as they become older expectations shift and strengthen around commitment to family and child rearing and so on.

Underpinning the correlation between age and terrorism is, Sageman argues, the 'ignorance' theory of terrorism. By this he extends the 'weak mind' argument to include all those who 'are too young to know better.' Nevertheless although the participants are not as young as often conceived, on average they are younger than middle age. There are a number of reasons for this, including less commitments,[29] more time, greater desire for excitement, less willingness to compromise than older generations, feelings of inverted ageism that results in blocked access to positions of power and influence, accentuated conflict between the generations and periods of transition as social restraints shift from familial to more ambiguous, less clearly defined constraints (Elias 1996).[30] Again though there is a danger of overstating the significance of age or to blur the boundaries. For example, Elias draws upon the opinions of the lawyer and influential RAF member Horst Mahler as representative of this younger generation of dissidents. Yet Mahler was in his 30s when he joined and had a successful career, characteristics which also apply to the group's female figurehead, Ulrike Meinhof.

In other words there is no terrorist profile. As Gill (2007: 152) points out with regard to suicide bombers and which applies across groups, 'Bombers are between fifteen and seventy years old, overly educated and uneducated, male and female, from all socio-economic classes, Christian, Hindu, Sikh and Muslim, religious and secular, single and married.' To understand and explain this variety requires, I argue, an appreciation of the relevant social processes which link experiences with ideas and behaviours. In so doing we are able to identify social commonalities which help to explain why distinct individuals become part of terror groups.

## Social processes

Impressions of terrorism are understandably influenced by the attacks and their immediate outcomes, especially death and destruction. Academics are not immune to the tendency to be affected by these images and can be distracted from wider factors. As Horgan (2005: 48) remarks, 'by focusing on ... the outcome of terrorist events, we achieve a distorted view of both the terrorist and the process of terrorism more broadly.' Thus terrorism becomes restricted to the act and its impact and terrorists become distinct forms of (in) humans, classified according to the devastation that they cause. The label of terrorist becomes all consuming, overriding and even disqualifying other roles and characteristics such as father, son, friend and lover.[31] This then tends to lead to analysis of why the acts are committed and the frequent underpinning of emotions that follow the aftermath. Understandably this impacts upon the explanations which often revolve around the type of person who can commit such atrocities. A more fruitful approach could be, as Horgan (2005, 2009) argues, to examine how people come to join, remain and disengage from groups, and to which could be added the formation of groups.

Overall though I am inclined to agree with Horgan (ibid.) and Taylor and Horgan (2006) who propose that exploring the mapping of pathways, their qualities and thus how people become 'terrorists' and behave accordingly is within the capabilities of social scientists. Multiple pathways into and through terrorism with surrounding social relations and activities are integral. These routes usually entail three key stages; joining, remaining and leaving (Gupta 2008, Horgan 2005, Ross 1999, Taylor and Horgan 2006). Social processes behind these stages are explored in the following chapters across a range of peoples and places. I will argue that individual and social identities develop within these processes and forms of We-ness emerge and shift within the interweaving of history and habitus. We-ness consists of particular traits, ideas, behaviour, tensions and solidarities. These help provide the basis for collective positive identification and negative dis-identification with the other which is essential to ground group superiority and moral justification while enabling the excluded and opposed people to be attacked.

Alongside constructed differences, terrorists share so many neglected similarities with people out-with their groups, not least their interdependencies with other individuals and institutions. Consequently as Elias and Scotson (2008) commented, unless research takes this into consideration, studies that examine groupings in isolation will ultimately be sterile. Hence individuals, groups and wider relationships and localities have to be examined to reflect the diversity within terrorism and between terrorists and individual experiences, socialising agents, group relationships and reasons for decision-making at key stages of the terror career. Comparisons across these variables will be undertaken throughout, identifying manifest differences and variations in ideology, actions, socialising agents and experiences. Furthermore, it will be argued, commonalities can also be identified in social processes, rationalities and emotions across different forms of groups. Hence some similarities can be highlighted both in 'objective' and 'subjective' reasoning behind an individual's involvement in terror groups, committing acts of violence, retaining commitment and ultimately leaving.

I am arguing that the processes through which individuals become terrorists are rarely rapid, particularly for the first generation that have to navigate routes from passive norms and values through to violent behaviour. The difficulties involved in this shift should not be overlooked. Managing individual ontological security during the transition is best achieved through careful phasing and connections with existing dispositions and historical precedents.

This does not occur overnight. On the contrary, pathways can be traced beyond the actual decision to broader radical layers of habitus where earlier stages of radicalisation occur. Pre-existing peer relations that formulate within mutual experiences are established and ultimately retrospectively mapped onto preceding generations where political violence was noticeable and never completely eradicated from social and individual dispositions.

Finally in this chapter I want to apply the concepts of emotions and rationality which underpin much of the above explanations. When examined separately the concepts can obstruct deep rooted insights into terrorism. Together they can help illuminate the social processes and surrounding appeal and purpose of terrorism.

## Emotions versus rationality

Much of the existing literature can be crudely divided into those that look for rational reasons to explain terror behaviour and those that rely upon emotions. They tend to concentrate upon the processes of terrorism as being either the outcome of emotional reactions such as excitement, frustration, guilt, humiliation and revenge which often have at least an implicit nod towards cognitive dissonance, if not mental illness, or through the influence of rational choice theory and Weberian axiological and instrumental rationality (Boudon 2003). In the latter category of explanations, the strategic purpose of terror tactics and individual goal-orientated participation based around materialism, relative deprivation and status opportunities or threats is emphasised. Again studies of social movements can help illuminate motivations behind non-material involvement. For instance, Marwell and Ames, (1979), Oliver (1984) and Opps (1989) have all identified the significance of values and group solidarities within collective action. By sharing social interdependence and a collective sense of identification amongst members, individual concerns regarding personal risks and consequences of their actions can be weakened.

Within the study of social movements the struggle over the emotional and rational facets within terrorism is more developed although, as Goodwin *et al.* (2007) acknowledge, emotions continue to be dismissed as too personal, too irrational or too inchoate. Since the 1960s debate has raged about the extent to which engagement within collective action is irrational (Olson 1963). In essence the debate can be condensed into a two part question; why does the individual participate within collective action, and how do they benefit? Stemming from the rationale within economics that identified clear goals and benefits to the individual through participating in the production of collective goods, the follow-up studies sought to understand 'what was in collective action for the individual?'

Forms of rational choice theory are located within explanations for terrorism and most easily applied within groups striving for national goals and a greater share of resources. Violence on behalf of such goals can be accommodated within Western analysis and the embedded understanding of materialism as a universal expectation. Nevertheless, if we look beyond the oversight that in many locations, ethnicity, religion, community, family and tribe[32] can be allocated primary significance then their commitment cannot be neatly attributed to personal gain. Explanations that focus upon relative deprivation seek to fill this gap. People become terrorists at least in part because the group provides them with income, status and/or they believe that through helping the group they will enhance their own employment prospects and participation in the allocation of resources. Under Max Weber's (1978) conceptual apparatus, this relative cost-benefit analysis would be goal orientated or instrumental rational action. Numerous examples provide support for this. There are also many notable instances where it does not apply; not least where members are well educated, middle class and with successful careers or the likelihood of such. Engagement within terrorism is actually detrimental to their career and material prospects, certainly in the short term. Moreover we are left with the same question that confronts the studies of social movements; namely, why do individuals invest time, effort and often financial resources into collective action when they bear all the risk and non participants would share the rewards if the collective goals be achieved? As Sageman (2004) comments with regard to terrorist involvement, this creates a 'free rider paradox,' and suggests that participation in terrorism may not be a consequence of utilitarian ideals. If individuals think terrorism will succeed, despite evidence from history which indicates otherwise, they could wait on the sidelines with no personal risk. After governments have been overthrown, the West repelled, blacks sent 'back to Africa' and the Jewish conspiracy destroyed, the 'sideliners' can share in the benefits. That many people do not is indicative of the presence of non-material factors. And of course this is particularly noticeable for groups who are not in pursuit of any immediately obvious collective goods. Conversely, rational choice is also unable to explain why there are fewer female terrorists than male. If we apply the generic logic of the conceptual model; women have more to gain and less to lose through involvement.

And as I mentioned above, in contrast to the invisibility of women within rational-choice models, they are all too apparent within explanations that emphasise emotional factors. Hence women are more inclined to be motivated to political violence by love, revenge, sacrifice, honour, disgrace, shame and humiliation, often under the umbrella of personal trauma rather than altruism, political awareness, discursive consciousness and national allegiance which can often be found in explanations for male engagement. As Patkin (2004) notes, the media, in particular, searches for alternative explanations for female involvement. In comparison with the media's tendency to accept male ideological statements at face-value Patkin argues that the women's accounts are sensationalised with the emotional given precedence over the discursive.

Emotional and rational approaches are therefore inherently flawed when examined separately; an observation which is supported by a cursory glance at most definitions of terrorism which tend to incorporate both affective and pragmatic, short-term and long-term intentions. In isolation both approaches share an inability to grasp the multi-dimensioned social construction of terrorism and processes therein, failing to comprehend why only a relatively limited number of people from seemingly generic groups become terrorists. Approaches that concentrate upon emotive factors are unable to explain the assessment of costs and benefits involved in joining, remaining in and leaving groups and the strategic use of emotion by terror leaders. By comparison, the emphasis upon instrumental rationality and self-interest fails to explain altruism within groups and the roles of feelings such as hatred and anger in determining decisions within the terrorist career. Here there are signs that the dichotomy within Weber's ideal types has been too closely adhered to.

For Weber (1978), value actions connect into 'ethics of conviction' and are based upon duty, honour or discourse. The cause or demand becomes the primary focus without regard for the consequences. By comparison, instrumental actions are about the means towards the attainment of calculated and purposive ends. Within Weber's typology these two forms are mutually exclusive alongside the other two ideal types; affective which is determined by the individual's affects and feelings, and traditional which is grounded by ingrained habituation. Yet these rigid demarcations are not necessarily appropriate or distinct. People can hold a binding conviction to an unconditional intrinsic value, emotions and calculative personal gain. Nor do the concepts inherently exist in their purest, ideal forms. For instance, it is arguably impossible to determine utilitarian reasoning without recourse to the values within individual and social habitus. Even utilitarian ideas are formulated through controlled learning methods and less regulated emotional interactions which inform their behaviour. As Epstein (1994) argues, processing information relies both upon logic and inference, emotions and associations. Equally feelings and values are affected by rational processes. As I shall explain in Chapter Three, the greater the perceived threat and level of risk, the more likely it is that feelings and emotions will influence decision-making. Moreover group members become involved for different values and instrumental reasons. For example, some 'foot soldiers' may be more likely to be concerned with short gain remuneration while leaders participate for more discursive and political reasons. Finally the parameters for the 'ideal-types' are by no means fixed or timeless. Values can become purpose and vice-versa according to the shifting figurations in which they are formulated and interpreted. Short- and longer-term planning requires foresight and hindsight, lessons to be learnt and consequences. For Elias (2000, 2005) this exemplifies that rationalisation is a process of cognitive and emotional change. In essence greater control over emotions and internalised self and social restraints over behaviour, that includes feelings such as guilt and repugnance, enables what we consider today to be instrumental rational action. Rationalisation is therefore a process of emotional change.

Studies of social movements such as Flam (1990), Jasper (1997) and Melucci (1989) provide a possible solution for terrorism. They have argued against over extending the rational criteria because many participants do not carefully select from a range of options according to a cost-benefit analysis that is underpinned by rationality. Instead they stress the need to incorporate emotions within an understanding about why people become involved in social movements. Studies such as della Porta's (1995) acknowledgement that affective bonds such as love, loyalty, trust and respect are especially important in consolidating terror groups are complementary. Emotions are thereby integral in the formation and continuation of groups. Equally with the reduction of expressive forms of actions comes the greater likelihood of the groups' demise. Nevertheless, it is apparent that some people are involved for materialist reasons and groups are strategic. Frameworks of explanation therefore need to integrate reason and emotion, the expressive and practical. Drawing upon these different perspectives and applying them to terrorism can provide a more holistic exploration of individual involvement. Hence, by highlighting ways in which groups operate and individuals react and behave at emotional and rational levels, I argue that rather than being mutually exclusive, the two concepts are coterminous. Both need to be embedded in order to fully illuminate routes into and through terrorism and the actions and appeal of groups. Crucially this interweaving is established within broader local and global processes that help to account for the construction and maintenance of terror groups and the acceptance of violence as a viable method of protest. Through this processual approach it is intended to comprehend people's and groups' terror careers.

Before looking at direct pathways through terrorism I initially want to explore their foundations, which are built upon social history. Consequently Chapter Two begins to ground the sociological approach, identifying facets of the past that have become relevant in the terror present.

# 2 History

## The legacy of political violence

### Introducing the past

Sociology has a proud history of exploring and identifying long-term processes which help in understanding contemporary relations and activities. Yet in this chapter I argue that historical sociology has largely been consigned to history. Studies of terrorism also neglect the importance of the past for the emergence and duration of groups. I am therefore contemplating throwing a few stones into this gaping sociological and subject-specific chasm. My particular intentions are twofold: to examine how terror groups utilise history to try to mobilise support and justify the use of political violence; and to investigate societies before the formation of terror groups to establish if preceding activities, policies and processes provide a legacy for subsequent political violence or residues within radical habitus.

First it is important to declare what I am not aiming to achieve. I am not intending to identify the absolute beginning of terrorism within societies. Pathways of terrorism are lost in the depths of unrecorded history like other forms of behaviour. Instead examples will be discussed that fit within a broader history of the related movement with identifiable connections between ideas, methods or aims. This is not to say that I propose a continuous trajectory of political violence within societies, or a continuum between tyrannicide and terrorism or nineteenth-century Russian anarchists and twenty-first-century members of trans-national militant Islamists. There are some differences alongside commonalities. Nor am I arguing that terrorism in the past begets terrorism in the future. Instead I am offering suppositions about patterns of development within particular nation-states that have contributed towards aspects of violence being retained or transformed within social and individual habitus. Crucially, this is despite, or possibly because of, the emergence of regional monopolies of violence and in many localities shifts towards greater individual restraints which accompanied the erosion of specific values and behaviour that were now deemed inappropriate.

As I shall explain in the following chapters, the passive norms and values that have contributed to the removal of non-sanctioned violence beyond the public gaze must be challenged if individuals are to confront individual and social restraints. Conversely, individuals are not uniformly immersed within webs of interdependence; nor do they empathise equally with all members of the population. On the contrary, individualised restraints can fluctuate, transforming according to interactions and experiences. For Elias (1996, 2000), distinct types of conscience formation control aggressiveness and potential violent impulses through the internalisation of feelings of guilt and repugnance. The overwhelming majority of people internalise restraints that severely limit the likelihood that they will kill anyone. In some environments these restraints can be overcome, and are noticeable by their absence or weakness. Roots for these differences can be located, in some instances, in the formulation of different norms and values that promote difference, superiority and insecurity and do not encourage mutual interdependence between ethnicities, religious denominations, discourse and so on. If Elias (1996: 196) is applied to case studies such as Ireland, Italy, Pakistan, Saudi Arabia and the United States it can be argued that 'In such societies, terror and horror hardly ever manifest themselves without a fairly long social process in which conscience decomposes.' Within some of these localities I will be arguing that the conscience has not been fully composed. Hence restraints are already weak and require limited decomposition. A timely dimension will enable the slow emergence of terrorism in these regions to be established.

Alongside the emergence of the reasons for implementing political violence, the timing for the adaptation of methods is also dependent upon the advent of technology and the availability of opportunities to either innovate or learn from others. Thrown dynamite, assassinations, hijackings, kidnappings, car bombs and latterly suicide bombs have all gained prominence within different asymmetrical conflicts. In this regard, ideological and pragmatic links have existed between obviously connected groups such as various anarchist organisations, 'red' urban groups and militant Islamists. 'Red' Italian terrorism can be traced from the anarchists back to the Young Italy successes in 1860 and in turn to the Carbonari of the 1820s. There are also many examples of more surprising cross-fertilisation. For instance, the Israeli group Lehi's Yitzak Shamir, and subsequent Prime Minister, held the Irish republican leader Michael Collins in such esteem that he selected the codename 'Michael' in his honour (Clutterbuck 2004, Sedgwick 2007).[1] Furthermore, as Sedgwick (2007) declares, grasping the history of groups is essential for understanding the transgression into terrorism, their origins, membership and dynamics.

In post-Second World War history the 1960s were to herald the emergence of what became categorised as 'new' forms of terrorism. Arguably, over the last 20 years it has been possible to witness the formulation of another 'new' form of terrorism associated with religion, in particular the Aum Supreme Truth in Japan and groups associated with al-Qa'ida. Conversely, alongside the distinct classification and demarcation of terror groups across periods of time, the past has been integral to understanding subsequent acts of political violence. This acknowledgement largely stems from the ways in which terror groups learn from predecessors across ideological and national boundaries.[2] Thus, concepts such as the 'vanguard,' 'propaganda by deed' and 'strategy of provocation' have antecedents in nineteenth century anarchism. The vanguard has since been the cornerstone of group strategies ranging from al-Qa'ida to Far Right groups in America. Allocating to themselves the role of visionaries, these terrorists aim to 'wake up' their respective populations to the atrocities, threats and injustices that they encounter. After being awoken the people will both realise the extent of the global, societal, national or religious problems and that the terrorists offer the only viable solution.[3]

It is often overlooked that for many countries facing terrorism today, the threat is not unique to the contemporary era. Following the outpouring of grief and shock that followed the 2001 terror attacks upon America, many people were subsequently surprised to discover that the country had regularly faced terrorism from 'enemies within.'[4] Americans could recall the 1995 Oklahoma bombing and older generations remembered the Weather Underground and SLA as the Left Wing descended into violence following the perceived failure of peace and student movements. Few people knew of early theoretical predecessors such as Karl Heinzen and Johann Most. Heinzen is an interesting character, not only for his role within America but his contributions to the practice of terrorism. Laqueur (1977: 26) described Heinzen as 'the first to provide a full-fledged doctrine of modern terrorism.' Following the failures of the 1848 European revolutions, which he attributed to a lack of resolution and ruthlessness, he migrated from Germany to the United States. Heinzen began to devise a doctrine of terrorism. Subsequent developments indicate that he was something of a visionary, anticipating both weapons of mass destruction and the potential of bombs, rockets and poisons in creating large-scale devastation. Despite the emphasis upon political violence, Heinzen did not engage, concentrating instead upon strategy. It may be that the lack of activity contributed to Heinzen's influence on the evolution of terror tactics fading from narratives. Yet Grob-Fitzgibbon (2004) emphasises the significance of Left-Wing terrorism in America through the adaptation of many of Heinzen's methods and ideas by another German migrant, Johann Most. Like his countryman, Most was also a teacher rather than a practitioner. Nevertheless Most was to become hugely significant to such an extent that Robert Hunter declared that 'The history of terrorist tactics in America largely centers about the career of Johann Most.'[5] His book *The Anarchist Cookbook* was adopted and published by the New Left in the 1960s and was to influence similar texts (Laqueur 2001). Most was one of the first strategists to appreciate media potential and also advocated indiscriminate attacks. When facing oppressive and powerful enemies, principles of chivalry had to be discarded if the terrorists' logistical disadvantage was to be overcome.

Despite links across terror groups and time, there has been a tendency to categorise terror groups into classifications. Rapoport's (2003) waves are probably the most prominent. Since the 1880s he identifies the anarchist wave; a colonial phase that emerged as groups sought to achieve independence from the 1940s, and the rise of the 'red' groups in West Germany, Italy, Japan and the United States were classified as the 'New Left Wave.' The surges in levels of religio-political activism in places such as Iran, Kashmir and the United States allied to the actions of the Aum Supreme Truth in Japan and Islamic groups have contributed to the classification of a religious phase.[6] By charting the history of terrorism Rapoport provides a useful counter-balance to those for whom September 2001 was the starting point. To a lesser extent the wave approach could also be utilised to challenge the clamour that a 'new terrorism' had emerged. The phrase was introduced by Laqueur (1999) and seemed to instigate a competition amongst many experts in the field to prophesise the bleakest, most devastating outcomes of the inevitable attacks that these new 'terrorists' would commit. The ever more destructive prophecies seem to have been largely based upon the potential for fatalities with little or no regard for the social processes and historical precedents which may lead to possible attacks. In a manner that those familiar with the Risk Society will recognise, the experts, rather than helping to address the threat, inflated the risk and with it the likelihood of detached, precise and appropriate reactions. This is not to argue that 'new terrorism' does not have validity. It does; important distinctions exist between generations aided and abetted by technological, communicative and scientific developments. Nevertheless as Neumann (2009) explains, it is too simplistic to divide into 'new' and 'old' terrorism, not least as some of the 'old' remain active alongside the 'new.' Instead he offers the more nuanced counter points of 'newer' and 'older.'

Although wave or phase approaches can be instructive, they are therefore not without flaws. In the haste to establish classifications other discursive groups can be neglected. For instance, although most studies tend to associate terrorism in the nineteenth century with anarchists, Rapoport (2003) acknowledges that nationalist groups were also active without achieving subsequent prominence. Sedgwick (2007) discusses Armenian, Bengali, Egyptian, Filipino and Macedonian groups. Arguably the limited direct impact of their activities upon the West has contributed to their isolation within regional histories and neglect within terror trajectories. Today the tendency to collate, consider and classify terror groups according to their threat to Western interests remains acute. The inner core of al-Qa'ida clearly calculated upon this when shifting their targeting from the 'near enemy' to the 'far enemy.' Reactions duly went from being regional to global.

Moreover, the formulation of difference between eras can result in commonalities being overlooked. For example, instead of the isolation of sacrifice as an Islamic phenomenon and which in turn became the tautological basis on which to explain the 'uniqueness' of Muslim suicide attacks, reference could be drawn to alternative examples of members giving up their lives for the discourse and/or group. The sacrifices of others have been integral in the mobilisation of generations and, of course, the reluctance to give up the struggle and gain a sense that martyrs have died in vain. By extending the parameters beyond the contemporary and religious, secular groups such as the IRA, Russian anarchists and Liberation Tigers of Tamil Eelam (LTTE) become incorporated. Within Irish republicanism, there are numerous martyrs from across the centuries and probably most epitomised by those who were killed either during the Easter Rising or subsequently executed by the British. For leaders like Pearse,[7] Plunkett and MacDonagh their actions and bloodshed would be 'a cleansing and a sanctifying thing' (McGarry 2010: 52). Following the implementation of penal systems, Irish republicanism was also to become associated with hunger strikes. Today, reflections tend to be dominated by the 1981 hunger strikers and the emergence of what became the ballot box and armalite campaign. Again, though, it is difficult to understand why the 1981 campaign was introduced, and in the first few months was widely supported, without recourse to history. Crucially the republicans were able to interweave Catholicism and a republican past in which hunger strikers had played an important role. For example, in the aftermath of the Easter Rising at a time when republicanism was rising, Thomas Ashe died when hunger striking after attempts to force feed him. At his funeral, the IRA leader, Michael Collins arranged for a demonstration of republican volunteers and over 40,000 mourners were reported as attending. The British Daily Express stated that the death and funeral had 'made 100,000 Sinn Feiners out of 100,000 constitutional nationalists.'[8] Suddenly al-Qa'ida becomes less extreme and unusual and part of both a history of terrorism from which they draw and emotional framings that they share(d) with other groups. Undeniably the numbers of casualties from attacks have increased over recent years but proclaiming religious fervour to be the reason fails to account for important distinctions. Duyvesteyn (2004: 448) provides a brief outline of the history of terrorism and raises a number of pertinent questions regarding changes in terrorist behaviour.

> Is the growth in deaths a consequence of terrorists consciously choosing to kill more people, of technological progress or increased effectiveness ... ? Is it not inherent in the logic of terrorism that the attacks need to be larger and more extreme in order to achieve the same effect? When the means becomes available, the terrorist expressions will inevitably become more extreme.

And, of course, religious groups have not monopolised attacks upon large numbers of people. The (secular) Real IRA's bomb in Omagh killed 28 people, more than any other attack in the province. Although the group quickly sought to dismiss the attack as a mistake, irrespective of the intentions, the death toll indicated capability. Nor is the intention for mass casualties or willingness to kill innocent civilians new. Karl Heinzen (2004) highlighted this when pronouncing in 1849,

> The path to Humanity will pass through the zenith of Barbarity. Our enemies have made this principle a law of politics and we shall either have to observe this 'law,' follow this 'constitutional path,' or be buried, and our freedom with us.

Similarly, terror groups are able to connect into deeply embedded fears and threats. For instance, declarations by the Japanese Aum Supreme Truth[9] regarding a looming apocalypse arguably were allocated greater credibility because they connected with wider concerns within Japan about world destruction. For Reader (2000) this is partly the legacy of the huge psychological, as well as physical, impact of the atomic bombs dropped upon Hiroshima and Nagasaki.

In light of these historical associations, it would be anticipated that the past features heavily within studies of terrorism. Any such expectations would be misplaced.

## Forgetting about the past

> For most commentators terrorism has no history, or at least they would have us believe that the 'terrorist problem' had no significance until the 1960s, when the full impact of modern technology was felt, endowing most individuals as individuals or as members of small groups, with capacities they never had before. (Rapoport 1989: xii)

With impressions of terrorism continuing to be dominated by acts and outcomes, underlying social processes have been under-explored. This is particularly true for long-term processes with even historical studies of terrorism tending to concentrate upon the emergence of groups and the transfer of knowledge and methodology to subsequent generations. At most there are underdeveloped discussions about the preceding mainstream movements from which groups emerge. By comparison the deep history of the societies in which terrorism emerges is ignored. In some respects this is understandable. Acts of terrorism are obviously motivated by recent experiences and emotions and as such are an obvious starting point. But not necessarily the end (of the starting) point. Such studies rarely consider the roots of violence or wonder why terrorism is adopted in societies where unauthorised violence appears to have disappeared from public spaces. Despite the reluctance to acknowledge the past of political violence, there is, certainly amongst sociologists, an appreciation that the origins of other forms of social behaviour precede us. As Elias (1996: 296) declared 'The living communicate with each other in a language that is to a large extent moulded by the dead.' This does therefore lead us to suggest that if other forms of communication, and we have already established that terrorism aims to communicate terror and discourse, are located in previous generations, the same could also be true for terrorism. Hence, can a study of the deep roots of these societies identify potential factors, activities and relations that remain embedded within the contemporary habitus and enhance the probability that terrorism will emerge? Drawing upon sociological explorations of history and in particular the contributions of Norbert Elias,[10] I will argue 'yes.' The sedimented past within the contemporary habitus is then explored within the following chapter.

Neglect of deep history within societies is a criticism that cannot be restricted to studies of terrorism. On the contrary, with the obvious exception of history, academic disciplines increasingly focus upon the present, even if it results in re-inventing the metaphorical wheel. Within sociology, historical studies were instrumental in the formation and acceptance of sociological epistemology. Sociologists theorised processes of continuity and change across historical trajectories. Some of the classic studies, including defining examples from Marx, Weber and Durkheim, have detailed the transfer of authority from localised and/or religious leaders to national, secular governments, the shift in social relations and activities, industrial development, technological transformations, political allegiances and fractures. Cohesion and control (or lack thereof) have been integral to many studies. Sociologists have grappled with understanding the increasingly complex interrelationships. These were accompanied by diminished local, personal relations and more impersonal, larger collective identifications and conversely greater expression and regulation of emotions and conformity amongst different forms of ideas and behaviour. Within these transformations, violence became heavily regulated, formally through state institutions such as police, army, prisons and legal systems and informally by more insidious agencies such as education and media.

During Goldthorpe (1991, 1994) and Mann's (1994) famous exchange over the nature of historical sociology there was general agreement about the necessity to incorporate the past within the discipline. For Goldthorpe (1991: 225) 'sociologists can never "escape" from history' and Mann (1994: 46) argued similarly that 'sociology which is neither parochial nor concerned to generate wholly abstract propositions about the nature of any human community must include the study of the past in its framework.' Today, though, the past, in the sense both of epistemology and long-term processes of integration and disintegration, seems to have been discarded or forgotten within large swathes of the discipline.[11] In part, the sociological challenge to evolutionary theory which united an unlikely alliance that ranged from Parsonians to Marxists, correctly contributed to the rejection of normative and teleological components. However, the verocity of the attack meant that the critique extended to incorporate the long-term processes of social development and a concomitant loss of enthusiasm for historical changes within sociological investigation (van Krieken 1998). By moving towards a more 'snapshot' approach sociology has contributed to diminished residues of collective memory. The evolution of conflict and competition from the past into the present is lost in contemporary concentrations upon perpetrators, victims and breaches of conformity and control. Arguably losing violence in history weakens not only academic study but policy application, in this instance counter-terrorism. Silke (2006) develops this point with regard to suicide terrorism and which applies equally to other forms. For him, historical examples are opportunities to enhance levels of understanding and responses. The distance of time allows for greater detachment and careful consideration, enabling objective insight into explanations, causes and processes.

## History of ideas

The above acts of terrorism and legacy of political violence are not free floating. They are embedded within habitus, individual and social disposition or make-up, interwoven with grounded realities and discourse. The precedents of ideas therefore also require consideration. Particular terror discourses may appear unique, very much products of their time. Conversely, there is a tendency to dismiss religious terror discourse as a historical throwback with ideas and forms of behaviour that are ill suited for the modern era. Populist evaluation of groups associated with al-Qa'ida is a case in point. Neither perception is strictly correct. Groups from the Far Left during the 1970s may have appeared innovative. Discursively they were a mix of influences contributing to a distinctive ideology, although the precise details were not always apparent. To varying degrees though, the 'reds' plundered history for inspiration. Marx, Lenin and Mao featured to some extent and it was also possible to locate contributions from Heinzen, Bakunin and Kropotkin, amongst others.

Religious groups obviously also draw upon figures of the past. The extent to which militant Muslims are applying the teachings of Muhammed is the source of considerable theological debate. Crucially the terrorists believe they are acting according to God's will. In support of this belief they also refer to the actions and traditions associated with Muhammed's immediate successors (*caliphs*) and subsequent inspirational characters. Hence Ibn Taymiyya (1263–1328) has been resurrected within contemporary militancy and his actions and rhetoric reapplied to contemporary injustices and humiliations. By tracking the evolution of religious and secular discourse, it is possible to interweave political and social changes with discursive transformations. Thus as the possibility of partition and the formation of Pakistan emerged, Muslims' sentiments shifted from the post Mughal despair over loss of Empire and infidel rule to a more positive, constructive dialogue for independence (Akbar 2004).

Similarly, nationalist groups also rely heavily upon historical connections to justify their ideas for independence. Irish republicans can point to a lineage that incorporates characters such as Robert Emmett, James Stephens, Arthur Griffith and the 1916 martyrs from a rich tradition of protest and uprising. What is often overlooked is that the French and American Revolutions, both in terms of actions and ideas, were also influential. On the reverse, Irish 'British' Protestants were influenced by changing religious beliefs and underwent evangelical revivalism in the 1850s which further demarcated sectarian divides across Ulster (Foster 1992).

Across discursive and nationalist terror groups there is therefore a tendency both to integrate ideas and behaviour from the past into contemporary rhetoric and strategies. The legitimacy of this approach and the likelihood of mobilising support will partly depend upon the extent to which it accords with peoples' experiences and their perceptions that the past continues to be relevant in helping to understand and rectify the present.

## The past as the present

The past for terrorists is mobilised for a number of purposes. In the dark corridors of history, examples can be located that support the legitimacy of terrorism in the present. Embedded within collective memories are continuums of injustice, brutality, dashed hopes and political failures. By drawing upon historical memories, terror groups seek to emphasise inherent problems that have existed across time.[12] The dynamics of control and ultimately change are often encapsulated within two sides of the same coin. Colonialists or governments are the cause of past and present problems and will continue to be so in the future unless confronted. Consequently, the only way to overcome this historical truism is to support and join the terror group. Relationships between collective memories and contemporary experiences have been illuminated particularly effectively by nationalist groups. Some of these groups have emotive stories to tell which continue to resonate with recent events and encounters. For example, the history of Russian and Sri Lankan atrocities is recalled by Chechen and Tamils respectively.[13] Irish republicans have also frequently drawn from the well of history incorporating the plantations that formally disadvantaged Catholics, Cromwell's ruthless campaign, nineteenth-century famine, 1916 Easter Rising, behaviour of 'Black and Tans' and Auxiliaries[14] and deadly rioting following partition. More recently Bloody Sunday and subsequent acts by the British government and army have been utilised to exemplify inherent and deeply embedded discrimination and violence within the dynamics of occupation. Similarly, the 1917 Balfour Agreement[15] and the failure of neighbouring Arab nations and international peace deals have been instrumental, alongside the more immediate experiences of Israeli policies and actions, in both surges of Palestinian terrorism and justifications for its adaptation.

Colonialism continues to cast a shadow over contemporary 'freed' nations with experiences under British governance; in particular, continuing to inform present day perceptions. Thus Western-inspired cultural and social processes of globalisation which are thought to threaten indigenous norms and values can be connected to preceding attempts at proselytising, which caused resentment across other religions. At a more brutal level, massacres of ethnic groups can also be retained within collective memory. Multiple examples can be located within the history of the British Empire in India. Numerous groups emerged to challenge the colonialists and contributed to a shift in the nature of the Hinduism, Sikhism and Islam. Within recent movements of radicalisation their legacy is apparent. For instance, the Islamic Deobandis began at a madrassa in Deoband, India, primarily to protect Islam against British incursion. At the time, Muhammad Qasim, the guiding force behind the emergence of the movement, declared in terms that could easily fit within contemporary Islamic militant rhetoric,

> The English have perpetrated boundless acts of tyranny against the Muslims for their fault, if at all it was a fault, of the uprising of 1857 and

their relentless endeavour for the independence of this country thereafter. They have left no stone unturned to plunder and obliterate the Islamic arts and science, Muslim culture and civilization.[16]

The transference of these 'difficult pasts' depends on numerous factors. In this regard, Vinitzky-Seroussi's (2002) conceptual model for commemorative outcomes can be applied because the relevance of the past to political violence is also influenced by 'agents of memory,' the relevance of the past to the present and the prevailing political climate. As Misztal (2010: 28) explains,

> memory helps in the construction of collective identities and boundaries, whether these are national, cultural, ethnic or religious. It can be seen as the guardian of difference, as it allows for recollection and preservation of our different selves that we acquire and accumulate.

## The past as a dark age

Fears over the past returning have also been instrumental within processes of radicalisation through into terrorism. Attempts by groups such as the Italian Red Brigades, West German Red Army Faction and Japanese Red Army tended to stress the continuity between the notorious recent past associated with fascism and government actions of the present. In West Germany, Elias (1996: 299) considered that,

> After a phase of almost boundless over-elevation of the national ideal, the rising generations saw themselves burdened not only with the stigma of defeat, but over and above this – and more difficult to overcome – with the stigma of a nation which had a tendency towards barbaric acts of violence.

For Elias (ibid.), in their search for meaning, younger generations of the middle classes seized 'on political ideals which stand in opposition to the great catchwords of this polluting past.' Contemporary life was being constantly monitored for signs that the past was returning and indeed in some respects it was considered to have never left. Despite the defeat of fascism in the Second World War, associated structures, principles and personnel were believed to have remained within power relations. According to former Red Army Faction member Astrid Proll (in MacDonald 1991: 211), 'They [the Nazis] were everywhere – every second person was a Nazi and they held powerful jobs in business and in the judiciary; the Nazis just continued their careers.' With older generations viewed as complicit within fascism, radicals felt that only they could be positioned as bulwarks against the explicit return of authoritarianism and repression. By comparison, older generations who had lived through the feared periods of history did not consider that their present experiences were indicative of fascism and therefore were generally not mobilised.

## The past as a golden age

Such portrayals of the past could result in a perception that history was always a negative source for mobilisation; it is easier to connect acts of extreme violence associated with terrorism with negativities. That people may kill under the rubric of terrorism for altruism or perceived discursive progression is more challenging to societal perceptions. However, the concentration upon the dark side fails to account for groups for whom history is also the source of magical memories, a period of highly regarded threatened or displaced precedents. A desire to replace the present with the past has long been associated with religious groups. Numerous examples can be drawn from religions where followers have considered the application of violence to be an appropriate method through which to reintroduce values and behaviour from previous eras. To varying degrees, emphasis is placed upon a 'Golden Age' and symbols and narrative that help to mobilise support for its return. Within contemporary terrorism, Islamic groups have gained the greatest notoriety.

Popular reasoning for contemporary actions by Muslim extremists is regularly conjoined with 'medieval' characters such as Muhammed ibn 'Abd-al-Wahhab (d. 1791), the founder of Wahhabism. In conjunction with the tribal leader Muhammed Ibn Saud they converted, often forcibly, much of what is today Saudi Arabia, to Wahhabism.[17] In the process they established a framework of religious and ideological systems with which to control the population. This is the Islamic interpretation which bin Laden internalised and so has understandably attained considerable attention. Clearly the austere nature of the interpretation and challenge to other practices and beliefs partly through *jihad*[18] continue to resonate. However, at the risk of appearing contradictory, history alone cannot explain the emergence of al-Qa'ida. Wahhabism has been influential but as one influence among many. Al-Wahhab would struggle to recognise his teachings within al-Qa'ida-related actions and discourse. And of course he was not the only fundamentalist wishing to return to pristine forms of religion; Niblock (2006) notes that even for the period, Wahhab was by no means unusual. For example, within England, Puritanism was prominent in the seventeenth century and was succeeded in the Victorian era by Christian fundamentalism. Neither was to inspire a terror movement within England. Yet traces through Puritan migration can be located within the American Far Right's adaptation of violence and religious underpinning for racial superiority. Sikhism has also been exposed to these processes of re-evaluation. The religion was founded around 500 years ago with the aim of addressing impurities within Hinduism. Gradually Sikhism became a distinctive collective identity and shifted from passivism to greater militarism resulting in the formation of a Sikh kingdom. Following annexation into the British Empire, ethnic consciousness diminished only to gradually regain significance. National consciousness rose during the struggle for independence in the Indian sub-continent. Following Indian independence, Sikh demands ranged from concessions over the holy status of the city of Amritsar to an independent

Sikh state to be called Khalistan. The more militant secessionists became vehemently opposed to Sikhs who were critical of their stance and began campaigns of violence that included political assassinations, plane hijacking and bombings.

Furthermore, and as the above examples indicate, the concentration upon Muslim radicals risks neglecting the ways in which other discourses continue to be embedded within processes of radicalisation which can result in terrorism. In the United States, acts of terrorism regularly emerge from interwoven networks of racialists, militias and Christianity, most infamously with the Oklahoma bombing in 1995 which killed 168 people. The perpetrator was Timothy McVeigh, a white American former soldier. Following the attack and the widespread anger and revulsion, the pre-attack hiatus for the broad racist coalition ended. Nevertheless, although the threat diminished, it never disappeared. Today, the Far Right has experienced resurgence. To some extent, this can be partly attributed to the election of Obama but this would be to ignore the gradual growth and embedded disillusionment and resentment felt by many white Americans. For instance, in 2005 the US Marshalls Service Chief Inspector, Geoff Shank, observed that 'Not a lot of attention is being paid to this, because everyone is concerned about the guy in a turban. But there are still plenty of angry, Midwestern white guys out there.'[19] Johnson and Frombgen (2009) argue that the historical legacy of white assimilationism and what they term 'creole nationalism' stems from white settlers, the crystallization of racial supremacy and relationship between the award of citizenship and race. Between the Civil War and the Second World War America was gradually transformed culturally from an Anglo-Saxon country to a white one. Despite the shifting political and cultural norms and values, racism continues to be embedded within American society.

Nor is the defence of the past necessarily associated with discursively extremist groups. For example, loyalist groups in Northern Ireland formed to protect their status and to prevent a united island. For them the past provided the justification for their actions, stemming from the formation of 'Britishness' following the migration of (Protestant[20]) Scottish, English and Welsh settlers particularly during the Plantations; sectarian victories such as the 1690 Battle of the Boyne; defiance of Home Rule between 1912 and 1914; the Ulster Covenant and episodes of sacrifice like the thousands killed in defence of Britain during the First World War.[21] The twentieth century rallying call of 'No Surrender' can also be traced to an earlier phase of Irish history. During the 1689 siege of London/Derry the surrounded Protestants issued the now famous slogan to the forces of James II. Ultimately the siege was broken and James defeated. These events are remembered within Unionist culture, most vividly during the 'marching season' when Orange Lodges parade the streets carrying a variety of banners depicting various scenes from the past. In so doing, memories are refreshed and renewed through commemoration and celebration. That, as Halliday (1998) points out, the marches and associated regalia emerged out of working class culture in the 1860s, almost two hundred years after the victory, was lost in the subsequent narration. Jarman (1997) has described the visual imagery as portraying an endless cycle of conflict, fear of betrayal and sacrifice. For Graham (2004: 488), 'most loyalists have a firm belief in the reality and objectivity of history and memory' and the historical accuracy of the images and accompanying narrative has become irrelevant. For those who believe the events to be true, to paraphrase W.I. Thomas (1928), they become real in their consequences. Alongside pictures of victorious Unionists, it is also possible to notice portrayals of atrocities committed against Protestants. For instance, the murder of around 100 Protestant children and adults in 1641 in Portadown by Catholics angry at the new settlements has regularly been vividly depicted (Kee 1995). Estimates for the number of Protestants killed in the wider rebellion across Ireland vary considerably. Irrespective of whether the figure was 12,000 or over 150,000,[22] the attacks confirmed the fear and insecurities held by Protestants about the threat from Catholics and continued to resonate within the 'Troubles.'

## Violent past

> 'Violence, both imposed and reactive, remains a chilling inheritance.'
>
> (Foster 1992: v)

History can also be the source to which direct reference is made in the application of violence. Under this version, violence was successful previously and under certain conditions can be again. There is some support to suggest that the extent to which violence can be drawn from collective memories influences the nature and duration of the terror struggles. Moreover, despite regular fluctuations in support, American Far Right discourse has been a prominent feature of extremist politics, often disseminating ideas and actions of political violence. Those responsible refer to the roles of religion, the founding fathers of America and militias. Individual freedoms and the right to bear arms are integral to these perceptions. Within Islamic groups, high priority has been placed upon the concept of *jihad*[23] and the legacy of confrontation. For these groups, military successes under the banner of Islam provide justification for their own adaptation of violence, whether those victories were during the time of Muhammed and the four *caliphs* as large swathes of Asia and Northern Africa were conquered, or in the Afghan war against the Soviet Union (1979–89). Again it is important to emphasise the fluidity of the concept of *jihad*. Heck (2004) details how various formulations during the first six Islamic centuries (7th–13th)[24] were embedded within particular socio-historical contexts. After Ibn Taymiyya's appropriation, the concept has continued to shift in meaning and application in response to colonialism, social and intellectual reform, and, Heck adds, as a pretext for terrorism.[25]

In Northern Ireland both loyalists and republicans were able to emphasise continuity between their acts and preceding periods of armed resistance. By establishing a historical framework, republicans were able to unite historical figures and groups such as Theobald Wolfe Tone[26] (1763–98), the nineteenth-century Fenians, Padraig Pearse and the 1916 Easter Rising martyrs[27] with the post-1969 republican movement.[28] Foster (1992: 162) argues that by the mid nineteenth century,

> The emphasis on past battles, and rebellions, and the high value put on 'dying for Ireland,' helped inculcate a verbal cult of physical violence; threatening to the Irish Protestant establishment as well as the British government and inseparably part of Irish nationalism from this time on.

Nor was the continuity restricted to republicans. A loyalist legacy of normative violence and group organisation also exists. Protestant concerns over weak central government were noticeable in the seventeenth century. As the dominant minority they protested about the lack of protection they were provided with against the excluded majority. With their concerns not addressed, Protestants formed 'bands' for mutual protection and thus began a tradition whereby security arrangements were self provided. With the onset of the twentieth century 'Troubles' (Miller 1978), these 'bands of protection' became increasingly visible. The historical precedents are indicative of subsequent loyalist terror behaviour. With the exception of criminalized activities and some particular incidents, loyalist campaigns tended to be categorised as reactionary in response to republican activism (Bruce 1992, Crawford 1999). Certainly this is an image that the loyalists wanted to portray; British stalwarts against long-standing secessionist enemies. Thus when the secessionists stopped using violence, the options for the loyalists continuing with their own armed struggle were seriously limited.

Conversely, the failure of violence as a tactic in contributing towards the mobilisation of populations can result in a re-consideration of strategy. For example, after the failures of the Irish Fenians in 1867, parliamentary agitation became the preferred tactic (Fitzpatrick 1992). Alternatively, government reactions can mobilise widespread opposition and strengthen the justification for asymmetrical violence. In 1979, radical Wahhabi Islamists seized the Grand Mosque in Mecca in a manner which Niblock (2006) remarks bore comparison with the *Ikhwan* rebellion during the late 1920s. The benchmark for the challenge was the principles of Wahhabism which the leader Juahyman al-Otaibi and his followers felt were being betrayed. Instead of religion, Western norms and values were considered to be permeating Saudi society aided by the considerable foreign presence within the country. At the time of the mosque takeover there was little popular support for the insurgents. However, the reactions of the Saudi government were to award greater prominence to the groups' issues and actions. In a similar manner to the British approach to the 1916 Easter Rising in Dublin, Ireland, the disproportionate use of violence by the government transformed the protestors into martyrs for many and helped shift perceptions both about the militants and the regime. In the Saudi example, as Niblock (2006) explains, the insurgence led to the re-evaluation and re-assertion of Islamic credentials. As the following chapter explains, the government's reactive strengthening of the association with Wahhabism further shifted levels of Islamic normative standards. From the militants' perspective, the 1979 incident indicated weakness at the heart of the kingdom. These views were provided with further evidence in 1990 when the monarchy incurred considerable anger and dismay when inviting the American army to defend the nation from possible Iraqi invasion. Despite vast military expenditure, the Saudi government had effectively declared it could not defend its people, thereby electing to share the monopoly of violence with the Americans. This was not a popular decision.

A different illuminating example with which to close this section is the variable level of mobilisation for the 'red' urban terror groups from Italy, West Germany and Japan. 'Red' terrorism in Italy was much more extensive than in the other two locations.[29] Neither Germany nor Japan had an established history of Far Left opposition and certainly not one that was legitimised by success. By comparison, Italy had a strong association with socialist and anarchist ideologies in the nineteenth and early twentieth centuries which had been influenced by discursive networks of revolutionaries, particularly of German and Russian origin, and inspirational figures such as Garibaldi and Mazzini (Drake 1984, Sedgwick 2007, Weinburg and Eubank 1987).[30] Indeed, the tradition of political violence in Italy preceded the emergence of anarchism. Bach Jensen (2004) details examples from the struggle for national unification, revenge attacks and tyrannicide. Words were translated into action. The twentieth century began with the assassination of King Umberto I and violent clashes between socio-communists and fascists in the immediate aftermath of the First World War (Pisano 1979). Violence to some extent gained greater legitimacy through the involvement of the Left-Wing in armed resistance against the Nazis during the Second World War (Pisano, 1987, Weinburg and Eubank 1987). Moss (1997) comments upon how both radical fascists and the extreme Left referred to the resistance. Within the post 1969 spirals of violence, the actions were a form of historical referent. For the extreme Right it commenced the period of prohibition, victimisation and discrimination. By comparison, for the Left it symbolised the possibility of uprising and revolution against national and international forces. Because the resistance was within relatively recent memory, oral histories and autobiographical accounts were directly available from participants who provided a sense of continuity between the past and present. Links were further strengthened through the close relationships between the first generation of Red Brigades' members and former partisans. The latter provided the former both with weapons and, when they designated them as heirs to the resistance, political credibility. Reference to the resistance was, however, to prove limited. There were a number of reasons for this which Moss (1997) identifies. First, the role of the Red Brigades as the primary links between the past and present meant that this connection was seriously weakened with the group's ultimate failure. Second, the symbolic capital of the resistance was also appropriated by the Communist Party and became celebrated within society as part of collaboration between Catholics, socialists and communists. As a consequence the radical Left lost its monopoly of the symbols and narrative of the past. Indeed its usage of history was questioned, the application of violence became closely scrutinised and the continuum from the resistance to the militants fractured. The loss of the past would seriously undermine the appeal of the Left terror groups.

The histories of religions are littered with massacres and discarded corpses. Such behaviour is much less common today but this does not necessarily mean that the potential has been lost from social habitus. Islam is an easy example from which to draw in this regard. Militant groups will recall earlier periods from the time of Muhammed until the present day. Saudi militants refer to Wahhab but also to more recent influences such as the *Ikhwan*. The *Ikhwan* emerged with the establishment of a kingdom by Ibn Saud (died 1953, a descendent of the earlier ruler) and his requirement for a regular, organised army. Ibn Saud created fixed settlements for Bedouins who were to renounce the nomadic life and spread Wahhabi belief and power through the kingdom and beyond. The new settlers were to become fiercely protective of Wahhabism and interwove past experiences of tribal skirmishes with utter conviction in the righteousness of their actions (Almana 1982). Through the application of the concept of salvation via martyrdom, what were once skirmishes became battles in the name of Allah for the right to impose his word and/or achieve individual paradise. Ibn Saud had sought to utilise the *Ikhwan* for his own ends and in the short term they proved invaluable in confronting challengers to the kingdom. Ultimately though, the relationship provided what could have been a cautionary tale for subsequent Saudi governments; by encouraging *Ikhwan* to defend the spirit of Wahhabism, the Sauds allotted power, authority and benchmarking to the Brotherhood. These were increasingly applied against the monarchy; the Sauds had effectively allowed the *Ikhwan* to establish the standards on which they were judged.

Yet the government's more secular nature was ultimately going to come into conflict with the *Ikhwan*'s increasingly rigid and rigorous Islamic interpretations. And so it proved. Vigilante groups acted as self-appointed religious police and dealt out harsh punishments to those deemed guilty of infringing their teachings. Travellers were attacked, pillaged and killed. With growing confidence, Wahhabis prepared to increase their control. At this point Saud acted and by 1930 the Brotherhood had been overcome. Perhaps surprisingly, when facing defeat the Wahhabis retreated as a beaten force. This is contrary to perceptions of fanatical Muslims being willing to die for Allah, witnessed most notably in suicide bombings. Certainly the Wahhabis could be considered to be fanatical in their behaviour and beliefs. Nevertheless Almana (1982) points out that fighting to the last man was not customary within desert wars. To fight against impossible odds would be viewed as foolhardy. Retreating allowed the possibility of regrouping and 'fighting another day.'

Fatalities were often limited as a consequence of this approach to warfare. Indeed, Almana largely attributes the relatively high number of casualties in this battle to the introduction of modern weaponry and, in particular, the machine gun. Although contemporary Saudi individual and social dispositions differ from the psyches of the 1920s, the legacy of history is apparent.

Incorporation within struggles against colonial rule has also provided an important legacy, particularly when it was interwoven with contemporary discourse. Republicanism in Ireland gained considerable credibility during the struggle for independence; a struggle in which terror tactics were widely implemented. Devji (2005), Hodgson (1974) and Lapidus (2002) detail examples of Muslim rebellion against infidel governance across colonised regions including what is today Afghanistan, Algeria, Chechnya, India, Nigeria, Pakistan, Somalia and Sudan. As Devji (2005: 35) remarks, 'many of the same places ... continue to provide both sites and recruits for *jihad* today.' Hence, today's insurgence and terrorism within the Muslim southernmost provinces of Thailand stem in part from the nineteenth-century assault upon Malay Muslim identity in the name of national consciousness, Muslim adaptation of violence and continuing unresolved tensions (Croissant 2007). Under British colonialism Muslims were exhorted by more militant leaders to rise up and overthrow the rulers or move to live in territory governed by Islamic law. Thus in India, a pamphlet was published in 1867 which declared, 'It is incumbent on Mussalmans to join together and wage war upon the infidels. Those who are unable to take part in the fight should emigrate to a country of The True Faith.'[31] Throughout the region there has been a history of rebellion and challenge to rulers. Violence has been endemic during periods of particular insecurity, fear, mistrust and uncertainty witnessed most gruesomely in the massacres that followed the partition of the territory into an independent India and Pakistan in 1947. Hundreds of thousands were killed and millions on both sides became refugees. Pakistan had a bloody birth. Moreover within what is now North West Pakistan and neighbouring Afghanistan, central control has never been fully implemented. The region has become renowned for armed rebellion against numerous invaders. By comparison with the above desert example, Allen (2006: 89) reports upon the willingness of Muslims on the North West Frontier to 'choose death rather than surrender' in battle. Akbar (2004) described the situation in Wazirstan during the 1930s. The region was so turbulent that there were more British troops stationed here than anyway else in the subcontinent. Even after defeats, Muslims would regroup and adopt subversive tactics, regularly calling upon *jihad* against the infidel invader. Even today, the implementation of Pakistani criminal and civil law is somewhat 'patchy,' gun ownership continues to be a symbol of local identification and the locality remains highly volatile.

Following on from this, it can be argued that preceding forms of political control leave behind multi-layered legacies which may support or undermine government or militants' discourse. In localities that lack central and comprehensive state authority, other forms of constraint are in place that often utilise violence as a restraining mechanism that imposes forms of control. When tensions arise between localised and national behavioural parameters, as Savigear's (1982) study of violence in Corsica exemplified, there is no guarantee that the latter will dominate individual behaviour. On the contrary, many people will continue to conform to the communal habitus and according to individualised disposition even if that should set them at odds with the nation-state and its security forces. Thus in Corsica, clan rivalries and loyalties, the self-declared 'rights to bear' arms and the custom of resolving their own disputes were not restricted to economic and social matters and could be extended into political conflict and challenges to French government attempts to impose its jurisdiction.

Saudi Arabia is also a good example of the impact of development upon social relations and constraints. With the discovery and massive extraction of oil post Second World War, the nation-state attained different credentials. Alongside the self-declared guardianship of the two holy sites[32] the kingdom also had considerable resources to protect. Internal security was strengthened with huge investment in military hardware and increasingly strong alliances with the West, and in particular the United States. The surge of resources created multiple problems for the nascent nation. Niblock (2006) discusses political and economic crises that emerged from the 1950s. Social and economic divisions widened and corruption became prominent. Arguably the intertwining of religion and politics that had been weakened following the conflict with the *Ikhwan* became solidified as the monarchy sought to legitimise policies and activities through recourse to religion. Lacking theological credentials meant that only the qualified ulema could provide the requisite legitimacy. Their approval came at a cost; namely, shifting the normative standards of religiosity towards more pristine applications of Wahhabism and exporting those interpretations. Both exporters and importers of Wahhabism continue to face the consequences and these are explored in the following chapter. Today the legacy is vivid. Niblock (2006: 31) argues that Wahhabism 'is integral to the character and dynamics of the state, underlying the legitimation of the political and social orders.'

Waldmann (2007: 594) in his study of Colombia explores different forms in what he describes as a 'culture of violence.' For Waldmann violence is a dependent variable determined by historical and contemporary factors. Here, 'with a history of civil wars and violence that goes back roughly 150 years, almost every aspect of life has been shaped and marked by these forms of violence in one way or other.' Without a comprehensive legally enforced system, restraints are imposed by a variety of state and non-state actors, in which violence and coercion feature strongly. Nor is this a recent development. Since the state was founded it has lacked a national monopoly of violence. Richani (2010) explains how the state's weakness in collecting rent and taxes was allied to the inability to enforce law, restricting resources and capabilities. For potential opponents, the opportunity costs of rebellion diminished. The propensity to violence is socio-culturally anchored across a multiple of government and anti-government criminal, guerrilla, terror and paramilitary organisations. Lacking taboos to prevent individuals from attacking or to restrain excess, the use of violence is prevalent. Potential constraints are further weakened by the bifurcation of Columbian society into friend and foe and affective loyalties and hatreds that accompany the demarcations. Sánchez[33] identifies historical continuity with existing enmities and patterns of behaviour and role models can be traced back in instances for generations. Remarkably these feelings have survived the transition from rural to complex urban society and from predominantly religious to secular values. For Sánchez, this can only happen through the forms of behaviour and associated feelings being embedded within cultural memories. The extent to which brutality is so prominent is reflected by the little regard that Columbians report feeling for life or death, levels of fatalism and uncritical and widespread acceptance of violence.

Preceding social relations are also instrumental within contemporary activities. For example, female terrorists are 'underrepresented' within terror groups. One of the main reasons for this is that despite their radical rhetoric, groups are largely representative of the norms and values of the societies in which they form. Hence the invisibility of women terrorists and gender relations within groups are reflective of relations outwith the group. For example, despite the long-standing involvement of females within republicanism in Ireland, men dominated political violence. And even when women were encouraged to become involved, indeed on occasion Whaley-Eager (2008) argues it was expected, they were to return to the domestic sphere when men became available following prison sentences, etc. The connection between societal gender relations and engagement of women within terror groups can also be true in cases where females are more actively involved. Speckhard (2008) examined Chechen female bombers and discovered that their involvement was a legacy of Soviet Union dominance. With some irony, the Soviet promotion of equal opportunities, female freedom of movement and expression and collaborative working between the sexes meant that females were willing and able to engage in the struggle against the Russian remnants of the empire. Involvement in terror attacks against Russian personnel and symbols was therefore influenced by the culture which enabled women to participate and social, familial and personal histories that emphasised firm roots for independence. Entwined with these influences were recent and more distant traumatic episodes and a desire for revenge that incorporates Stalin's forced deportations and modern day atrocities committed by the Russian army. Although less closely exposed to the immediacies of war, Speckhard (ibid.) comments upon similar patterns of recruitment within Uzbek militant groups. The willingness of females to become suicide bombers was also influenced by their relatively liberated roles within society. Furthermore, across the Muslim Caucasus, conflict with Russia far precedes the Soviet Union. Akbar (2004) discusses the nineteenth-century opposition to the Russian army. A popular belief that originated from the period declared that Chechen females would only marry those who had met a number of criteria, including killing a Russian soldier. The extent to which romance also featured is less well documented.

## Conclusion

That the past continues to live on in the present is unsurprising. That there is a legacy of political violence that has been communicated and reinterpreted across generations and frequently through narrative, behaviour, memory agents, symbols and songs is perhaps more surprising. Within societies that are commonly associated with terrorism today such as Pakistan, Ireland and Saudi Arabia and those that we do not, but perhaps should, such as America and Italy, throughout the last couple of centuries there has been a lurking possibility of violent death more generally and killing for political purposes in particular. Historical configurations have existed causing communities of uncertainty, fear, unpredictability and danger. Such emotions are not conducive to pacification and levels of self-restraint are less well embedded and robust than in some other societies where terrorism is not an indigenous problem. In this regard it is illustrative to compare levels of internal terrorism within countries in which British migrants were integral to national development. Of these 'European countries overseas' (Mennell 2007) it is the United States with the neo-nationalist threat and not other locations such as Australia. This is despite, or perhaps because of, the distinctly unpromising batch of early British migrants to Australia. With different contemporary attitudes to violence that are reflected within national habitus, many Americans are less sensitive to the use of weapons, and aggression is normalised across more contours of social behaviour. The following chapter elucidates upon the significance.

In nations such as Pakistan and Saudi Arabia, internalised controls are fragile, formed during periods of uncertainty with regimes more reliant upon state restraints for compliance that are often brutal. Processes of internalisation are also relatively short-term, with historical memories of the traumatic, frequently brutal, formation of the nation-state; experiences that also help to explain the situation in Ireland. At this point it is important to stress that neither the fragility of restraints nor histories of political violence necessarily mean that terrorism will subsequently emerge. However, the possibility becomes greater when weak restraints intersect with violent sediments from the past and processes that contribute to the formation of radical habitus within contemporary societies. It is therefore to the habitus that I now turn.

# 3 Habitus

## Terrorism and violent dispositions

### Introduction

In the previous chapter, long-term processes, the pacification of populations and accompanying internalisation of social constraints were discussed. The duration of uninterrupted processes of pacification of behaviour, norms and emotions (Bogner 1992) are instrumental in the extent to which they are deeply engrained within the habitus and the degree to which taboos over the use of violence permeate through societies. The greater the numbers of generations that transmit passive norms and values to children, the more normative, robust and uncritically internalised they become, and the less likelihood there will be of these people becoming terrorists.

All forms of violence are affected by these processes yet rarely have they been completely eradicated. Emotions such as fear, insecurity, anger, rage and hatred remain embedded within social relations and activities and humans retain the biological capacity for aggression. Within societies, this potential is largely curbed through learning and internalising techniques of self-restraint. Thus there is an increase in 'the social constraint towards self-constraint' (Elias 2000: 365). However, in particular environments emotions can prove more powerful than incomplete processes of self-restraint. Violence in Western social spaces is legally restricted to sporting occasions and cultural exhibitions yet remains a feature of school, gang and nightlife cultures. In other words, although there has been a substantial shift in the extent that violence is acceptable, and the locations where it can be practised, residues remain within mainstream societies despite generations of pacification. Particular concentrations of aggression are located within specific habitus. Conversely, in 'failed states' associated with endemic aggression and chaos such as Somalia, violence is deeply embedded within social relations and activities. Since colonialism, chains of interdependence have regularly been interrupted, social and self-constraint mechanisms have been displaced and previously controlled hostilities and tensions have burst loose alongside new forms. Traumatic periods with shifting alliances, resources, power relations and socio-economic opportunities and threats inhibit the reformulation of stable habitus in which behaviour can be sufficiently restrained by self and social constraints. Armed robberies, tribal attacks, kidnapping, murder, political assassination and widespread acts of terrorism are commonplace. People are living with greater danger and uncertainty and as a consequence react to events and experiences more emotively. Violence is an accepted form of response to the surroundings.[1]

Perhaps surprisingly, extensive and widespread levels of violence are not essential for terror groups to form. On the contrary, terror groups emerge in societies which appear at first glance to be pacified. That political aggression does occur suggests that beneath the passive façade, residues of violence remain embedded within social and individual personality structures. Adopting the concept of habitus, in this chapter I examine the extent to which violence is entwined within feelings and behaviours in communities and dispositions. Reasons for the violent past remaining resonant within the present are discussed. The chapter concludes with a brief examination of some of the ways through which related ideas, feelings and behaviours are transmitted. I should acknowledge that this is not an exhaustive critical evaluation of the concept. Instead my ambitions are more restrained, orientated towards the application of habitus to processes within terrorism.

## Establishing habitus

Through the contributions of Bourdieu and Elias, habitus has become an influential concept within sociological studies that seek to understand conformity and change. Prior to their applications Van Krieken (1998) draws attention to the neglect of dispositions and habits within sociology. As with history, habits also seem to have been disregarded. Yet as Jenkins (2002) and van Krieken (1998) detail, Durkheim, Hegel, Husserl and Weber identified the centrality of habits within traditional and modern forms of behaviour.[2] Subsequently, habits became subsumed within the application of the concept of socialisation while 'folkways' largely disappeared from sociological syntax during the 1980s. Through this incorporation, van Krieken argues habitus as a concept has become immersed within the wider debate over the extent to which socialisation is deterministic. What Weber (1978) described as the 'inner habitus' has slipped from sociological consciousness.

Building upon the previous chapter there is an obvious overlap between history and habitus. If we are to understand the latter today we must possess knowledge about the social activities and ideas that have re-formulated over generations and which are largely accepted uncritically. Social memory is narrated by legitimised agents of memory and reflective, symbolic practices. Representations of the past are entwined within individual and social habitus and 'the fortunes of a nation over the centuries become sedimented into the habitus of its individuals' (Elias 1996: 19). As such historical narrative helps to shape contemporary meaning and behaviour. The past lives on within collective memory, albeit subject to transformation, intersecting with recent experiences and reflections. In the examples of Golden Ages conversely history is both re-energised and frozen in the present.

By adapting the concept, both Bourdieu and Elias sought to overcome the individual and society dichotomy that has bedevilled sociology. For Elias (1991: 182), 'The social habitus of individuals forms, as it were, the soil from which grow the personal characteristics through which an individual differs from other members of society.' Pierre Bourdieu (1977: 189–90) considered habitus to be,

> The product of the work of inculcation and appropriation necessary in order for those products of collective history (e.g. of language, economy, etc.) to succeed in reproducing themselves more or less completely, in the form of durable dispositions ... each *individual system of dispositions* may be seen as a *structural variant* of all the other group or class habitus, expressing the difference between trajectories and positions inside and outside the class.

It is thus both structured and structuring, product and producer of social worlds (Crossley 2003). Elias also draws together the inherent interrelationship between individual and social and in the process helps to explain individual and social commonality and difference. Social habitus refers to learned dispositions that are shared by people in a group, community or society. Individual habitus describes a person's learned and particular emotional and behavioural dispositions.

Following on from these points, I am arguing that studying historical processes will enable greater insight into the experiences of social life as they are lived today. Habitus is not, however, a rooted, immutable point in human development. Just as individual personalities will change over time, as people learn from others, mature, have different experiences and exposure to transforming agents and conditions, social habitus shifts. Personality structures change in accordance with the nature of the contexts and transitory human activities and interactions. Norms, values and habits continue to re-formulate within modern societies meaning that individual and social habitus are located at particular periods of history and represent personality structures of a particular social figuration. Crucially though, the complex nature of increasingly convoluted social processes and activities mean that the outcomes of actions and policies will have unintended consequences; the more people who are affected, the more difficult the outcomes are to control. This creates problems for individual and social personality structures; namely, what happens when the dynamic of social processes is rapidly transformed and the habitus is lagging behind? Does the habitus shift to accommodate the changes or do people seek to protect their identities and resist or challenge the broader processes? Elias (1991: 211) describes this as a 'drag effect' and argues that responses to the unplanned development processes will depend,

> on the relative strength of the social shift and deep-rootedness and therefore the resistance of the social habitus whether – and how

quickly – the dynamic of the unplanned social process brings about a more or less radical restructuring of this habitus, or whether the social habitus of individuals successfully opposes the social dynamic, either by slowing it down or blocking it entirely. ... One has the impression that the solidity, the resistance, the deep-rootedness of the social habitus of individuals in a survival unit is greater the longer and more continuous the chain of generations within which a certain habitus has been transmitted from parents to children.

To some extent, the remainder of the chapter, and part of the following chapter, explore restraints within different habitus and shifts according to intersections with social, cultural, economic and political developments. Social habitus is more closely examined here and developed through an exploration of individual shifts within processes of radicalisation in the next chapter.

Within the contributions of Bourdieu and Elias there are considerable similarities, including the emphasis upon learned dispositions and the acknowledgment that 'the habitus is a product of history' (Jenkins 2002: 80). Inevitably there are also differences and aspects of underdevelopment. I have tended to be more sympathetic to Elias' application because of its fluidity and greater emphasis upon historical continuities and legacies of earlier forms of conflict.[3] In this chapter I seek to draw together historical and contemporary forms of habitus that are instrumental within the formation of terrorism.

## Violence and restraints within habitus

Across nation-states there have been noticeable shifts in levels of restraints as governments have become more powerful. And if nation-states are to be defined at least in part by the protection and control they provide, then, as Weber (1978) identified, a monopoly of the means of violence within a designated territory is essential. Providing leaders have sufficient power, this can initially be achieved against the wishes of the population. If, however, the regime is looking at legitimacy and longevity, its prospects would be enhanced if the social habitus incorporated norms and values that contributed to a shift away from public violence and the need for socially imposed constraints. Instead of excessive and costly displays of military threat that insist upon obedience, individuals internalise constraints over generations. With the demise of religious institutions, covert and overt responsibility is shared across a multitude of agencies including legal systems, public education, government departments, the mass media and cultural industries. Prohibitive threats are only effective when they are in place and the personnel, armaments and accompanying bureaucracy are expensive. By comparison, when lengthening chains of mutual interdependence are in place and sufficient restraints have been internalised, the state can more confidently reduce levels of physical security. Nevertheless, no state can be completely confident in the balance of self and social restraints. Both are vulnerable to fluctuation according to events and experiences and the durability of passive social relations and activities. For instance, as Bourdieu (2000) discussed with regard to rising levels of protest in France, some assumptions and habits that are embedded within everyday life can quickly become out of step during moments of crisis and are replaced by more critical forms of social agency.[4] As Crossley (2003: 49) comments in his critical application of Bourdieu to social movements, considerable emphasis is placed upon the emergence of 'protest repertoires' during times of crises: 'protest behaviour tends to draw upon a stock of historically and culturally variable "techniques" of protest which agents learn: for example, petitioning, marching, occupation, tunnelling and bombmaking.' Thus, as Elias outlined above, there is a process of adjustment during and following interactions between habitus and the social environment and accompanying threats, opportunities, freedoms and controls.

Violence can therefore be part of protest repertoires particularly during crises. Clearly the stock of techniques to be learnt is crucial to the evolution of terrorism. Attention must also be placed upon the synchronic attitudes towards, and practices of, continuing acts of violence within mainstream society. Areas that are associated with Islamic terrorism today have long been associated with violence. At an international level, Saudi Arabia is one of the most prominent nation-states within perceptions of terrorism. Out of the 19 bombers in the attacks upon America, 15 were Saudis. Furthermore, Niblock (2006) reports that in 2004, 25 per cent of Guantanamo Bay detainees were Saudis, and 10,000 of its citizens were estimated to have been recruited into al-Qa'ida forces in Afghanistan, 2001.[5] Within Saudi Arabia there have been regular bursts of political violence, including terror attacks, throughout the first decade of the twenty first century. The immediate forerunners of the late 1990s and 2000s militants were the Wahhabis who seized the Great Mosque in 1979. Their historical lineage can be located with the *Ikhwan* who had fought since 1912 for the formation of the Saudi state. The *Ikhwan* committed thousands of violent killings and mutilations (Allen 2006) until they were defeated by forces loyal to Ibn Saud after challenging his authority. The 1979 militants shared the same Nadji heartland as the *Ikhwan*. Moreover, the association of the region with violence long predates contemporary fears over al-Qa'ida. For instance, in 1863, William Gifford Palgrave, when travelling through the region declared it to be 'the genuine Wahhabee country ... the stronghold of fanatics, who consider everyone save themselves an infidel or a heretic, and who regard the slaughter of an infidel or a heretic as a duty, at least a merit ... .'[6] This may at first glance seem to connect into Weber's (1966) argument that warriors seeking to conquer the world were the 'primary carrier' of Islam.

For Weber, violence within Islam was embedded within the religious discourse as evidenced by the use of force by Muhammed and his successors. Today's application of *jihad* could be considered to be an inevitable component stemming from the discursive foundations, part of an aggressive continuum. For the purposes of this chapter, this is problematic at three levels. First, Turner (1993) points out that Weber's characterisation of Islam grossly overlooks the vicissitudes within Islam, historical transformations and instrumental roles of diplomacy, trade, commerce and conversion within the dynamics of expansion. Second, today as in the eighth century, the overwhelming majority of Muslims do not engage in political violence. Third, Islam becomes both discourse and causal factor for violence and the social processes that contribute to aggressive behaviour are neglected or oversimplified (Sutton and Vertigans 2005). Nevertheless, despite these inaccuracies, the warrior tradition continues to permeate both within Western fears and militant reinterpretations. For example, members associated with al-Qa'ida exemplify this when describing themselves as 'holy warriors.' Hence the contemporary militant memory contains the narrative of the warrior tradition.

Violent pasts are, of course, hardly unusual. Aggressive struggles over discourse, resources and power feature throughout history and across societies. Yet terrorism is not a feature of all societies that have encountered a violent past. Therefore I am not arguing that an aggressive heritage inevitably results in subsequent terror. My central argument here is that ongoing and recent terrorism emerges out of environments where the pacification of behaviour, norms and emotions has been interrupted, partial or lacks longevity. In other words processes of pacification are not robust and normative, uncritically internalised over generations. Numerous illustrative examples can be found within South America where terrorism has been, and continues to be, prominent.

The history of violence and civil wars in Colombia, Waldmann (2007: 594) suggests, extends 150 years: 'almost every aspect of life has been shaped and marked by these forms of violence in one way or another.' Without a secure nationwide monopoly of violence and with ineffective law, Colombia's system of order is based upon fluid, unstable coalitions of civilian, criminal and government agencies. For Pécaut (discussed in Waldmann), violence and coercion are fixed components within social and political systems and the pursuit of aims. With limited restrictions upon the use of violence, aggressive behaviour becomes normative. Waldmann (2007: 596) argues that in Colombia this has resulted in escalations into 'orgies of violence' within 'a cult of annihilation of enemies.' Other factors to consider within this culture of violence include the rigid demarcations between friend and foe, a celebration of machismo of which violence is an integral component and fatalism within a 'live for today' approach to life.

In Peru Poole and Rénique (2003) identify the continued presence of violence within employment and economic practices, state abuses and opposition tactics. The terrorism of the 1980s and 1990s extended the usage of violence both in terms of targets, in particular civilians, and the nature of attacks which included torture, rape and executions as military and paramilitary 'death caravans' toured competitively through rural areas. The Peruvian Communist Party – Sendero Luminoso (PCP-SL) or Shining Path – were heavily involved within the spiralling political violence. The adoption of terror tactics by the Far Left was not unusual. Groups had undertaken economic sabotage and military engagement with government forces. The 1980s marked a shift in tactics as the Shining Path built upon the perceived failures of lesser forms of violence and extended targets to include all those who did not support the group. Spiralling violence was marked even by the standards of preceding generations[7] to such an extent that it was described as the 'manchay tiempo' or time of fear (ibid.). In essence the previous forms of violence informed the group habitus and became the benchmark by which to measure the likely effectiveness of actions. Thus, revolutionary violence was considered to be the only mechanism that could defeat state-sponsored violence. With this hypothesis, the nature and breadth of terror that is unleashed becomes an integral measure towards revolution. Reform programmes reallocated land, created massive agricultural co-operatives, fuelled massive migration to urban areas and,

> hastened the breakdown of Andean society. ... When, after 1975, the military government went into a crisis ... the great associative enterprises were left like semi-abandoned and demoralized garrisons, scattered in the power vacuum left by the state's retreat from the countryside. (Degregori 1997: 40)

The demise of the old oligarchical order, a previous history of authoritarianism and failure of the government to embed regional and national democratic reforms in the late 1970s meant that the appeal of totalitarianism rose as a solution to the disorder and decay. When developed within the culture of violence, the nature of the discursive consciousness and conviction led to a further diminution of social and individual restraints. The spiralling effect within these habitus is particularly striking. Moss (1997) compares the level of violence within Peru (25,000 deaths) and Sri Lanka (between 70,000 and 90,000) with Italy, around 400 murders. Clearly the amount of killings is heavily influenced by regimes' tactics and the number of insurgents capable of political violence. In Peru there were around 25,000 insurgents compared with a few hundred Italians involved in clandestine violence. Yet the figures fail to explain why violence became so brutally endemic in Peru. In part this can be considered to be a consequence of the correlation between the numbers of insurgents and levels of fear. Simplistically the number of insurgents is reflected in the level of fear amongst the population and government forces contributing to a higher density of violence. In turn this contributes to increasing levels of uncertainty, insecurity and hatred, which further weaken social restraints against the use of violence. This may partly explain why widespread civil conflicts generate greater numbers of deaths and atrocities than many other locations experiencing more clearly demarcated forms of terrorism.

Across other regions, numerous other more explicitly terror groups have emerged following the demise of norms and values based around family, community, customs and religion and prior to the internalisation of a new comprehensive system within individual and social habitus. Italy is a very good example with the situation compounded by malfunctioning political systems, weak national consciousness and migration from southern regions to the north and from rural to urban areas (Pisano 1979, Vinci 1979). The shifting populations placed unbearable burdens upon social services within the popular locations while simultaneously the dispositions of significant numbers of people were lagging behind the social and economic transformations they were experiencing. Moreover, existing discursive frameworks were in crisis through association with Mussolini's fascism, post-Second World War political stagnation, instability, corruption and the gradual weakening of Catholicism's hold upon morality. In these circumstances, groups that offered explanations and solutions found appeal (Jamieson 1989, Lumley 1990, Silj 1979, Tarrow 1989, Weinberg 1986).

## State and civil spillover

The centrality of the state in the monopoly of violence and shifting restraints has already been established. Despite the gradual transformation towards pacification, episodes of terrorism indicate that processes are incomplete. In some locations it is possible to argue that nation-states' approaches to violence are contributing to aggression becoming, or remaining, integral within some layers of habitus. Spillover theory suggests that there is a relationship between the extent that a state legitimises violence in certain situations and more illegitimate forms of violence such as armed robbery and murder. Although the state only permits violence within demarcated spheres the accompanying values and justification 'spillover' into other social contexts. Thus to declare that people in favour of the death penalty will be less constrained to support other forms of violence would be a reasonable supposition. Equally in societies where capital punishment is public, members of the civilian population are likely to have a different perspective towards the application of violence. Thus in Saudi Arabia and other Muslim systems of jurisprudence which implement a literal interpretation of Shari'ah law violence is a more integral method of punishment. Chopping off right hands, stoning adulterers and beheading murderers in public both reflect and reinforce habitus and the acceptance of violence as a solution.[8] For Bowers' (1984) brutalisation thesis, the death penalty and, by extension, capital punishment desensitises people to killing. Human life is devalued and the policy provides the rationale to attack those who cause offence to the individual or collective identification. The boundaries for spillover become particularly blurred when the same concepts are both implicitly supported by governments and utilised by the opposition to legitimise acts of political violence. Thus the interwoven teaching of *jihad* as a form of attack and sacrifice/martyrdom permeates through Muslim societies alongside the emphasis upon submission to religious leaders. The repetitive and widespread acceptance of the literal necessity and compatibility between both applications has become part of absolutist narrative and the benchmark for behaviour within political circles and beyond. Compromise and achieving the potentially contradictory standards becomes increasingly difficult. As a consequence, government discourse is often challenged against criteria they helped to formulate for its un-Islamic nature.

Within the West, the United States provides an excellent example of the prevalence of violence and associated ambiguities within even the most modern of nations.[9] Mennell (2007: 1) illuminates this when observing how 'the laws and customs only weakly restrain people from doing harm to themselves and others by the use of guns, and the murder rate is about four times as high per capita as in Western Europe.' The widespread availability of guns is allied to the integral symbolism of weapons within We-images of (white[10]) America. In essence the gun is symbolic within lifestyles of large segments of American society and arouses heightened emotions within the pro and anti lobbies (Crothers 2002, Karl 1995, Levitas 2002). The coinciding huge surges both in gun ownership in the mid nineteenth century and homicide rates would seem to endorse a possible connection. Alongside the individual's right to bear arms, formal levels of pacification are further challenged by state-sponsored violence. The death penalty continues to be carried out within particular states. These states were part of the confederacy that fought to retain slavery in the American civil war and included regions where, rarely punished, lynching of black people continued well into the twentieth century. In these locations, honour between whites continued to be emphasised before and after the civil war. Quarrels were often resolved according to informal codes and violent responses to particular provocations were considered appropriate.[11] White dominance over black people had been normalised throughout slavery and beyond. Power was asserted within daily life in the nature of social interactions and physical, social and psychological demarcations between white and black zones. Violence against black people was a prominent mechanism both in reinforcing perceptions of white dominance and imposing social restraint upon blacks. Aggressive attacks like these were largely ignored by law enforcement agencies.[12] In comparison with this neglect, today there is considerable public support[13] for the application of the death penalty. However, this apparent contradiction reflects a shift within those same states from popular support for 'extra judicial' murder of overwhelmingly black males to state sponsored killing of black males who are significantly over represented amongst those who are executed (Zimring 2003). Arguably the continuation of these policies has meant that ritualised violence has remained embedded within largely Right-Wing layers of dispositions which Mennell (2007) notes is more strongly represented in America than in most other Western nation-states.

Alongside the incorporation of violence within national habitus, governments also contribute to the interweaving of aggression, ideas and feelings. This has been particularly noticeable within many Muslim nation-states as governments have either utilised anti-American sentiments to generate support or sought to overcome the perceptions of themselves as USA stooges.

Thus governments that are considered Western allies such as Egypt, Pakistan and Saudi Arabia have publicly or complicitly encouraged anti-Western rhetoric. Abdallah (2006: 46) draws upon the 'paradox of Mubarak's regime ... [in] an era in which Egyptian–American relations were consolidated at economic and military levels although political discourse and media exposure were more anti-American.' Arguably such sentiments are even more pronounced in Saudi Arabia where distinctions within Wahhabism between 'loyalty and disassociation' encourage distance from infidels (Hegghammer 2009). Demarcations are further reinforced through perceptions of superiority and lack of social contact with non-Muslims which tend to result in portrayals of Westerners being somewhat crude and stereotypical. That terrorism by Saudi nationals has been directed more towards Western targets than the regime is perhaps not surprising in light of this.[14] The fundamental problem with this political manoeuvring is therefore that it contributes to the further normalisation of aggression within the national habitus.

National symbolism also features within sedimented feelings towards violence. Symbols of destruction and aggression are noticeable throughout many leading nation-states with military apparatus integral to the dominance. Power has been secured regularly through political violence or military coups across South America, Asia and Africa. Furthermore, major conflicts continue to threaten or engulf regions in places such as Indonesia, Algeria, Philippines, Rwanda, Chechnya and the Middle East. There are two particular examples of militarism that in part reflect regional uncertainties that I wish to draw upon. Over recent years Pakistan and Saudi Arabia have invested heavily in armaments. Both have experienced substantial episodes of terrorism within their nation-states. I am not arguing that there is a ludicrously simple causal relationship here. The amount of money spent on tanks does not correlate to the number and magnitude of terror attacks. Nevertheless, this is another facet of the respective societies that further reinforces the incorporation of violence within social and political relations which contribute to the justification of terrorism within particular locations.

Bandura's (1976: 128) observation provides an apt summary for this section: societies with 'extensive training in aggression and [which] make it an index of manliness or personal worth' spend greater 'time threatening, fighting, maiming and killing each other' in comparison to 'cultures where interpersonal aggression is discouraged and devalued.'

## Community layers

Contrary to the popular portrayal of the 'evil' terrorist who by implication is innately wicked, and thus beyond redemption, radical discursive consciousness forms within social interaction. This is not restricted to intergenerational acts of political violence but also the ideas and forms of behaviour which are retained within the broader habitus. These social personality structures do not inevitably mean that all people who hold the related values become violent generally and terrorists in particular. The following chapter aims to detail how complicated and difficult this process is. Nevertheless, the broader communal habitus does contribute to processes of radicalism and provides the normative standards for feelings and behaviour. Immersion within particular social habitus contributes to the internalisation of particular beliefs and values and adaptation of forms of behaviour. Arguably this habitus is instrumental in determining the likelihood that individuals will be exposed to, and internalise, radical discourses and the legitimising experiences.

Nationalist communities are the most obvious example of this. In some instances these are not widely dissimilar from radical ideas within the habitus of terrorists. Such pathways into terrorism often commence with the complimentary discursive consciousness that is acquired within, and shared with, communities. For instance, the code of honour and racial supremacy continues to be sedimented within American regionalised characteristics. When this is intersected by the acceptance of armed civilians, complicit allowance of militias and vigilantes and 'ethic of self-help' (Spierenburg 2006: 110), there is a shift to racially inspired political violence 'in defence' of white rights. However, these factors will only become instrumental if processes of pacification and individual restraints are not well embedded. In America, as Mennell (2007) explains, the higher incidence of affective homicides when compared to West European nations, indicates that '"the muting of the drives" (Elias 2000) has been less effective than in equivalent parts of Europe.' Obviously easier access to guns is also a factor and arguably is indicative of the different approaches and levels of control. Conversely, when restraints are imposed such as New York's drive to reduce gun crime, they can be effective. Nevertheless, the extent to which emphasis can shift over the longer term from government to individual controls will depend heavily upon the restraints becoming sufficiently embedded and robust within individual and social dispositions. As I explained earlier, this requires security and trust which cannot be formulated and deeply embedded over the short term. Challenges over the monopoly of violence allied to the insecurities, threats and fears that were prevalent within slavery and subsequent racial structural arrangements inhibited the shift towards self-restraint. Today heightened fears over employment, immigration and insecurities stemming from crime and terrorism have connected into the history of self-defence and militias. 'Citizen volunteers' such as the Minutemen, many of whom are armed and supported by white supremacist groups, in Arizona have worked alongside border patrols in seeking to stem illegal entry. And because of the blurred boundaries between volunteer and extremist groups, the incorporation of the Minutemen provides formal legitimacy to the racial underpinning for the immigration patrols that extends into radical ideas within habitus.

Within communities that are demarcated according to nationality, ethnicity or religion, interaction across the boundaries is usually restricted. Limited social interactions contribute to the foundation of stereotypes which become embedded both within 'We' identification and stigmatisation of the 'Other,' following what Fanon (2007: 81) described as the Aristotelian logic of the 'principle of reciprocal exclusivity.' Collective memories abound with narrative and images that are associated with particular spaces and contribute to the demarcation. Agents of memory create and re-create representations with place, time and peoples. The Palestinian territories and Northern Ireland provide illuminating examples with divisions accepted, encouraged and contributing towards collective forms of identification and detachment. For instance, in 1968 just prior to the 'Troubles,' two thirds of all families lived in the streets of Belfast, Northern Ireland, where 91 per cent of households belonged to the same religion (Arthur 1997). Urban interfaces are strategically marked with opposing flags, emblems, murals and graffiti to reinforce collective memories and consciousness. Historical images are utilised to connect with the present; with the gradual demise of previous generations who had participated in the Somme, Easter Rising, war for independence, partition or civil war, agents of memories have been essential within the utilisation of historical images in the maintenance of common memories. For loyalists, Jarman (1997) argues, Unionist iconography tends to depict the past in terms of blood sacrifice, Catholic duplicity and fear of betrayal (by the British). Sacrifice also features prominently within nationalist iconography. These help to reinforce positive perceptions of the in-group. By comparison, the 'Other' is an established figure of hatred with accompanying feelings and emotions inculcated into individuals from childhood. Social exchanges between the opposing groups are restricted to verbal and physical forms of violence. Symbols become integral in reinforcing negative emotions about the 'Other' and with limited interaction, there is little opportunity to offset the stereotypes with contradictory experiences. Thus, thirteen years after the Good Friday Agreement physical and psychological divisions remain between the respective We groups and the possibility of more widespread forms of reciprocal political violence remains.

Alongside physical barriers, social and cultural boundaries have reformulated distinctions with habitus. For instance, the Gaelic challenge to Anglicization within Ireland towards the end of the nineteenth century re-energised the Irish language, poems, songs, legends, folk tales and clothes (Foster 1989). In this regard there was a reconnection with the traditional interconnection between literature and politics that has often been described as a 'bloody crossroads' (Kiberd 1992). Folk songs and music could be added to the catalogue. Although initially cultural, Gaelicisation was to raise awareness, confidence and assertiveness in a sense of being Irish and related achievements that were to feed into and become interwoven with the republican movement. Michael Collins, the IRA leader, declared that 'We only succeeded after we had begun to get back to our Irish ways.'[15]

As I discussed in the preceding chapter, previous violent experiences as both aggressor and victim can remain integral to the contemporary. The involvement of females (and males) within Chechen militant groups was heavily influenced by 'a mass societal trauma that still lives on in group consciousness' (Speckhard 2008: 1027). Recent actions by the Russian government are viewed through a continuum that incorporates confrontations between Chechens and infidel Russians since the eighteenth century. Mobilising history includes episodes under the rubric of *jihad* and mass deportation during Stalin's regime (Johnston 2008). When these actions are considered within a habitus that incorporates a duty to revenge, less constraints and greater liberation of women, feelings can transcend into behaviour which in Chechnya has meant women becoming terrorists and attacking Russian targets. However, as the preceding chapter also indicated, women can become terrorists within environments that could, with some justification, be classified as patriarchal. In the Palestinian territories, there has been a shift in restraints as females were, initially begrudgingly, allowed to participate within terror attacks. Again if we examine forms of female behaviour that preceded the attacks, females of all ages were centrally located within the first *intifada*. Prior to that, women were involved within the secular precursors of today's more religious terror groups. Leila Khaled is the most notable example. Consequently, although there has been a subsequent shift in gender balance towards further male dominance, the legacy of greater female participation remains within the habitus. Compared to other Arab societies and while acknowledging that the society remain male-dominated, Copeland (2002: C1) argues 'Palestinian women have been the most liberated.' Similarly women continue to acquire higher education and pursue professional careers. For instance, Speckhard (2008) details the achievements and experiences of a couple of female suicide bombers which challenge the popular perception represented by Victor (2004) and the centrality of employment, educational and social restrictions to motivations. Speckhard and Ahkmedova (2006) also challenge the tendency to categorise Muslim suicide bombers, noticing that support for such attacks[16] and the 'cult of martyrdom' are much less noticeable within Chechnya than in the Palestinian territories.

In the studies that draw upon gender involvement, numerous similarities between the sexes in terms of experience and motivations were overlooked. This is symptomatic of most studies of gender which Fausto-Sterling (2000) argues continue to search for differences and not similarities. In terms of habitus, girls also attend kindergartens and school where they are exposed to a curriculum laden with declarations of Palestinian heroism, sacrifice, Israeli brutalities and the religious obligation to fight for Palestine (Burdman 2003, Oliver and Steinberg 2005).

By comparison, if the emotions within the group are more detached from the community, they will be more isolated. Shared historical memories and commonality of feelings between communities and nationalist groups like IRA, ETA, HAMAS, Islamic Jihad and Chechen militants were arguably factors behind their considerably greater levels of support compared to ideological groups such as Red Army Faction, Red Brigades and Japanese Red Army which failed to connect across their respective societies. Within these cultures of opposition or resistance (Foran 1997), there can be resources, traditions and symbols that stimulate feelings of endurance, determination and sacrifice in circumstances in which victory is by no means guaranteed. Instead, groups may adopt a long-term strategy to which members contribute. These individuals may never witness the achievement of their goals and may never expect to. Yet their contributions to the possibility of an eventual victory provide sufficient satisfaction. Nevertheless, these commonalities cannot be assumed to invariably provide the basis for nationalist support. Wieviorka (1997) details how this is contingent upon militants and populations sharing the same aspirations and, I would add, fears. Basque nationalism was seriously eroded by democracy alongside stability and prosperity: conditions which undermined the broader demands for independence while contributing to the acceleration of terrorism. Subsequent attempts by trans-national groups such as those associated with al-Qa'ida have also failed to recruit in massive numbers (Vertigans 2009). Arguably this is in part because the internalised historical memories and collective forms of national identification of potential supporters provide a defence against the appeal of radicalism. There is a bounded restraint that is hard for alternative emotions to penetrate. Certainly people are angered by Western policy, outraged by Israeli incursions and morally repulsed by the deaths of women and children. Nevertheless, the social constraints they have internalised and collective loyalties prevent these emotions from becoming triggers into terrorism. Within national settings such as Chechnya, Northern Ireland, the Palestinian territories and Sri Lanka, the emotions were more inclusive and representative of the communities. By comparison the feelings of the ideological and trans-national groups were more exclusive, not engaging with non-participant's experiences.

Further important distinctions can be located within demarcated public spaces in localities such as Northern Ireland, Sri Lanka, Palestinian territories, Kashmir, Philippines and Chechnya, where large numbers of the respective populations share opinions about the nature of the problems (inequality, repression, poverty) they encounter, the cause (governing nation) and solution (independence). They also tend to share a reconstitution of history with narrative that affirms ethnic unity, heroism and cultural and political demarcations. This has enabled associated terrorists to largely be embedded within the communities. Emotions, discourse and strategic goals continued to be shared with family, friends and neighbours although not necessarily the adoption of violence. Within these localities conflicting beliefs become normative. They became sustained and reinforced by contemporary experiences, common history and discourse that groups such as the IRA, HAMAS, UVF and Tamil Tigers (LTTE) have been able to utilise in order to recruit members and retain wider support. In her study of political violence in Italy, della Porta (1995) identified the importance of police brutality, state authoritarianism and indiscriminate attacks against demonstrators and activists. These events and experiences contributed to an atmosphere in which violence was considered to be an appropriate, indeed the only, appropriate response to violence. Within these dynamics, spirals of hatred accelerate as state and non-state actors become embedded within reciprocal forms of violence. If groups and surrounding 'civilians' continue to share sufficient emotions and experiences within these settings and the former are widely considered to be acting in support of the latter, then the extent of detachment is restricted. This is not to say there is none; the clandestine nature of terrorism means that even within supportive communities, those participating within actions are unable to share their experiences and feelings with non-members. By comparison, with the exception of the above Italian example, groups such as the 'reds' of the 1970s and 1980s did not share dispositions with most of their societies and the emotional distance between them was greater.

## Broader movement

Forms of discursive consciousness feed into norms, behaviour and emotions, providing frameworks of explanation both for problems faced and solutions. The more successful groups tend to be part of a broader ideological movement with which they share a number of norms and values and which are explored in greater depth in the following chapter. Thus terror groups have formed at the extreme of numerous nationalist, Marxist and religious movements and multiple locations including South America, the Middle East, Western Africa, South and Southeast Asia. With regard to religiously inspired terror groups, Ranstorp (2003: 124) notes that 'Almost all the contemporary terrorist groups with a religious imperative are either offshoots or on the fringe of broader movements.' Today, it is possible to notice a shifting and blurring between ideological demarcations. Hybrids are forming between the discourses as singular forms become discredited by failure or pragmatism. Thus religion and nationalism is interwoven within diverse groups such as the Christian Far Right in America, Hindu Tamil Tigers in Sri Lanka, HAMAS and Islamic Jihad in the Palestinian territories, International Sikh Youth Federation in India while Marxism and nationalism can still be located within South American terror and guerrilla groups.

The foundations of pathways into terrorism very often occur within the community or nation. For instance, although groups such as The Covenant, the Sword, the Arm of the Lord and The Order were to some extent physically and psychologically detached from mainstream America, there was considerable overlap between their discourse and those of the dominant political hegemony of the period. As Hamm (2007) outlines, during the early 1980s the Christian Right was in the ascendancy and became interwoven within patriotism and conservatism. In this regard, the new movement should be considered as part of the legacy of Puritanism. This is rooted within American conservatism and provides the moral framework with which to establish boundaries between good and evil. Populist campaigns that concentrated upon immigration, scarce public services and crime were implicitly underpinned with racial and migrant connotations. Through these relationships, the national religious curriculum within schools shifted in content, and the traditional family was promoted as the cornerstone of American life. By comparison, matters such as abortion,[17] pornography and homosexuality were widely denounced as immoral, the fallout from the 1960s permissiveness and counterculture. Radical groups 'were marching in lockstep with the Reagan-era zeitgeist' (Hamm 2007: 97).[18] These issues were happening alongside the 'great transformation of American society with regard to matters of race' (Omi and Winant 1994: 94) as white supremacy has been challenged from the early 1950s and ultimately replaced by the concept of 'racial equality.' Within the transformation, barriers to political and social participation were formally removed, much to the consternation of white racialists. For them, as for other members in positions of perceived dominance, the changing nature of the relationship became a challenge to their super-ordination and the basis for their identified superiority. This is because,

> Even under the most favourable circumstances ... a chain of several generations is usually needed in the life of a people for completion of the transformation of personality structures which facilitates the secure functioning of a multi-party parliamentary regime. (Elias 1996: 294)

Moreover, earlier adoptions of violent behaviour can then become the best predictor of subsequent behaviour. Post *et al.* (2002) outline the predisposition within groups to become involved in violent campaigns when leaders and/or members have previous experience. The recruitment strategy of the Real IRA which targeted disaffected members of the Provisional IRA is indicative of this. Arguably this can also apply when other discursive groups have practised political violence during a preceding period as outlined in the previous chapter.

Groups not connected to broader social movements have tended to be, as Hewitt (2003: 61) remarks, 'small, short-lived and responsible for only a handful of incidents.' Within Europe it is illustrative to further compare the intensity and extent of 'red' terrorism in Italy and West Germany. In the previous chapter, I outlined historical reasons why terrorism was more extensive in Italy. There were also contemporary issues with which they interacted. Both countries experienced unrest. In Germany this was largely restricted to the student and counter-culture movement. By comparison, the wave of unrest that spread within Italy during the late 1960s incorporated both students and workers within uprisings, protests and strikes (Pisano 1979).

## Threats to the habitus and solutions within

Within ideologies such as those associated with militant religious groups, the Far Right in the United States and, to a lesser extent, loyalists in Northern Ireland and pro-government groups, death squads and Right-Wing extremists in Central America such as Mano Blanco (White Hand) in Guatemala, principles, beliefs and standards are embedded that stem from the past. To varying degrees, these are ideals that are rooted in perceptions of greatness, a 'Golden Age' when the discourse was implemented in its pure essence accompanied by actions of heroism and devotion that continue to be the source of pride within contemporary forms of identification. Long-lasting fragments from previous forms of social habitus usually incorporating symbols and customs prove durable within modern dispositions. That these are socially constructed and the accuracy of the synchronic narrative questionable has become irrelevant with the passage of time. 'All traditions are created ... through shared practice, and they can be profoundly and consciously modified and manipulated under the guise of a more legitimate earlier practice' (Eickelman and Piscatori 1996).

Ahmed (2004) and Akbar (2004) outline how the origins of Pakistan proved instrumental in subsequent fears over challenges to (Sunni) Islam from neighbours, other religions and Islamic denominations, most notably Shi'a.[19] For instance, experiences under British colonialism, the gruesome massacres committed during partition of India, impressions of Muslims being under threat, the usage of Islam as the one unifying form of consciousness and subsequent politicization and incorporation of religion by governing regimes, most notably during the leadership of General Zia ul Haq,[20] have all become interwoven within national and trans-national habitus. Akbar (2004) suggests that Zia's policies led to Islam being radicalised with contours reformulated. Hitherto, Christians had largely avoided the outbursts of violence. Now they became incorporated within the revised and extended demarcation lines between the Sunni Muslim 'We' and the remaining groups loosely categorised as the 'Other.' Although they had not been involved with the violence of Partition, the refocused targeting of enemies included the West and merged with the bitter local history under colonialism.

Comparing the contemporary mundane with the extraordinary past can contribute to wistful longing for tradition and a detachment from the morals and principles of the present. And as Elias (1996) identified with respect to the rise of Nazism in Germany, the appeal of idealised aspects of belief rises during times of crises. Thus Left-Wing surges of support in South America, shifts in racial laws in the United States and re-evaluation of political boundaries within Northern Ireland have all been accompanied with a competing and challenging We resurgence in symbols and slogans that connect to a preceding habitus. If the struggle over issues such as inequalities, political representation and lifestyles becomes sufficiently significant then as Stuart Hall (1985: 113) explained with reference to race, 'social reproduction becomes a contested process.' In these environments, social and political consensus is seriously undermined, mutual interdependence and empathy becomes weak. Crucially all the above forms of social protest have transcended into terrorism partly, I argue, because the perceived shifts in national consciousness left the militants feeling like detached outsiders. Consequently, they were less emotionally attached to the nation and its peoples. Elias has pointed out that greater functional democratisation is accompanied by enhanced levels of empathy and the likelihood of inter-group tensions diminishes. This does not appear to apply in the above examples. On the contrary, these groups chose to attack when national functional democratisation became more substantial. Greater incorporation of ethnic minorities within power relations and economic opportunities is considered to be at their expense.[21]

## Competitive habitus

Situations with two competing terror groups provide different dynamics. For instance, as Chapter Six outlines, sectarian terror killings were often instrumental within spirals of violence in Columbia, Iraq, Italy and Northern Ireland. A common perception held by one 'side' is that very often they are an extension of the state on whose behalf political violence is committed. In Northern Ireland, loyalists defended their actions as being in accordance with British identification even if the government was not necessarily appreciative of their efforts. Under this reasoning violence can only be justified as part of a defensive, reactive strategy to republican aggression. When loyalist groups appeared as aggressors then they became detached from the role as defenders of the community and public support diminished. By comparison, as Hayes and McAllister (2005) explain, republican violence was embedded within Irish politics to such an extent that it had been enshrined within the Irish republic's constitution which in turn had been heavily influenced by preceding phases of violence. These historical and strategic reasons for the justification of political violence were, Hayes and McAllister (2005) argue, instrumental in understanding different sectarian attitudes to decommissioning.

Exposure to alternative discourses or lifestyles can also contribute to a strengthening of individual and group beliefs. One such example is the emergence of new religious movements and counter-cultures during the 1960s in America which led to a shift in more conservative forms of Christianity. In the 1970s and 1980s this culminated in a surge in the New Christian Right's cultural and political activism (Dawson 2006). Similarly, rising visibility of secessionist and Marxist guerrillas groups have activated pro-state groups in Northern Ireland, Guatemala and El Salvador while the emergence of fascist and pro-government groups in Germany, Italy and South America during the 1960s and 1970s were strongly linked with the formation of Far Left groups. By comparison, the damaged German national consciousness and collective feelings of guilt that were internalised by subsequent generations contributed to a lack of positive We-images. For the children of the Nazi generation this contributed to a restricted collective consciousness and certainly a reluctance to express national sentiments. Without nationalism to help bind the defeated nation, emphasis was placed upon development and consumerism without addressing the void within levels of We-ness. Many within the younger generation sought alternative discourses to explain the feelings and fears they were experiencing. In this regard, the decision to reformulate extreme Left discursive consciousness was unsurprising (Elias 1996).

From the waves of student protest across Western cities in the late 1960s in America, Japan, Italy and West Germany people became committed both to non-violent direct action within social movements and political violence. The relative youth of those involved contributed to a lasting impression that terrorism is for the young.[22] For those who became engaged in violent action, peaceful protest was considered to have failed and terrorism was considered to be the only solution. The terror (and non-violent) leaders and members possessed cultural and social capital with which to critically oppose and formulate alternative discourses and groupings. In the West German example, the above characteristics of the younger generation are, for Elias (1996), given added resonance by the national habitus. He examines the legacy of the German military tradition which was so instrumental in the emergence of Nazism. What is, however, less immediately apparent is that the sediment of those same values existed within the habitus of the Left-Wing groups that were so vehemently opposed to the possibility of fascism returning. Thus characteristics such as absolute conviction, determination and unwavering loyalty to principles alongside a portrayal of compromise as a betrayal of ideals are noticeable across a trajectory that stems from the aristocratic militarism of the nineteenth century. For Elias, strategies of compromise make for more difficult navigation for individuals across social landscapes. Proscription and prescription provide clearly demarcated routes. Navigating through compromise is much more complex, with both means and ends open to negotiation that requires insights into tact and sensitivities that can only be acquired through exposure. In this regard there was a clear lag between the democratic arrangements adopted by the post-Second World War West German state and the more rigid absolutism that continued to reside within layers of social habitus.

## Migrant international habitus

Thus far I have concentrated upon figurations and habitus transforming around clearly demarcated areas. Throughout history, individuals have consciously sought to change their habitus through relocation for social, cultural, economic, political and legal reasons. Elias (1991: 236) describes the demand for a change of social habitus which people aim to achieve through migration. Yet the choice of destination, transition and accommodation are all restricted by the pre-migration habitus. Processes of modification and reinterpretation abound during, and after, migration. Particularly pertinent examples can be found both within Pakistan and Pakistani immigrants to the UK. Migration from rural to urban areas or to different countries can contribute to what Roy (2004) refers with respect to Muslims as 'deterritorialised communities.' For migrant Muslims, Roy argues, the process of resettlement or uprooting leads to a reassessment of their beliefs and often a subsequent reconstruction of Islamic identity. Migrants and subsequent generations caught between cultural norms and values from the country of origin and those of the new home country can experience a process of de-culturation as the 'pristine ethnic culture' fades with each generation. Communities become places of shelter from recurrent problems that migrants encounter (Elias 1991). For second and third generations different problems arise as they acquire the social habitus of their parents and language, customs and morals of the host country. Personal, generational, ethnic and nationalist tensions arise as individuals seek to reconcile values and forms of behaviour that are often contradictory. There are a number of alternatives:

1 Some members of the later generations remain integrated within the habitus of their parents.
2 People can become detached and shift towards the dominant mainstream culture. However levels of discrimination, racism and defined contours of national identity may limit this option.
3 Of most interest here, individuals can formulate hybrid responses to the situations in which they are located. For these people, religion and ethnicity become sources of shared commonality and solidarity, proving feelings of unity, beliefs, rituals and prescriptions amidst displaced collective memories and discarded, outmoded forms of behaviour.

Transnational movements, allegiances and explanations can appeal to these people through a form of international habitus. The attraction of global *jihad* and the al-Qa'ida franchise should be considered within this broader movement and habitus. Both Gunaratna (2003) and Sageman (2004) have identified the disproportionate involvement of migrants within major terror attacks since the late twentieth century. Again though, it is important to stress that there are historical precedents. For instance, Akbar (2004) notes how, in the late twelfth century, responses to Saladin's call for a *jihad* against Richard the Lionheart[23] came from as far away as India. Of course this was long before the emergence of processes of globalisation that are often viewed as inherent within forms of international Islamic militancy.

Yet what the studies of the impact of immigration upon radicalisation often overlook is that it is male centric. Female migrants do not feature prominently within terror groups in the West. The lack of women in contemporary Muslim groups is all too easily explained by patriarchal, traditional families and communities. Certainly there are elements of this. Nevertheless for the 'traditional' to be a universal feature we would expect male British Muslim bombers to originate from such families. This has often not been the case. Moreover, as Speckhard (2008) explains, the experiences of first to third generation females differ from males, not only in the potential restrictions that are placed upon the behaviour of many women, limiting opportunities for radicalisation. Unlike males, female migrants do not suffer the drop in status that many men experience on arrival. In short, these women had already been awarded secondary status. Speckhard (2008) argues that many girls are more flexible in their approach to learning and study harder at school than boys who struggle to adapt to the family's drop in status. As a consequence they are able to extend their knowledge and interests beyond de-territorial experiences and become more integrated into the host society. Hence, unlike females who do not become radicalised because of their restricted enclosure within familial safeguards, the incorporation of some of the other women within societal employment, political and cultural spheres can diminish the likelihood of their radicalisation.

## The political solution: Freedom or suppression

Political arrangements can also be instrumental in radicalising layers of habitus. Shifts in balance between social and self restraints with greater emphasis upon the latter can create spaces for terrorism to emerge particularly within democracies. There is a long standing belief that terrorism emerges when movements are denied other political forms of expression. However Hafez (2003) and Rashid (2002) have identified a number of recent instances of the 'successful' repression of opposition in Algeria, Central Asia, Egypt, Syria and Tunisia. In situations such as these, personality structures are aligned with the dictatorial regimes and there is a greater willingness by individuals to accept orders and be guided by external constraints and hierarchies of constraint. If people do not obey they are quickly encouraged to adapt their personalities or are constrained by state forces of surveillance and correction (Elias 1996). Numerous historical instances of this can be drawn upon. Anarchists in Germany and Russia were largely eradicated through persecution, imprisonment and execution (Aydinli 2008, Bach Jensen 2004). Thus these radical groups were suppressed. However, the underlying processes that led to their formulation were not addressed. Consequently systemic problems remained and anarchism was to be replaced by other powerful forms of radical discourse, namely communism, socialism and fascism.

By comparison within some democratic arrangements, militant movements have become incorporated within mainstream society over generations and contribute to the internalisation of pacification. In Woodcock's (2004: 917) study of anarchism, one anarchist is included who wrote about the lack of anarchist fervour in northern Europe. This was, at least in part, because the anarchists enjoyed 'the prestige that in northern lands is granted to those voices crying in the wilderness, which form the conveniently externalized consciences of peoples largely devoted to the acquisition and enjoyment of material prosperity.'

Nevertheless, democracy is not a universal panacea. Terrorism occurs across a multitude of political arrangements including democratic (Gurr 1998 and Lutz and Lutz 2005). Functional democracies across Western Europe, North America, Japan and on occasion within some South and Central American states such as Guatemala, El Salvador and Chile have all witnessed prominent terror threats.[24] Therefore, terrorism can be operational within countries where the state's monopoly on violence is tenuous such as Colombia and Somalia, where it is all embracing like some of the above examples and perhaps more surprisingly to Western perceptions, in liberal democracies. Under repressive regimes, challenges to governments are often curtailed within extensive apparatus of control. Therefore as Elias (1996: 235) argues, 'human groups usually revolt against what they experience as oppression not when the oppression is at its strongest, but precisely when it begins to weaken,' which, in this instance, also accords with the political opportunity structure thesis. The actions of Euskadi Ta Askatasuna (Basque Country and Freedom) or ETA are a case in point. Although ETA formed during the Franco dictatorship, their actions intensified as the Franco regime weakened. With the transition to democracy, 'it became more violent and more separatist. ... Terrorism escalated just as democracy had indisputably established itself' (Wieviorka 1997: 295). Furthermore, migrants from authoritarian regimes to liberal democracies have also reconstructed discursive consciousness and become more radical. The most notable example was the Hamburg cell that was instrumental in the September 2001 attacks on America. Members appear to have consciously decided to adopt political violence as a form of behaviour after arriving in Germany from more authoritarian regimes.

Further distinctions within the spectrum of dominant political arrangements need to be drawn to accommodate groups such as the loyalists in Northern Ireland and Far Right in America. Other groups may denounce oppression, injustice and police brutality but the reported incidents lack the extensive, pernicious nature of the constraints imposed upon preceding generations in Germany and Italy and contemporaneous Egypt, China and Russia. At this point, there is a danger of apparent contradiction as all three latter countries have encountered terrorism[25] and of the former two countries, Italy under Mussolini experienced episodes of terrorism, including attempts on Il Duce's life. Consequently, I should stress that there is not a political system that can be guaranteed to incorporate potential radicalisation and prevent attacks of political violence. The likelihood of this eventuality is heavily influenced by the duration that self-restraints have been internalised and levels of mutual interdependence, functional democratisation, stability and security. Democratic institutions and accompanying civil liberties, security, pathways for consensus and compromise and self-controls must become developed and embedded within dispositions and behaviour before tensions can be contained within the democratic framework. Therefore, in situations where authoritarian regimes are overthrown and replaced by democratic institutions there will be a lag between the new political structures and individual dispositions which are more attuned to formal processes of decision-making and visible forms of external constraint.[26] For Elias (1996: 291), the long process of attunement in Britain has contributed to it being 'one of the few countries in which, so far, a parliamentary state structure and an individual personality structure have become attuned to each other in a comparatively friction-free way.'[27]

## Conclusion

In summary, just like other forms of behaviour, political violence is part of individual and social dispositions. As with other forms of social behaviour, the forms did not emerge in a vacuum; nor could the roots be unearthed within the soiled minds of crazed individuals. Terrorism is learned, it relies upon communication, shared and competing norms and values and levels of social and self-restraints. Processes of social control and interwoven forms of collective identification and functional democratisation were insufficiently developed or in some instances had become threateningly over-developed at the expense of the previously self-declared dominant groups. In other words, processes of pacification are partial, incomplete or can be undermined. For terrorists this has meant that violence as a form of behaviour can be adopted because radical norms and values have proved more influential or the restraints they have internalised are not considered to apply within particular settings. In some instances violence has been encouraged by communities within these localities. Nationalist struggles would be such an example.

That pathways into terrorism so often emerge in places with histories of political violence, state-sanctioned capital punishment or the normalisation of aggressive behaviour is not coincidental. As this chapter has shown, contemporary habitus in these locations contain violent sediment from the past or in other words dispositions are 'soiled' with aggressive ideas and forms of behaviour or history. Through the intergenerational transmission of narrative, mythology and symbols, violence has been retained and is expressed as a form of political action during the intersection with particular conditions. These include perceived threats to, insecurities of, and uncertainties within, the habitus which contribute to challenges to the opposing 'Other.' The habitus therefore becomes both the source of protection and protectors. In the following chapter, processes through which groups form and individuals join and thus become 'protectors' of habitus or intended creators of new forms of disposition are explored.

There is a danger here that this emphasis upon dispositions could be read to imply that identifying the responsible habitus will enable counter-terrorism to be more precisely targeted and ultimately victorious. Or in other words, I have created the sociological equivalent of the psychological profile. I hasten to add that this is not the intention. Within the remainder of this book I reiterate, with almost repetitive regularity, that just as there is no single profile nor is there one habitus in which terrorism forms. On the contrary, the multiple locations, ideas, emotions and forms of behaviour are indicative of distinct forms of habitus. Such differences should not, however, preclude investigation. The study of individual processes of radicalisation did not end with the realisation that Osama bin Laden and Leila Khaled have fundamentally different personalities. Much can be learnt about individual pathways into terrorism. Similarly, considerably more information can be obtained about the social figurations in which people's journeys in and out of terrorism occur. Consequently, in the following chapter, the socialising agents that interweave the history and contemporary habitus and broader movements and terror groups are explored. Through this exploration we can postulate the processes whereby people join and form groups.

# 4 Becoming a 'terrorist'

## Processes into groups

## Introduction

In *Distinction*, Bourdieu (1984) demonstrates important differences in the extent to which the educated middle classes are more inclined towards engagement in the public sphere in comparison with the working class. Just as the middle classes' habitus enables them towards greater involvement and higher levels of attainment, in the previous chapter I explained how the social dispositions of terrorists and social layers in which they are immersed means that they have a greater propensity for political violence. Nevertheless it is not inevitable that people who share common memories based around symbols, sites and narrative alongside accompanying exposure to recollection of past, or exposure to present, forms of political violence, will become terrorists. Individual and social restraints have to loosen or be part of incomplete processes of pacification resulting in less effective controls than in societies not challenged by terror groups. At the same time, there has to be a synchronic shift away from the nation, institutions and peoples who become the targets of attack. Thus feelings of attachment and interdependency towards the enemy must be sufficiently weak if individuals are to become willing to be part of groups that seek to injure, scare or destroy. The likelihood of this happening depends on a number of 'how' and 'why' factors including the existence of terror groups, their recruitment policies, pre-existing connections with members, peer dynamics that can contribute to groups forming their own terror cells and the impact of triggering events. Although as Dawson (2010: 7) explains,

> Normally we are not in a position to explain the actual reasoning of individuals who join NRMs [new religious movements] and *jihadist* groups. Their choice is shrouded in an element of mystery no matter how hard we press. But the research to date has a funnelling effect, in the sense that we can progressively restrict the range of potential converts, and the ways in which their conversions were managed.

For individuals to join terror groups, funnelling indicates that emotions have to be transformed. During radicalisation, the potential terrorist has to disengage from social restraints postulated by agents such as family members, friends, employers, many media outlets and school teachers. In other words they cannot join groups when holding consensual views that conflict with radical ideas and behaviour. Hence existing affective ties have to weaken, alternative social relations become tighter and the appeal of the terror group is greater than other potentially contradictory forms of relationship. Through socialisation new or revised social bonds are (re)constructed and internalised. The formulation or extension of beliefs and distinctive patterns of behaviour and accompanying cognitive and affective transformation often begins, at least for the first generation of terror groups, within the wider movement.

## Broader movement

The significance of the social habitus within the broader associated movement was discussed in the previous chapter. In this section I want to explore this in greater depth, in particular the ways in which the wider entity helps the individual to accommodate the shift towards political violence. Once again, studies of social movements are instructive in this regard, explaining how participation within protests or movements can create a disposition towards further political activism or what Crossley (2003: 50) described, in his application of Bourdieu's perspective to social movements and rational action theory, as an 'activist' of 'radical habitus.'[1] Individual radical dispositions are obviously closely connected to biographical experience; but following on from Bourdieu, the biography is interwoven with, and influenced by, their structural locations and broader historical processes. Crossley (2003: 52) provides a number of salient points that are also pertinent for processes into terrorism. These include:

1 'Perceptual-cognitive schemas which dispose agents to question, criticize and distrust political elites and processes.'
2 'Political know-how to transform this distrust and criticism into action.'
3 'An ethos which encourages engagement.'
4 'A "feel" for protest and organizing which allows agents to derive purpose and enjoyment from it, to "believe" in it and to feel "at home" doing it.'

   'Only some people protest, according to this point of view, because ... only some have enjoyed biographical exposure to the formative experiences that increase one's probability of acquiring the disposition to do so' (ibid.).

These processes are noticeable within the formation of terror groups and individual decisions to join groups. Within broader movements, participants internalise schemas, acquire political know-how, learn about how to engage and the purpose and pleasure of protest. McAdam, Tarrow and Tilly (2001) explain how these experiences can help to facilitate reform or contribute to destabilising processes in which extremism emerges. These aspects are developed in this, and the following, chapter along with the more condensed processes for subsequent generations. Certainly there is a strong connection between broader movements such as student groups, resurgent Islam, civil rights movements, Christian Identity and 'red,' Muslim, Republican and Far Right terrorism. The movements were instrumental in mobilising broad support, for informing and forming networks that were to contribute to the subsequent emergence of terror groups and recruitment therein. These movements had already challenged the dominant discourse while simultaneously 'proving' the justification and potential of political protest. Movements and organisations such as the Northern Ireland Civil Rights Association (NICRA), Students for a Democratic Society (SDS), ANAPO Socialist Party, the Christian Identity and militia hybrids in the US, alongside associations such as the John Birch Society and the first *Intifada* in the Palestinian territories, were all to varying degrees successful in raising the profiles of social, economic and political problems and the legitimacy of challenging the status quo. The shift to radicalism was indicative of participants' relative detachment from national state structures. As Paz (2002) noted with regard to radical Islamic groups, wider movements contribute to an atmosphere of heightened levels of extremism that provide greenhouses for the germination of terror groups. Today similar processes can also be observed within the United States and the Right-Wing populist rebellion epitomised by 'tea parties' (Potok 2010). The blurring of boundaries between social, religious and political movements across concerns about the federal government, economy, immigration, healthcare and abortion has contributed to a greater sense of opposition and collective identification as part of a manifest shift in Right Wing politics. Although normative levels are not extreme they have incorporated strands of radicalism, conspiracy theories and racism. In the process they become legitimised by their prominence, interwoven within contemporary habitus that more extremist groups connect into. Moreover, the recent evolution of this opposition shares a number of similarities with the movement from which Timothy McVeigh, the Oklahoma bomber, emerged in the 1990s.

Without the more passive protest groups initially challenging the hegemonic dominance and transforming emotions of apathy, disillusionment, frustration and shame into pride, anger, hatred and hope, it can be difficult to contemplate terror groups emerging. Conversely the failure of these movements to achieve the aims of the more radical supporters following a period of raised hopes and expectations (Davies 1971) led to splinters emerging and some disillusioned members disengaging from social and political protest. Groups such as (Columbian) M-19, (Peruvian) Shining Path, (American) Weathermen, (German) Red Army Faction, (Italian) Red Brigades, Japanese Red Army, (Palestinian) Islamic Jihad and HAMAS, Irish Republican Army and (Spanish) ETA emerge from the fragmentation with members' emotions re-directed. Political violence was to be become a consciously selected tactic directed towards achieving their aims (Degregori 1997, Florez-Morris 2007,

Pisano 1979, Vertigans 2008, Zaroulis and Sullivan 1984). In essence violence is adopted because other political alternatives are considered either to have failed or to be unlikely to be successful.

That the groups emerge out of broader movements[2] is also important when seeking to establish levels of broader support and thus the likelihood that greater numbers of people will be radicalised. Despite the fracture or breach across the movement's discursive spectrum, there are shared ideas and beliefs. Movement members' decisions not to join terror groups in part reflect a disagreement over the use of violence; they are often broadly sympathetic towards the terrorists' aims such as national independence or greater re-distribution of power and resources.[3] It is this commonality that terror groups seek to extend and governments seek to contract. However, the actions of the latter are often instrumental in surges in the former's popularity. Subsequently terror groups utilise government acts and policies to help mobilise opposition, often adopting similar campaigns to social movements such as 'public awareness' and 'issue awareness campaigns' with particular attention placed upon shifting the consensus through media coverage. Obviously, as I discuss below, the task is much more difficult for terror groups because mainstream media operators are more inclined to be supportive of government actions and opposed to seditionists.

At a practical level engagement with broader social movements also allows for gradual radicalisation that is easier to accommodate within ontological security. For Crossley (2003), the social movement field[4] provides a 'home' for individuals radicalised during particular crises. Within this field, rules, networks and forms of activity help to stave off disillusionment, thus maintaining what Bourdieu referred to as the 'illusio.' By this he meant participants recognise that the stakes of the game are worth competing for. The decision to join a terror group and the site of struggle can be extremely difficult or costly in emotional terms, often involving deception of family members and friends alongside possible arrest and risk to life (Moghaddam 2004). Individuals also have to be willing to directly support or to be willing to kill in the name of the group. Discursively this requires what Bandura (2004: 140) referred to as an 'evolvement process' as individuals' beliefs shift towards greater allegiance with those that share the same collective identification and away from people holding rival alternatives. Involvement can follow a trajectory that becomes noticeable initially through attendance at demonstrations and meetings, before members are involved in more integral, yet relatively safe, roles such as distributing leaflets and fund raising[5] and, in the case of members of groups such as HAMAS, participating in funeral marches (Asal *et al.* 2008) and low level militant activities (Hafez 2006). Through long and more immediate processes of socialisation individuals are orientated towards radicalism and ultimately terrorism. A member of the Italian Prima Linea Vincenza Fioroni reflected the experiences of many terrorists when declaring that 'For 10 years I had been engaged in social struggles in unions, in school and in my neighbourhood. It seemed to me that nothing had changed and so the armed struggle was the last resort.'[6]

In this sense, Bourdieu's application of Weber's elective affinity has relevance. There is a certain fit between particular individuals' values and terror groups that contributes to people wanting to join and being accepted. From the group's perspective the gradual progression can also be informative, enabling greater opportunities to establish the individual's suitability, monitoring reliability and trustworthiness (della Porta 1988, 1992). The matter of elective affinity is also noticeable within the number of female members participating and the nature of their roles. For instance, female participation across different levels in the Western 'red' groups was striking. Although as I mention elsewhere this did not indicate egalitarianism, it was reflective of shifting perceptions of the roles of women and rising levels of female empowerment across the affected societies. In the case of Italian groups, Cunningham (2003) observed how women were overwhelmingly attracted to Left-Wing organisations and not the fascistic. These groups' ideological messages for political and social change were attractive. Despite continuing forms of sexism, perceptions of gender equality did permeate throughout the groups including leadership levels. Hence, the ideas that were being promoted were to some extent being practised within. Consequently there were fewer barriers to women being involved across organisations and within leadership roles than in most other terror groups.

## Shifts into terrorism: The emotional and rational

If, for now, we artificially detach the emotions surrounding terrorism, the long-term intention behind the strategy can largely be viewed as a demand for significant political change, whether that is the introduction of far Left and Right discourses in South and North America, a global *ummah* across Muslim societies, national independence for the Basques or national unification for (northern) Irish republicans. Terror groups are therefore mechanisms for collective political action and in this section I want to discuss how and why people become involved. There has been a tendency to assume that recruitment has been a top-down approach, led by manipulative leaders who target the vulnerable and susceptible. In this regard, studies of social movements are informative.

At the most noticeable level, individuals who often want change are dissatisfied, encountering injustice, inequality, discrimination and relative deprivation, and consider peaceful protest to have failed.[7] Within early studies, relative deprivation theory was influential. Subsequently, as I explained in early chapters, resource-mobilisation theory, new social movement theory and rational choice theory were particularly critical of this approach. This was largely because most people tend to have grievances and do not become involved. Consequently, other studies sought to understand why people joined groups and incorporated other factors within the decision-making of participants such as the extent to which they thought the situation could be changed to their benefit. Hence, this is part of an instrumental paradigm in which individual resources and perceptions are incorporated. Although rational choice theory in particular has been subjected to considerable criticism, the paradigm has become more nuanced and individual decisions and interests have been embedded within social networks. The depth and intensity of these relations helps to explain the extent to which individuals become involved (Kim and Bearman 1997). Klandermans (2007) also points out that for those involved within movements, material costs can often outweigh benefits. Consequently other factors must be involved such as collective identification,[8] the benefits to the individual of group membership and the opportunity to be involved in the expression of ideas. As McAdam (1986: 64) observed with high-risk activism in the Freedom Summer, 'an intense ideological identification with the values of a movement disposes the individual toward participation ... .'

Conversely, studies of other movements such as converts to religious cults discovered that, although processes of recruitment were often gradual as individuals were introduced to ideas and ways of behaving and participated in discussions, many new recruits had much to learn about the new religion. These believers effectively join before a fundamental shift in their beliefs and world-view (Robbins 1988). Similarly Bjørgo (2009) explains how in most cases young people who join racist groups gradually adopt extreme views when they are part of the group. Somewhere in-between these accounts are Bakker (2006) and Sageman (2004), who discovered that the levels of faith of *jihadists* increased in the months prior to them joining or forming groups. And as Bjørgo's (2009: 32) analysis of Neo-Nazi groups showed, there are multiple reasons behind involvement. These include perceived threats, feelings of provocation and anger, protection, thrill seeking, attraction of violent and militaristic elements, search for substitute families, father figures, friends, community, status and identity. Irrespective of both initial motivations and levels of discursive consciousness, Taylor and Horgan (2006: 594) suggest 'that explicitly (through training) and implicitly (through attribution of meaning), political ideology and organisational factors become increasingly influential in determining the individual's behaviour and the choices made ... .'

Thus boundaries between rational, emotional and discursive influences begin to blur. Emotions of participants within social movements are also constructed through interweaving with cultural and historical processes (Goodwin *et al.* 2001). To encourage recruitment, movement leaders strive to interweave emotions with moral, cognitive and instrumentalist attitudes. For the first generation of participants in the terror group decision making largely occurred over several stages. The shift for subsequent generations is, however, often different. Their emotional journeys are often condensed, connecting into an explanatory and moral framework that group founders had established as they sought to overcome moral ambiguities (Silke 1979, Vertigans

2008). The different stages in group evolution at which individuals join are also reflected in their motives. Crenshaw (1983) notes how first generations can be united out of a collective sense of deprivation and grievance. Following the introduction of counter-terrorism, subsequent generations are in part reacting to government approaches. In the face of intense confrontation and seeking to maintain groups they gain support through calls for revenge and brutality. Certainly this seems to be indicative of 'red' groups where time also allowed for subsequent generations to make better informed decisions. In Italy Weinberg and Eubank (1987) discuss the significance of cognisance with the preceding generation and their successes and failures. Through this knowledge later groups were better able to judge the costs, risks and opportunities. However, I would add that this would depend upon the stage in the spirals of violence at which they joined and the extent that attacks was motivated by emotional demands for retaliation. These periods of insecurity and threat can hinder the detached rational approach that 'lessons learned' requires.

Consequently processes into groups are not lone pathways. Instead there are multiple routes into and through extremism. Motivations identified within other studies range from altruism on behalf of the nation,[9] religion or people, to addressing injustice, overcoming discrimination, to revenge attacks and egoistical self-interest associated with opportunities to change personal circumstances, to increase material income, levels of power, personal salvation, pleasure, status[10] and excitement.[11] For women, reasons provided also include love, romance, the need for male approval,[12] sexual disgrace,[13] avenging their lover's deaths[14] or because they have been drugged, blackmailed, kidnapped or raped.[15] As von Knop (2007: 400) remarks, in many studies there is a suggestion 'that female subordination is linked to female participation in terrorism.' If we move beyond the tendencies to reduce female involvement to male manipulation or to domesticise their reasons for joining and instead acknowledge that both men and women are influenced by social and individual factors, then as Speckhard (2008) argues, a variety of similar emotions are integral across processes of radicalisation.[16] Of course, the emotions impacted upon how 'everyday life' was viewed. As a former IRA member explained, time with the group 'gave a strange edge to my life: I lived each day in a heightened sense of alertness. Everything I did, however trivial, could seem meaningful. Life outside the IRA could often feel terribly mundane' (Collins 1997: 158).

## Triggers

Within individual shifts into terrorism the impact of particular events is well documented. People are reported to be recruited to terror groups after witnessing or hearing about particular attacks, experiences of degradation and humiliation[17] and emotions of hatred and anger. These are triggers or what Silke (2003) calls 'catalysts,' della Porta (1995) 'precipitating factors' and

Lofland and Stark (1965) described as 'turning points' in their study of processes of conversion to a (cult) 'deviant perspective.' Personal accounts for the motives and related events behind joining groups should be, as C. Wright Mills (1940) noted, with regard to underlying causes of the act, treated with caution, not least because they are often relayed 'after the act.' Nevertheless a regularity and consistency of responses can be identified across case studies which contribute to greater confidence in the 'memories' of those involved. For instance, della Porta (1992), Jamieson (1989) and Silj (1979) discuss how actions of 'red' and 'black' terror organisations tended to be reciprocal as each group sought to avenge attacks by the other in spirals of violence. Similarly in Northern Ireland aggression between republican and loyalist paramilitaries tended to be within spirals. The threats from rival groups and reactions to attacks proved instrumental in surges of recruitment to both republican and loyalist groups (Bruce 1992, Crawford 2003, Taylor 1998, 2000). During times like these, emotional and cognitive (re)framing can occur. When this happens, people can be disposed to become part of wider groupings in which they find frameworks of explanation and purpose that are often lacking during periods of uncertainty and crisis. Within particular habitus, it can be argued that the higher perceived levels of crisis, threat or insecurity the greater the demand and appeal of terror groups. For example, at the onset of the Troubles in Northern Ireland and during particular periods of heightened tensions such as the Republican hunger strikes in 1981 there was rapid growth in recruitment for both 'sides' (Taylor 2000, Vertigans 2008). As the following chapter discusses, the subsequent challenge for terror groups is to retain these new members when this collective effervescence dissipates.

At the level of the individual, many have reported being motivated by the actions of national security forces as witnessed by the anger and mobilisation of support following the deaths of Left-Wing protestors and subsequent transformation into terrorism, death of activists in terror actions (Ayers 2003, Jacobs 1997, MacDonald 1991), rival terror attacks (Jamieson 1989, Taylor 1998, 2000) and the killing of Right-Wing militants by American federal agents which led to them being declared martyrs within the broader movement. The deaths were seen to be symptomatic of the threat of the US government (Berlot and Lyons 2000, Dobratz and Shanks-Meile 2000, Flynn and Gerhardt 1989). From the 1990s, concern over controls over gun ownership was heavily influenced by emotional attachment to the American constitution and the right to bear arms. Crucially the historical legacy of American independence has become interwoven with rising fears about a 'New World Order' and the need for individuals and militias to be able to protect themselves from the threat of international armies and in some accounts, the American administration (Crothers 2002). These fears were set against the backdrop of federal government armed raids that were framed as part of the war against individual rights. Thus the constitution seems to have been influential in the radicalisation of Timothy McVeigh (Michel and Herbeck

2001). At an international level, American involvement in Afghanistan, Iraq and Saudi Arabia and complicit support for Israel has contributed to rising levels of anti-Americanism which finds expression at the violent extreme as declarations of revenge for Muslim deaths that the administration has been held accountable for. Conversely the perceived international failures of America have, Dees (1996: 75) argues, 'left millions [of Americans] angry and unsure of America's role in the world.' The challenge to American hegemony whether from communists outwith or liberals within has become central to Far Right discourse over the post Vietnam years (Vertigans 2008).

Numerous accounts of the factors behind the mobilisation of men and women in the Palestinian and Chechen struggles for independence refer to Israeli and Russian actions. These attacks impact to such an extent that revenge is sought for the arrest or killing of family members and friends (Kimhi and Even 2004, Speckhard and Akhmedova 2006, Victor 2004). Alongside these emotional factors, more materialistic causes can be considered. For instance, Beg and Bokhari (2009) detail how al-Qa'ida and the Taliban are reported to have 'purchased' *jihadis* by the promise of three meals per day and a life of honour now and in the afterlife. There are also numerous accounts of payment to Palestinian suicide bombers.

Clearly these accounts are important and cannot be easily discarded. Nevertheless events such as the hunger strikes or various American examples, from above, have to be rooted within the underlying processes that interweave history and habitus in order to explain why some people are motivated to become terrorists and others are not. These events interact with particular habitus and individual dispositions that result in some people joining or forming terror groups.

## Roles of socialising agents

Alongside the existence of a broader movement and triggers, involvement with a terror group can only occur through contact with a recruitment agent. There are signs that the form of these agents may be changing in accordance with advancement in IT and related forms of communication. Nevertheless other, more 'traditional' forms remain influential. Overall, socialising processes are hugely significant to such an extent that Silke (2003) suggests that becoming a terrorist is primarily a consequence of socialisation. Although this may be overly deterministic and neglects some of the other historical and contemporary factors outlined here, the role of socialising agents requires considerable consideration. In essence, socialising agents transmit the history and are integral in the internalisation of habitus. Just like other forms of social interaction and the internalisation of norms and values, socialising agents are essential in the (re)formulation of dispositions. At a basic level, communication between terrorists is usually in a shared language with common symbols and meanings that have largely been acquired during formative years or deliberately inculcated. The same processes of understanding and identification are also apparent within the moral and ideological basis for adopting terrorism as a strategy. If groups are to form they too must formulate discursive consciousness and be able to communicate with each other in person, by telephone, via email and across chat-rooms.

In this regard, as Chapter Five in particular outlines, the terrorist field becomes instrumental in the shift from non-violent tactics to acts of political violence. At this stage, it will suffice to point out that despite similarities within the wider habitus, individuals are exposed to a variety of different forms of activities and social interactions that help shape alternative networks and cognition. This is in part because the nature and roles of socialising agents have shifted, and will continue to evolve in order to accord with the changing experiences and expectations embedded within economic, political and social transformations. Thus in many instances the expansion of larger public institutions such as education, social welfare and social control agencies has been at the expense of the family. Accompanying the shift in responsibilities have been different forms of social restraint and greater emphasis placed upon the individual. Regardless of the changes, people continue to learn about radical ideas and behaviour from agents that they associate with or are exposed to. Crucially, in the overwhelming majority of cases, individuals already know the people that effectively recruit them to the group.[18] The following section therefore explores a range of relevant agents such as education, peers, media, family, religious institutions and prisons.

## Education

At present the most notorious agencies associated with terrorism are madrassas. The dramatic growth of these religious schools across Muslim societies and communities has contributed to shifting levels of religiosity.[19] Pakistan provides a clear example with their madrassas achieving international prominence following the rise of the Taliban. Thousands of recruits had attended religious schools where they acquired a seminary type education that often consisted of a literalist interpretation of Islam (Allen 2006).[20] Akbar (2004) refers to a parallel state as Islamists, who were excluded from power at the inception of the country, introduced madrassas as a way of generating greater religiosity and thus support. Despite their high profile, though, only a small percentage of schools are believed to teach militant interpretations (Beg and Bokhari 2009). Nevertheless, the failure of the Pakistani government to rigorously monitor curricula has meant that over recent years schools have been teaching radical norms and values to children.

The involvement of 15 Saudis in the September 2001 attacks also meant that the Kingdom's religious schools have been subjected to external enquiry (Admon 2007, Kepel 2004). Hegghammer (2009) reports on the subsequent heavy criticism that the education system attracted including emphasis upon Saudi superiority, ethnocentrism and relative neglect of other cultures. Internationally the Saudi government's huge investment in the establishment of religious schools, mosques and Islamic materials in other countries has contributed to growing numbers of graduates from madrassas. At one level this has contributed to radicalisation within other countries. Croissant (2007) details the situation in southern Thailand where upon returning from studying abroad graduates have become involved in teaching within local communities. In the process they share their more radical ideas and forms of behaviour which becomes normalised across school cohorts who in turn graduate and pursue their own opportunities. Consequently the depth and breadth of religiosity continues to increase.

Within many schools across the world *jihad* has been repositioned as a central pillar of the faith, other religions and weaker Muslim interpretations are regularly denounced as immoral and 'irreligious' regime actions and policies are condemned as apostate. That the benchmark may be to the benefit of ideologues who lack theological credentials and who issue religious edicts with limited or no historical precedents is neglected as dispositions quickly become ingrained and accepted. In this manner, the burqa becomes the norm, the morally justified form of females' appearance.[21] *Jihad*, the abode of war and martyrdom become uncritically accepted expressions within daily discourse.[22]

Despite the importance of religious schools in exposing pupils to religious discourse and the formulation of literalist dichotomies, there is little evidence to directly connect these institutions with terrorism and related skills. Sageman (2004) argues, for instance, that this type of 'top-down' ideological indoctrination is less important than the bottom-up networks in which groups tend to form. Nevertheless Magouirk (2008) suggests that at the more radical madrassas, individuals are provided with a meeting place. The schools are a focal point for others with similar ideas and where, I would add, these ideas can be developed. In essence, within the madrassas social networks can form that will be instrumental in the formation of terror groups.

Although religious schools have tended to receive the most attention, more secular schools can also be instrumental in normalising demarcations between groups. In Northern Ireland the separation of children on sectarian grounds immediately divides pupils into two distinct groups. Opportunities for breaking down the psychological barriers and processes of stigmatisation are therefore minimised. Instead the schools compound divisions with separate curricula that connect with their respective populations. Thus in Palestinian schools, children are taught about the virtues of Islam and martyrdom alongside anti-Semitic and anti-Zionist statements (Burdman 2003, Oliver and Steinberg 2005). Protestant schools in Northern Ireland tend to have an ecumenically sympathetic religious ethos and teach a version of Irish history that emphasises Britishness (Irvine 1991). Equally Catholic schools are sympathetic to their denomination and imbibe an Irish nationalist version of history. Across the schools different sports, music and literature are taught and practised, further reducing opportunities for commonality (Brocklehurst 1999, Gallagher *et al.* 2003).

These demarcations are not only created or reinforced within conflict zones. Within the United States there is a growing trend towards home schooling or small collective learning centres as parents remove their children from 'godless,' 'liberal' education systems. Many of the parents belong to the Far Right and teach their children about the violent roots of the nation, the central role of early white settlers and subsequent citizens and (white) Christianity (Bushart *et al.* 1998, Singular 2001, Sonder 2000).

Although learning institutions are clearly important for many people who become terrorists, their impact cannot be examined in isolation. The increasing prominence of the media has also attracted considerable attention over the possible impact on recruitment.

## Media

The media is often a tool for recruitment and is integral to contemporary forms of communication, unintentionally helping terror groups to achieve their primary short-term aim, namely to terrorise. Today, without media coverage this would be markedly more difficult. Extensive coverage provides groups with platforms that are denied non-violent groups, enabling levels of fear and insecurity to be inflated and awareness of the group to be magnified. Although most media operators tend to be opposed to terrorism as a form of political behaviour and the accompanying discourse, they are interested in terrorism as an event. First and foremost terror attacks, particularly within the West and/or against Western targets, are highly newsworthy. Moreover, with the monopoly of violence the cornerstone for their existence, governments tend to allocate considerable significance to acts of terrorism which the media reports, often in a manner which inflates the extent of the threat. Governments are also quick to disseminate information relating to successful counter-terror strategies which again tends to attribute terror groups with being a credible threat and to raise the status and profile of particular leaders who are targeted for attention.[23]

Groups also develop their own media strategies that seek to communicate directly with supporters and potential followers. Through their own cultural resources they try to insert their 'own voice' into the debate. Methods range from more basic methods such as graffiti and posters to journals and websites, DVDs and podcasts (Bushart *et al.* 1998, Bunt 2003, Lumley 1990, Sonder 2000, Weinberg 1986). Within the Palestinian territories this is particularly overt as television channels transmit programmes and music for both adults and children that promote and symbolise political violence and martyrdom (Burdman 2003). Posters and murals are also noticeable within nationalist struggles to attract support and justify actions. Whaley-Eager (2008) notes how the LTTE used posters that predominantly featured female cadres that were intended to overcome families' traditional reluctance to send daughters to join, to provide credibility for their group's claims for gender equality and to incite men through comparable challenges to their bravery.

Occasionally individual actions and sacrifices become immortalised within songs. Such a tradition is particularly noticeable within the history of Irish republicanism.

The advent of the Internet has also provided terror groups and potential recruits with new opportunities. Today suffering can either be personally experienced or virtually witnessed. Within the radicalisation of contemporary Muslims, Burke (2006), Khatib (2003) and Sageman (2008) have detailed the impact of videos and the Internet. Images of atrocities and humiliations have been instrumental in mobilising terror opposition to the responsible forces although, following on from an earlier section, it should be stressed that these are triggers and not causes. One of the most cited examples of virtual suffering and anger followed the killing of a twelve-year-old boy, Mohammed al-Dura, by an Israeli soldier during exchanges with the Palestinians. Sageman (ibid.) reports that the incident has become one of the most watched Internet videos and was reported to be instrumental both in the second *intifada* and processes of radicalisation beyond the territories. Emotions tend to be heightened when watching videos like this and are associated with moral outrage and desire for retaliation. In this particular example, the youth and innocence of the victim further inflamed feelings and demands for revenge.

The potential impact of the Internet is not restricted to emotional arousal. Within what Weimann (2006) called the 'online terrorism university' it is possible to acquire considerable knowledge about different discourses, groups, strategies, methods of activity and techniques in order to be able to commit acts of terrorism. In so doing, websites become portals that enable potential terrorists to become part of networks, to be self-taught and form their own groups. Nevertheless, as Stenersen (2008) observes, there is little evidence that terror cells have become 'virtual-only.' Instead the Internet tends to be a resource bank that is utilised alongside other more traditional training that requires personal contact. Consequently, rather than describing the Internet as the university it is more accurately considered as a 'pre-school of *jihad*' in that it provides the basics on which to develop. In the same way individuals rarely become terrorists just by accessing militant websites. They have been actively searching for the information and images. Therefore they wanted to witness particular events, read certain insights, communicate with militants; they were already shifting towards radicalism before accessing the site. Sageman (2008) explains how these sites tend to reinforce impressions rather than create them. Rather than assuming that those involved are passive within processes of radicalisation he points out that the anonymity of websites and relative security enables bolder, often more aggressive forms of expression than they would express in person. Within the virtual network, discussion forums become integral, providing opportunities for debate which is instrumental in transforming opinions. In essence, Sageman is challenging impressions of the passive, gullible young Internet user who is virtually manipulated. Instead they select their forums, learn and review the debates that can often rage between opposing websites and which in turn they discuss on-line and/or with friends and relatives. For Sageman it is this exchange that is crucial in the shift to *jihadism* and not simply witnessing particular atrocities. This is not to argue that militants are not manipulating individuals on the web. Potential recruits can be groomed, with individuals from open forums carefully selected and invited to participate in more secure, closed sites that are more likely to have ties with violent organisations such as those associated with al-Qa'ida.

Finally, the Internet could be anticipated to feature prominently within the roles of migrants who were shown, in the previous chapter, to have been highlighted within many studies of processes into terrorism. Migrants are very much embedded within popular conceptions of terrorists who are recruited, and recruit, through virtual communications and join trans-national groups alongside individuals from around the world whom they never meet. Not for the first time, the popular perception is misplaced. Certainly some individuals do become engaged through electronic relations; however, Bakker's (2006: 34) study of migrant *jihadists* in Europe details similarities within networks in terms of homogeneity. People who became involved tended to share 'age group, country of family origins and the country in which they live.' As Sageman (2004) and the following chapter explain, terror groups generally recruit participants through lengthy processes that require personal interaction. The focus therefore shifts to an agency which perhaps best provides this interaction, namely peers.

## Peers

Just as pre-existing friendships have been identified within studies of recruitment into religious and social movements,[24] their significance within processes into terror groups is becoming increasingly recognised. As McAdam (1986: 80) declared, when discussing pathways into 'high risk' activism within the 1964 Freedom Summer movement, 'Having a close friend engage in some behaviour is likely to have more of an effect on someone than if a friend of a friend engages in that same behaviour.' Indeed Diani (2007: 342) argues that 'the more costly and dangerous the collective action, the stronger and more numerous the ties had to be in order to support decisions to participate.' Certainly this seems to be borne out by numerous studies of terrorism that argue that recruitment through friends and kin is generally more successful than recruiting among strangers. For instance, della Porta's (1992, 1995) research stressed the importance of friendship in the recruitment of West German and Italian Left-Wing militants. Sageman (2004) identified that pre-existing friendships were important in 68 per cent of cases of individuals joining terror organisations. Interaction within peer groups can contribute to the formulation of strong inner bonds and synchronic weak(er) extra-group relations. Closer emotional ties result that unite members and detach them from those that they increasingly oppose. This also applies within processes that result in the formation of groups. Silveria Russo, an

Italian 'red' member, declared that 'Prima Linea came into being ... out of a group of friends who used to meet in a bar in Sesto and wanted to be Robin Hoods.'[25]

Within nationalist communities, childhood associations often continue to resonate and provide links between friendships and paramilitary organisations. As 'Alan' explains to Horgan (2009: 53),

> And some of the guys that I had grown up with had taken that course [joined UVF] quite a number of years before I eventually joined, so it was ... I probably socialised with some of them, and so it was just a matter of them, ah, making them aware that you were interested in becoming involved with them.

Again similarities can be drawn within more general processes through which friendships tighten and familial ties are less binding. As the child matures and encounters different generational experiences, these provide commonality within the peer group and distance from older familial generations. Sageman (2008) has also commented upon the importance of friendships at an earlier age among Muslim migrants. For instance, five of the seven bombers involved in the 2004 Madrid attacks and who subsequently collectively committed suicide were discovered to have been childhood friends. Individuals leave their countries of origin and often search out old friends and associates in the new locations. After making contact migrants quickly become immersed in the wider social networks. If these groups are radical, for Sageman, there is a distinct possibility that the migrant will adopt similar ideas and forms of behaviour.

Inner dynamics can also help explain the association between migrants and terrorism (Bakker 2006, Leiken 2004, Sageman 2004, 2008). For instance, the Hamburg cell that was integral in the September 2001 attacks on America was radicalised in Germany. They were educated migrants encountering discrimination, feelings of alienation and disillusionment whose principal source of commonality was Islam. During the early stage of their relationship Sageman (2008) points out that the individuals involved would conform to conversational courtesy and discuss shared interests and traditions. In so doing they formed a micro culture and collective identity. All had originated from societies in which communal relations were given greater priority and We-feelings were more clearly defined. Relocating to Hamburg with its greater 'I' emphasis and individual physical detachment from the source of We-ness meant that the migrants had to accommodate these changes. Religion therefore seems to have become a central component of their initial search for companionship and subsequent friendship, the prism through which other relations and experiences were viewed and the framework for ontological security.[26] It was Islam that became the discursive form of expression through which their dissatisfaction with the migrant experience and international relations was relayed.

Consequently, comradeship and friendship is integral to processes of recruitment. Khaled al-Berry (2005: 8) draws upon this when explaining that when he joined a radical Egyptian group, 'I wasn't attracted to their brand of religion: I was attracted to them as people ... it's like a new group of friends. At that time you already like them and want to be one of them because you like their courage and sense of devotion.' Analogies with the family are also drawn when militants discuss the appeal of the group and their experiences within. For one of della Porta's (1992) 'red' respondents, the 'comrades became my family ... it is the sense of a family.'[27] These dynamics are not unique to particular discursive groups. Horgan's (2009) interview with a former member of a Norwegian Right-Wing extremist group, who was convicted of bombing a mosque, exemplifies the appeal of social networks. During their meeting 'Lars' referred to the sense of isolation he felt after moving to Oslo. Through social events held by racists Lars gained a sense of belonging and developed friendships. Following on from an earlier point, members of these different groups tend to share common localities and experiences that prove instrumental in their radicalisation. Certainly discursive consciousness is important but group dynamics are instrumental in processes of internalisation.

## Family

Just as with the other agents, the role of kinship in transmitting radical norms and values and engagement in processes of recruitment varies. Some studies of urban 'red' groups such as those by Ferracuti (1982) did not discover any instrumental links between parents and their children in decisions to join or form terror groups. By comparison, Zahab (2008) identified the significance of the family whose explicit blessing was often critical if individuals were to join the militant group *Lashkar-e-Taiba*. Members of other nationalist Islamic groups in Palestinian territories[28] and Lebanon (Davis 2003, Post *et al.* 2003, Reuter 2004, Victor 2003) and transnational global *jihadis* (Bakker 2006, Sageman 2004) have also reported the importance of family support in their decision-making. Post *et al.*'s (2003: 177) interview with a Palestinian terrorist is indicative in some ways of the intense and widespread penetration of norms and forms of violent behaviour. For this Palestinian, 'the entire family did all it could for the Palestinian people, and won great respect for doing so. All my brothers are in jail, one is serving a life sentence for his activities in the Izz a-Din al-Qassam battalions.' When socialised within these environments, it is often more surprising when people do not join the groups rather than when they do.[29] Highlighting different possible pathways, Gerges (2005, 2006) documents Islamic militants who hid their involvement from their families and often ran away in order to make more substantial contributions.

Nor is the socialising role of family members restricted to Islamic groups. Kinship is often instrumental in the early stages of radicalisation and in deciding whether to join nationalist groups such as the IRA and INLA in Northern Ireland (Horgan 2009, McDonald and Cusack 2005) and ETA in Spain (Reinares 2004). For example, a former IRA member Marion Price mentioned to English (2003: 129) that she had been 'born' into a republican tradition on both sides of her family 'so we always grew up with republicanism.' There are numerous similar quotes from both republicans and loyalists. The struggles and discursive consciousness 'were the kind of things that you learned very, very young about … .'[30] The transference of familial emotions based around resentment and stereotypes was pronounced. Indeed, group members are often integrated within communities and are part of organisations that are held in relatively high regard as defenders of the community. Harking back to the study by Tönnies, within closer community relations we will usually find closer kin ties. Thus it is much less surprising that, where children and parents feel emotionally close and live in communities considered under threat, there is support across the generations for the actions of those who are viewed as their legitimate defenders. Moreover these connections are more likely to become apparent during long lasting tensions and conflicts. Florez-Morris (2007) explains how lengthy conflicts can often mean parents and subsequently their children become involved. Within Colombia the duration seemed to impact upon the extent to which younger generations were influenced by the earlier participation of older generations. Again similar observations have been made about other diverse groups such as Northern Irish republicans[31] and German neo-fascists.[32] If we were to crudely demarcate between the studies that did not identify family connections and those that did, we could argue that those in the latter tend to be from groups that are more representative of wider communities who are what Silke (2003: 39) described as 'marginalised at birth,' while the impact of peers was more marked for ideological groups.

In addition to the intentional influence of the family, processes of recruitment can also be unintentionally affected by antagonistic relations. Florez-Morris (2007) discusses how parents can be both intentionally and unintentionally involved in processes of recruitment within Columbian terror groups. By design, parents' ideological convictions contributed to their offspring joining the armed struggle. Alternatively, some children from families that were opposed to the armed groups joined as a form of rebellion against their parents. Similarly, West German 'red' groups (MacDonald 1991, Varon 2004) and Islamic militants interviewed by Gerges (2005, 2006) talk about their rebellion being both against government failings and their parents passivity.

## Religious institutions

Yet another controversial agent associated with the formation of terror groups and individual radicalisation has been the religious institution. And because terrorism connected to Islam is currently most prominent, the mosque has become integral to perceptions of processes of radicalisation and or brain-washing as the 'popular' press like to describe it.

Prior to September 2001 there was considerably more transparency within Islamic militancy. Radicals would openly meet and recruit at mosques, be involved in information centres and charities, promote books, organise rallies and distribute leaflets. Post September 2001, public spaces associated with Muslims have been subjected to surveillance and numerous militants have been arrested, deported and placed under house detention. Subsequently militancy has gone underground or relocated to virtual realms. The impact on mosques in the UK has been illustrative. Once closely associated with radical religious leaders such as Abu Hamza and Abu Qatada, today's mosques have largely been sanitised. Nevertheless they continue to be places to meet people in similar situations and in some regards this has not changed. Indeed, the explicit impact of mosques and preachers has often been exaggerated, not least as it is easier to target resentment at identifiable enemies, especially those like Hamza who fit the role of pantomime or vaudeville villain so effortlessly. Radicalism also occurred beyond the prominent stage performers whose presence was always a distraction and easily monitored within these theatres of extremity. With the end of these public shows militancy has gone further underground and infor-mal religious study groups have become more influential and interwoven with friendship (Gerges 2006, Hegghammer 2006 and Stemmann 2006).

Of course religious institutions have featured within the shifts towards other forms of terrorism. Within nationalist struggles religious denominations have become interwoven. For instance in the Basque region, collective identification and violence were cultivated in school, the Church and through family and cul-tural forms of expression (Wieviorka 1999). However, the different institutions do not agree upon the means to the ends of independence. Despite the view that the conflict in Northern Ireland was a 'religious war,' in reality religious institutions tended to be restricted to roles supporting the community. Although loyalists believed that 'the Roman Catholic Church ... dominates Irish politics and social life' (Davis, 1994), republicans considered the institution to have been their strongest internal opponent. Nevertheless religion does have an influ-ence upon habitus. Institutions from both denominations contribute to the maintenance of sectarianism through processions, rituals, roles within the community and the interweaving of nationalist, loyalist and religious symbols and rhetoric (Irvine 1991, Morrow 1995, Vertigans 2008). By comparison, the influence of religious institutions in the Palestinian nationalist struggles is much more explicit. In the territories, despite surveillance and some restrictions, with many mosques, especially in HAMAS controlled areas, imams will lam-baste Israel and the West while advocating the fight for Islam (Tamimi 2007).

## Prisons

The role of prisons within the radicalisation of individuals is becoming increasingly prominent. During the 1970s and 1980s it was apparent that both republican and loyalist prisoners in Northern Ireland were utilising their periods of imprisonment to develop and refine tactics and ideologies. However, these prisoners were already largely members of paramilitary organisations. Today there is growing concern about the radicalisation of Muslims in prisons. Unlike the Northern Irish examples, these individuals arrive in prison as 'common criminals' and leave as potential terrorist recruits. The potential for radicalisation can be greater in prisons. In the Palestinian territories Abu-Amr (1994) noticed the ways in which Islamic Jihad recruited within such institutions. Similarly deportation can also result in concentrated radicalism and heightened emotions which strengthen support for terrorism. Tamimi (2007) examined the expulsion of Palestinians to Southern Lebanon where they were able to take advantage of opportunities that had not previously been available such as freedom to meet, formulate and share ideas and develop strategy. By comparison, incarceration within spaces that are less densely populated with people who share similar discursive consciousness raises other possibilities. Stripped of layers of their 'civilian' identity and physically removed from family and preceding friendships contributes to what Goffman described as the 'mortification of the soul.' Individuals feel vulnerable in the new environments and possess limited social relationships. They often lack awareness of the nuances of prison life and possibilities of, in some instances a demand for, cognitive restructuring. In Trujillo *et al.*'s (2009) study of prisons in Spain *jihadi* radicalisation was connected to psychosocial and contextual conditions. Levels of social support alongside Islamic ideology and credibility of violence contributed to processes of radicalisation. Between Muslims, group solidarity was recorded as being quite high. By comparison, communication with non-Muslims was relatively low. Consequently opportunities to overcome racial divides and stereotypes were limited and the Muslim We-image was strengthened.

## Multiple agents

Again it is important both to avoid overstating the roles of particular socialising agents and to consider the social processes in the formation of terrorists' dispositions as being fundamentally distinct from other layers of habitus. Just as individuals who possess more moderate ideas and forms of behaviour internalise norms and values through complex and convoluted processes and experiences, people become terrorists through the internalisation of different agential influences. Agents like the people who compose them do not operate in isolation and do not act independently of each other. Thus in many instances, individuals become involved through a mixture of socialising agents and who in turn are influenced by other agents and their members. For instance, Florez-Morris (2007) details the significance of friends and family in recruitment processes into Colombian groups. The same combination is also noticeable across Palestinian groups (Post *et al.* 2003), ETA (McCauley and Segal 1988), Irish republicans (Horgan 2009, Taylor and Quayle 1994), Italian

Red Brigades (della Porta 1995) and global *jihadists* (Bakker 2006, Hamm 2007, Sagemen 2004).

Moreover the interweaving of government agencies helps to explain what at first glance appears to be the surprising fact that Muslim nations that have most rigorously incorporated religion within state institutions, including law and education, encounter some of the most significant terror threats. In addition to Pakistan, Saudi Arabia, the self-declared Guardian of the Holy Sites, is the most notable example. The incorporation of *ulema* within government, the legitimacy they can provide for secular policies and their role as a counter-balance to radicals following the 1979 uprising, has provided them with considerable negotiating power. In turn they have utilised this opportunity to increase the prominence of Islam within the kingdom which in turn further enhances their responsibilities and capabilities so that they effectively have become the guardians of morality. Consequently there have been extensive mosque building programmes, religious education has increased markedly and prominent Islamists, often in exile from less receptive regimes, most notably Egypt, have secured influential positions within universities and other state institutions.[33] The policies[34] have contributed to an acceleration of Islamification. Of course, from a sociological perspective, this is not necessarily problematic. The resurgence of Islam indicates a desire for explanation and a framework for behaviour that other institutions, nation-states and international agencies are failing to provide. Where this does become problematic is when normative levels of religiosity shift towards radicalism and forms of behaviour and feelings associated with militancy are part of the social habitus, uncritically accepted as the benchmark for behaviour. The visibility of adherence to these Islamic standards is quickly noticeable within attire. The extent to which females are covered and male facial hair and behaviour accords with rigid and narrow moral parameters contribute to these perceptions being confirmed, reinforced and easily monitored. In other words, the gap between the religious layers of the majority and that of terrorists shrinks.[35]

## Capital requirements

At this point it is important to reiterate that I am not arguing that becoming a terrorist is an inevitable outcome when particular dispositions and networks intersect with socialising agents. There must also be a demand from groups or others willing to form a cell and a certain amount of 'luck.' The types and levels of capital that individuals have accumulated such as knowledge, prestige, influence, relationships and body behaviour (Bourdieu 1984)[36] will consequently influence both the likelihood that individuals will want to enter the field of terrorism and the extent to which they will appeal to the agents of recruitment, thereby gaining access.[37] Thus the types and levels of capital accumulated by people and their aggregate within individual habitus will both dispose entry into terror groups and the roles they then adopt. Alongside the more obvious practical resources, social capital[38] is an indicator of relationships and the ways in which friendships and acquaintances are instrumental in opportunities for group membership. For prospective terrorists the networks of associations and especially the type of people they are involved with provide, as I discuss below, the requisite connections and credibility. In other words, terror leaders recruit like other types of organisation through existing networks. Hence people who share social capital and are connected into these relationships through family, friends and acquaintances are more likely to be provided with opportunities to join. This is one potential reason why female members are proportionately underrepresented. In essence and somewhat simplistically fewer women are interconnected to these networks and hence have reduced opportunities to join.

Leaders also look for characteristics which will enable chosen individuals to contribute towards the achievement of aims and objectives. Terror groups require a range of skills and dispositions if they are to prosper. Alongside the most obvious roles of shooter, bomb maker and bomber, there is a requirement for strategic leadership, couriers, logistical planning, recruitment, website design and criminal activities. The last task is often fundamental for groups that have little or no funding and includes credit fraud, counterfeiting, armed robberies, manufacturing firearms and acquiring false identities. Hamm (2007) argues the reliance on these types of illegal activities has been instrumental in domestic terror groups specifically recruiting individuals with criminal capabilities. And if we return to the issue of gender representation, the skills that groups require are associated more with men than women. This can be a consequence of stereotyping and/or a reflection of the types of capabilities the different sexes learn through social expectations and conformism. Either way, men are probably viewed as being more appropriate both in terms of temperament and technique. Moreover, just like other forms of organisation, supply and demand influences the rigor and criteria within terror groups' decision-making processes to select potential new recruits. Thus if they are short of members and only a limited number of people want to join, then the level of capabilities requested can be anticipated to be lower than groups experiencing considerable demand to join. In a manner similar to labour shortages during war-time and the mobilisation of female workers, terror groups have also sought to encourage or permit women into groups during periods when there was a shortage of available men, such as particular points in nationalist struggles in Northern Ireland, Sri Lanka and Chechnya.[39]

Because terror groups operate within societies and, as I explain in the following chapter, members share tremendous similarities with the populations in terms of ideas, behaviour and restraints, what recruits learn within societies is also crucially important for the success or otherwise of terror groups. For instance, within state learning programmes individuals both internalise the formal curricula and forms of capital that are valued by terror organisations such as critical analysis, planning, IT aptitude, communication skills and social awareness.

Groups want a range of skills and aptitudes that require, as a former IRA member told Horgan (2009: 81), arrangements whereby 'people were evaluated and put into certain roles. ... 'Cos every large organisation is going to have that challenge – how do you fit people into things?' Within the UFF a more rudimentary approach seems to have been adopted on occasion. 'Doug' informed Horgan (2009: 104) in response to a question about identifying potential recruits, 'I was just looking for someone who had the balls to f****** kill someone. That's it in a nutshell. There's no real training, basic training needed.' Therefore the aggregate of capital internalised within individual personality structures will heavily influence the likelihood that they will want to be part of a terror group and that the terror group would want them. Hence the appeal of the aggregate of capital that people possess will vary across groups and time according to the requirements of the field they want to join. Thus both loyalist and republican groups in Northern Ireland were much less discerning at the onset of the Troubles when numbers were required urgently in order to defend locations and present impressions of solidarity and strength. Subsequently, as the Troubles became established, the need for longer term strategies and more military-styled operations meant that the criteria for recruitment became more rigorous. Arguably the loyalists, in particular, subsequently struggled to overcome problems that stemmed from these early less well disposed recruits attaining positions of responsibility.

## Conclusion

For people to join or form terror groups requires them to hold or be willing to acquire forms of behaviour, norms and values that collectively will enable them to support or participate in acts of political violence. Individuals must become detached from contradictory cognitive and normative patterns and competing socialising agencies. Just as socialising agents are instrumental in the cultivation of individual restraints and internalised pacification, they are also integral to the shifting of restraints within particular settings, most notably with regard to political violence. For people socialised within environments with limited or no interaction between their group and the targets and for whom there is a legacy of political violence within the social habitus, the dispositional shift is less marked than for people with higher levels of mutual identification. For these individuals the transition is more dramatic[40] and very often occurs gradually through engagement within the broader movement before funnelling down into radicalism. This allows greater order and continuity, enabling ontological security and the changing balance in levels of restraint and pacification/aggressive behaviour and meaning to be accommodated. Conversely as an Italian 'red' militant informed Neuberger and Valentini (1996: 114), 'Those who joined the armed struggle too fast ... cannot have had the time to experience the failure of peaceful avenues and so they went into armed struggle and, hence, into the possibility of killing, without a sufficient level of conscience.'

Shifting forms of We-identification are crucial, enabling justification both in terms of protecting the group and associated ideology, community and nation and attacking (as a form of defence) the enemy with whom individuals no longer identify. As members tend to consider terrorism as a form of warfare, just as in conventional warfare the emphasis upon We-identification becomes stronger and I-images weaken. Thus the social takes precedence over the individual and the collective norms and values become integral across the group, community or nation (Vertigans 2009). Because terrorism will inevitably be challenged by counter-terrorism, this creates feelings of fear, insecurity, incalculability and concerns over the survival of the collective entity. Within these spirals, which are discussed in greater detail in Chapter Six, levels of hostility among existing members towards the 'Other' rise. Broader support can become radicalised and more inclined to experience a shift in their own levels of restraint that enables less passive behaviour to become normative within particular demarcated spaces.

The extent to which wider support and new members could be attracted by the deeds of terrorism is obviously strongly influenced by the extent to which militant rhetoric connects with individual realities and interconnects with history and habitus. Terror tacticians have to assess levels of public anger, dissatisfaction and frustration against intended targets. They must also determine whether these emotions connect into existing habitus regarding political violence or if feelings are sufficiently powerful that they enable a shift in restraints towards support for terrorism. Therefore the American militias can only attract support if they connect into perceived threats from a New World Order, globalisation, Islam and federal government and fears over job losses, house repossessions, bankruptcies, crime and immigration. Equally, nationalist groups such as HAMAS, ETA and the IRA struggle unless the communities on which they rely are also experiencing injustice, military brutality, arbitrary arrest and restricted mutual identification with the 'Other.'

Moreover, altruistic reasons associated with the particular ideology abound and cannot be discounted. Equally emotions are integral to the processes of joining, ranging from anger, resentment and hatred through to excitement, comradeship and enjoyment that can be experienced within related social networks and related activities. Although there is a tendency to associate female terrorists more with personal issues than discursive, emotions and rational, individual and social factors apply to both males and females. Consequently joining terror groups is in some ways similar to becoming members of other types of social and new religious movements. Members of terror groups also tend to be mobilised in figurations that vary in intensity and functions and not within a mobilisation of isolated and dislocated individuals. These people must want to become members and be part of at least one network or related field and by extension gatekeeper, who will help in the process. Processes of recruitment are therefore very often 'bottom-up' most explicitly in the case of female members of the Chechen Black Widows who actively sought resources and training (Speckhard and Akhmedova 2006).

Although terror groups have, and continue to, target(ed) particular locations such as universities, prisons, religious institutions, gun shows and virtual sites, overall processes tend to connect into existing levels of interest which they seek to develop and radicalise. The pre-existence of these networks and their relative intensity can help to explain how individuals are able to negotiate the transition with ontological security as members make a shift from passive citizen to recruit of a violent organisation.[41] Consequently, the perception of passive members and exploitative leaders is fundamentally misleading. This is not to say that such individuals do not exist, but it is to declare that they are much less prominent than perhaps governments and mass media would like. Instead individuals are recruited through interaction within social networks and processes of negotiation that incorporate the appeal of the individual to the group and vice-versa. As Sageman (2004) commented, in many instances people are more inclined to join groups rather than being actively recruited. In essence they approach the recruiters.

The development and refinement of these relations are essential in maintaining members and by extension, the group. Consequently it is to dynamics within the terror group that enable social bonds to be tightened and restraints weakened and yet controlled that I turn to in the following chapter.

# 5   Group dynamics

## Trusting terrorists, secrets and ties

## Introduction

In the preceding chapter the roles of socialising agents were identified as fundamental within pathways into terror groups. Yet on joining groups individuals are rarely 'fully formed' terrorists. Very often their ideas and behaviour have to be further radicalised and emotions created, replaced and transformed. This occurs within the group, an observation that is supported by the relative rarity of terrorists acting alone without affiliation to a social entity.[1] Groups establish characteristics, processes and structures which provide the normative framework for norms and values. If individuals are to remain, and be successful, these have to be internalised and individual affective and collective experiences integrated. By establishing aspects of commonality, 'I'/'We' boundaries become blurred. Furthermore, new members must also be integrated within the wider group or movement, sharing layers of habitus that will provide the bonds of solidarity and conformity that terror groups require. The interplay between trust and secrecy can be integral to social integration and meaningful relationships. In essence groups and social capital help shape dispositions and generate activities that will contribute to individuals becoming active members within processes of terrorism. Hence, group dynamics are the focus of this chapter, commencing with the processes through which recruits become, and remain, members.

## Solidifying We-ness: The outsiders

Group dynamics within peer relations were established as being fundamental within the shifts into terrorism, and they continue to be extremely influential in the subsequent phases. For Horgan (2005: 162), 'the group plays perhaps an even more obvious role in terms of sustaining involvement and promoting engagement in violence.' Affective relations within friendships prior to the transition to terrorism often subsequently become stronger through talk, gossip, narrative and positive forms of identification and negative classifications. Irrespective of the extent to which the group is entwined with wider social relations, inner relationships will gain greater significance and reliance upon other group members will become prominent. Gilio (1972: 137) interviewed the imprisoned leader of the Uruguayan Tupamaros who explained that 'the most important thing is to create in him a feeling of dependence on the group. He has to be aware of the fact that he cannot be self-sufficient—that the others are essential to him.' The existence and continuation of the group has to matter to the recruit. The nature of the role means that even when individuals continue to live within communities, with their families, are in paid employment and engage in sporting and cultural activities, being a 'terrorist' will influence how other people and institutions are viewed. This tends to mean that the only people with whom they can discuss their 'terrorist lives' and the impact on the everyday are members of the group, which again provides further sources of commonality and shared emotions. For members living a clandestine existence, the Italian Susanna Ronconi mentioned that there was a seamless unity of purpose to their lives.[2] In turn, the intense relations within groups contribute towards individuals reporting that members become 'your family. The organisation defined who you were, it gave you an identity, a purpose.'[3] For reasons of security and comradeship, members such as those in Northern Ireland would frequently meet in bars and clubs to discuss experiences and make plans, reinforcing commitment through engagement to the 'cause' and socialising.[4]

Within groups, individuals have commented upon feelings of devotion and enthusiasm alongside the sense of meaning, self-esteem and heightened status that involvement within particular groups can confer (della Porta 1992, 1995, Elias 1996). These emotions are frequently heightened within internal affective bonds because as one respondent informed della Porta (2009: 82),

> I am unable to cultivate relationships outside the organization. With comrades from the organization, these are also relationships for life; they are, above all, friendships. The first embryo of the BR [Red Brigades] was formed by friends, people who lived more or less in the same part of town.

In order to achieve this, groups must strive to create positive inter-group identification that revolves around shared meanings and common cognitive frameworks and which interplay with, and are reinforced by, external differences. Thus individuals need to identify and be attuned with the group's ideology, goals, methods and members and be aware of their position within the field. For participants who had been socialised within radical families, sharing similar values, the discursive distance to travel was less extreme by comparison to recruits with limited knowledge and experience. In this regard, the range of levels of preceding involvement and discursive insights within the American Weather Underground[5] group are typical. Here there were members deeply steeped in the history of Left-Wing radicalism and activism joining alongside recruits with little awareness of the fundamental issues and solutions (Braungart and Braungart 1992). Hence as Crossley (2003: 59) observed with regard to social movements, 'the field entails a variety of mechanisms for educating neophyte radicals; affording them knowledge of struggles and issues, as well as "training" (formal and informal) in the skills of protest.' Newly formed groups establish boundaries based around accentuated moral, cognitive and affective differences which are interwoven with behavioural parameters. If groups become well established, such as HAMAS, the IRA and ETA, boundaries can become reinforced and routine, normative forms of identification become uncritically internalised, with which subsequent recruits are expected to identify. Simmel (1965b) comments that 'the wider the social circles in which individuals participate and the larger the groups of which they are members, the greater will be their individual differences.' The reverse is also true. Greater emotional involvement within one relationship is often accompanied by a reduction in other social relationships. For terror groups, the emphasis upon inward relations and looser relations with other social entities means that individual differences will diminish and as a consequence inner group commonalities will increase. The former member of the Italian Red Brigades, Adriana Faranda, illuminates upon this when explaining 'When you remove yourself from society, even from the most ordinary things, ordinary ways of relaxing, you no longer share even the most basic emotions. You become abstracted, removed. In the long run you actually begin to feel different. Why? Because you are different.'[6]

The emphasis groups place upon crisis, war and danger helps to generate what Durkheim (1984 [1893]) referred to as collective effervescence. Shared beliefs, practices and heightened emotions provide definitions and meaning. When attachment is strong there will be greater commitment to prevailing collective beliefs and commonalities between individuals. In a similar manner to peoples threatened by more conventional warfare, terrorists also acquiesce to the We-image and the need for survival which overrides sectional interests that may exist within the group. Moreover, the asymmetrical nature of the terrorist struggle usually means that insecurity and risks are omnipresent. Contrary to Durkheim's argument that legal codes will provide the basis for common behavioural codes and by extension the We-image, for the terrorists it is the breach thereof and specified sanctions which are instrumental in their collective consciousness.

Through evaluation, members and groups are able to underpin the basis for collective inner charisma and outer stigmatisation which helps generate reciprocal attacks as the following chapter demonstrates. For recruits making the transition into terror groups, these boundaries, the intense relations within and familiar social networks help to provide ontological security and reduce dissonance. On the reverse of intense feelings such as loyalty, pride and togetherness that the We-image and group dynamics invoke, people who do not share the same beliefs are excluded. This happens across multitudes of groups but is given added resonance for terror groups.

Furthermore, cohesion is partly determined by tensions with competing groups which add to feelings of threat, fear and insecurity within the social habitus. Difference becomes an integral component of We-ness, partly constructed and asserted in opposition to them and the construction of a 'They-image' about other groups of people or nations and the development of associated feelings and identifications (Mennell 2007). 'The more pressure there is on communities to change ... the more vigorously boundaries will be symbolised. Difference will be constructed and emphasised and we-ness asserted in opposition to *them*' (Jenkins 2004: 114). Psychological, social and military attacks upon group ideas, members and infrastructure can help solidify participant and group identification and levels of commitment.[7] For instance, Bjørgo (2009) describes how the stigmatisation of neo-Nazi groups has contributed to the severance of outside ties and stronger in-group relations.

In turn, the aroused emotions can contribute to groups' progression across the spectrum of radicalisation and help in demarcating between the group and the 'Other' who are to become the 'legitimate' target of attacks. Synchronic with the emphasis upon the inner group is the negative characterisation of the 'Other.' The construction of these in-group-out-group memberships enables the development of what Blumer (1939) described as an *esprit de corps* among broader movement members. Collective charisma and concomitant stigmatisation help to specify distinctive characteristics with particular norms, morals and codes of behaviour associated with the 'Other.' These help both to accentuate the in-group commonalities and coherence and a partial framework for understanding which helps provide behavioural and ideational boundaries and a sense of collective identification and solidarity. When combined with a discourse that vehemently emphasises the superiority of group ideas and the inferiority of rivals, rules for the moderation of behaviour are overridden or disregarded.

Elias and Scotson (1965, 2008) identified similar processes in their study of social tensions within neighbourhoods in an English town and which can easily be adapted to provide insights into the onset of political violence.[8] Their investigation into social processes between communities detailed how the interactions influence, and are influenced by, group dynamics. For the 'established' dominant group there was a tendency to select attributes, people and forms of behaviour that were considered to provide evidence for their superiority and 'group charisma' even though in practice they were representative of the 'minority of the best.' These attributes provided the basis for social identification and other practices and behaviour that contradicted this image tended to be ignored. By comparison the 'outsiders' group was categorised according to the traits and forms of behaviour associated with a 'minority of the worst.' Through 'elevating the group's own members, the group charisma automatically relegated members of other interdependent groups to a position of inferiority' (Elias and Scotson 1965: 104). Through regular inner group communication, charisma and stigma became routine, interwoven within habitus, accepted and over time transmitted uncritically. Adherence to these perceptions and dispositional barriers contributes to further strengthening of inner bonds while simultaneously weakening connections to the 'Other' whose actions by comparison could arouse hostility, disgust, anger or contempt. Group charisma was thus both a weapon of defence and attack.

In Elias and Scotson's example, the outsiders lacked coherence and collective identification and tended to internalise the images of the established. This does not apply to influential terror groups. Hence when the 'established' (in this instance governments, international agencies and media operators) instigate similar processes of stigmatisation against the terrorists, and often the people with whom they are most associated, the reaction is very different. Instead of internalising and reinforcing inferiority and becoming embodied within personality structures, the established discourse tends to confirm and strengthen the terrorists' collective identification. Rather than passively internalising the established's rhetoric within weak levels of group and self-esteem, the coherence, power and challenging dispositions contribute to terror outsiders utilising the rhetorical attacks to strengthen their own charisma and appeal in part by counter-stigmatising the established. Much therefore depends on the balance of power between the established and outsiders and the extent to which the former is held in regard by the latter. In the case of the terrorists, the former is held at best in contempt. Thus by their collective strength and unity they can deflect, subvert and transform government attempts to blame them into self-declared group praise.[9]

When both sides possess sufficient power, confidence and collective, coherent identification, reciprocal processes of stigmatisation further exacerbate tensions and as I discuss in the following chapter, contribute to the spirals of violence and selective examples both of group charisma and the others' disgrace. Moreover the broad brush approach to stigmatisation found within terror and counter-terror strategies that classifies together governments and anyone who does not support terror groups, and terror groups and anyone who does not support the government, diminishes boundaries that existed within the two, initially distinctive, groupings. Thus categorising all Tamil nationalists as being part of LTTE and Muslims as members of al-Qa'ida tends to create shared emotions that extend across the demarcations. In the process counter-terror strategies and the wider populations contribute unintentionally towards collective experiences and support for the terrorists' discourse if not their methods.

## Trusting terrorists: Secrets and ties

Because the transition into terrorism is accompanied by varying degrees of detachment[10] from other social relations, the group assumes magnified importance and becomes the main source of both political and social allegiance. Both for the individual and group this can be potentially dangerous, not least because as Simmel (1906) commented, one person can never absolutely know another person or group. Impressions therefore become based upon insights into the other person's disposition and how this is interpreted through the interpreter's own conceptions of appropriate norms, values and forms of behaviour. Groups need individuals who are able to become part of an integral unit and the likelihood will be enhanced if they share layers of disposition.

In order to try to minimise risk and maximise effectiveness a balance has to be achieved between secrecy and trust. These become integral to the inner relationships and the interplay between affective emotions and cognitive processes.[11] Hardin (2006: 18) suggests that, 'As a rule, we trust only those with whom we have a rich enough relationship to judge them trustworthy, and even then we trust only over certain ranges of actions.' Terror groups require what Putnam (2000) called 'thick trust' which is embedded within highly personal relations. Hence terror groups have to try to generate deep trust both within the group and across members. New recruits require evidence about whom to trust and whether they have enough confidence in the group to risk the dangers that come with engagement. Equally other members need to know enough about the recruit to be confident in their morality, capabilities and temperament, thereby reducing the risk of indiscretion, betrayal and discovery. Questions to be answered include: will the individual be discrete, what skills do they possess, how useful will these be for the group, to what extent do they support group aims, will they conform to discipline and how will they fit into the group? This contributes to recruits being gradually inducted into the group or as Simmel (1906: 488) described it a 'graduated process of admission.'[12]

As the loyalist example in the preceding chapter showed, this is not necessarily universal. When groups desperately require someone to undertake terror attacks this potential capability can be overwhelmingly significant, although even in this example, groups must be confident in the ability of individuals to perform required actions. The extent of the perceived risk and the degree to which the individual is already known within the group will heavily influence the level of trust that is awarded. Within neo-Nazi groups, for example, Bjørgo (2009) details how some groups tend to be careful with new recruits, restricting their involvement and activities until they are confident in their trustworthiness and dedication. Once trusted the recruits are expected to internalise similar restraints that revolve around group processes and a sense of honour and morality that stems from discursive and social attachment. In turn, they must develop security consciousness that means topics for discussion and the details within must be carefully vetted according to levels of trust. Bjørgo (2009) argues that the threat of infiltration and attack can mean that this cautionary approach is justifiable. Nevertheless it also serves to strengthen group consciousness, cohesion and loyalty through security and the threat from surrounding enemies to the small in-group.

Equally, existing members will be looking for signs that new recruits are reliable, competent and can be trusted both on cognitive and affective grounds. The abstract nature of trust for Simmel means that reciprocity and constant renewal is required, even if as he suggests the bases for trust can be weak. As with other forms of group membership these impressions and emotions will often be heavily influenced by how we feel about the individuals and the extent to which they share our ideas, beliefs and general disposition (Hardin 2006). Hence recruits who share similar habitus with other members are more likely to be accepted on account of common pre-existing norms, values and forms of capital. Trust is therefore awarded based upon interpretations of the information provided and the social relationship between the members (Fine and Holyfield 1996). In this regard terrorists are no different, if possibly more thorough and conscious in their deliberation. And as Simmel (1906: 484) explains with regards to secret societies, when other people are excluded this can raise the value of the excluding criteria. Knowing that other people are denied participation and are not aware of their own involvement accentuates the significance of the group for members.

> The always perceptible and always to-be-guarded pathos of the secret lends to the form of union which depends upon the secret, as contrasted with the content, a predominant significance as compared with other unions. (ibid.)

When applying this quote to terrorism I would suggest that the content has considerably more significance than for some of the secret societies which Simmel describes. Nevertheless the application is certainly appropriate when considering the significance of the secrets for group allegiance. Secrecy is essential for protection and longevity. Groups dedicate considerable attention to discipline and concealment through informal social constraints and the distinct possibility of violent retribution to anyone who betrays their confidences, intentionally or otherwise, or in some instances refuses to participate within attacks.[13] Arguably membership of groups that are part of grounded networks with surrounding communities and predated relationships provide a more robust basis for these forms of collective identification and in all likelihood strong levels of commitment and mutual interdependence. In these settings, Lewis (2007) and Sageman (2004) refer to small dense networks that are based upon friendship, camaraderie, similar backgrounds and beliefs.[14] Within these loosely organised yet coherent groups 'from below,' collective identification and emotional commitment can be easier to generate. Moreover flexible forms of structure make penetration harder. Historically groups often sought to replicate their opponent's insignia and structures in miniature with clearly demarcated hierarchies, designated military-styled roles and, in the case of 'liberation' armies such as the IRA, arrangements that reflected local neighbourhoods. On realising that these structures were relatively easy to identify and disrupt, terror organisations have shifted to more opaque, fragmented arrangements and in the case of the IRA, a policy of positioning members outwith their neighbourhoods. Consequently, rather than the popular portrayal of characters such as the late bin Laden manipulating from afar, contemporary structures tend to be amorphous, with cells operating often semi-independently and certainly known only through the leader to a limited number of people within the chain of command outwith the group. In some instances, such as groups within the American Far Right and some of the activities committed in the name of al-Qa'ida, there are indications that these were undertaken by autonomous groups acting on behalf of, but not under the instructions of, the broader discourse or movement. This greater emphasis on secrecy restricts the potential damage that could be caused by informers or the arrest of cell members. And this greater security has an overlooked, possibly even unintentional beneficial consequence for the groups; namely, social bonds are also strengthened.

All this attention to secrecy has hitherto hidden one of the central contradictions within terrorism. As Erickson (1981: 200) pointed out with regard to secret societies, to 'pursue their goals, they must engage in behaviours that cannot always be disguised or buried in the stream of mundane activities.' Hence terrorists must reconcile the requirement for secrecy and the need for publicity. They are secret groups who must act publicly. Within the group, secrecy is stressed yet new recruits can only become trusted if they are able to provide enough information about themselves and their connections. Only the release of personal knowledge can overcome initial concerns about concealment and duplicity that are applied to members with limited preceding social ties with existing members. For Simmel (1906: 466), 'Secrecy sets barriers between men, but at the same time offers the seductive temptation to break through the barriers by gossip or confession.' This can bring about a profound irony with groups consisting of close intimacies. Within this type of social formation, Simmel (ibid.: 467) argues for members 'every peculiarity of being, acting, or possessing the persistence of which requires secrecy is abhorrent to it.' For terror groups this is probably overstating members' abhorrence to secrets. Nevertheless, this is a dilemma for terror organisations and there is little doubt that boundaries between participants are much more porous and fragile when members are emotionally attached. Knowledge of the secrets that they share can further increase confidences within the group; providing the disclosure of secrets within the group does not impact upon security, then this may not necessarily be problematic. However, if any members are captured there is always a danger that they will provide information about colleagues. A further risk is that deep empathy, even devotion, will hinder individual objectivity. Members become restrictively concerned about the well-being of other participants which reduces their effectiveness and possibly contributes to a significant reduction in risk taking.

The advent of the Internet could be considered an opportunity to reduce levels of risk. In the preceding chapter, the utilisation of the Internet for spreading propaganda, training and communication was discussed. Even to the technophobe the potential for increasing levels of security and secrecy and thereby restricting risks is apparent. Virtual communication can, providing safeguards are introduced, enhance levels of secrecy and security, not least as meetings in person, and thereby chances of being identified or remembered, can be reduced. As the House of Commons' (HOC, 2006: 31) *Report of the Official Account of the Bombings on 7 July 2005* reported, the Internet is enabling visible contacts between militants and potential recruits to be reduced and thereby there is less opportunity to detect networks and possible members. Yet further to the preceding chapter, the completely virtual terrorist is largely a figment of populist media's imagination; face to face communication remains an integral component within group arrangements and the solidification of boundaries and cohesion. This is partly because, despite the huge potential for terrorism, and the planning for the September 2001 attacks is indicative of this, the Internet can be insecure. For instance, it is easier to establish if counter-terror forces are monitoring your residence from a neighbour's house across the street than it is to grasp that IT security experts have cracked the codes behind your Internet account. And just as personal communication is extremely important in establishing levels of trustworthiness, despite the addition to social capital, the lack of such contact means that terror groups are very reluctant to trust individuals who only become known through the Internet. Without social networks that can be validated and levels of conviction that can be confirmed there is a reluctance to trust the unknown. Hardin (2006) explains that Internet relationships generally lack the structure of trust relations, being neither embedded within preceding relations or as part of overlapping networks. Consequently relationships that only exist on the Internet tend to be 'relatively thin' (Hardin 2006: 105) and lack the norms and sanctions of thicker, social relationships. If we apply this to terror groups and insights into processes of recruitment outlined in the preceding chapter, it can be seen that virtual-only relations do not provide individuals with the required authenticity if they are to be recruited. Within these thin electronic interactions there is very limited scope for individuals to prove they warrant trust. Doubtless there are incremental steps that can be taken but at some point the potential recruit would have to meet with the potential recruiters in order to be, in essence, interviewed. As part of the personality test they would have to provide evidence in support of their application that could not be achieved virtually. Certainly recruiters seek to utilise the Internet to attract members but this is not an unconditional drive without controls. Terror groups are notably cautious within this ongoing cyber war and rival strategies of virtual grooming and counter-terror virtual infiltration. Thus the Internet has enhanced both the risks and social capital capacity of terror groups and potential effectiveness and efficiency, providing members have the requisite skills and knowledge to exploit the potentialities.

## Ritualising ties

Belonging to high-risk groups, sharing threats of arrest, imprisonment, possibly torture and death, provides shared experiences and empathy which heightens forms of identification with each other. Eyerman (2005) and Klandermans (2007) detail how participants in social movements develop mutual empathy through collective actions such as demonstrations and symbolic markers such as items of clothing, badges, flags and placards. Although the largely clandestine nature of terrorism hinders such overt expressions, symbolic identification through rituals, meetings and common codes helps to solidify group relations. When groups have opportunities to build upon these forms of identification they will often seek to utilise them. Within Far Right groups such symbolic capital is integral to actions and image. Weaver (1997: 128–29) discusses how for Far Right German groups,[15]

> it is through a violence of re-enactment – the strutting, the uniforms, insignia, and the discourse … punctuated by atrocities, walls smeared with hate slogans, immigrant hostels burned, individuals beaten – that the return of the Übermensch and the master race is signaled.

Although there is a tendency to consider social capital and community relations in a positive manner, Hardin (2006: 97) reports upon groups such as the Nazi Party and Ku Klux Klan. They 'have substantial social capital that enables them to accomplish the grim results they produce.' Hamm (2007) details the attempts by Robert Mathews, whose use of symbols was integral to impressions and subsequent mythology surrounding The Order or Silent Brotherhood. Through the use of codenames, choice of name, regimented actions, racial references and Silent Brotherhood medallion, Mathews aimed to formulate member and group identification around a narrative of American Aryan warriors. Across American Far Right groups, myths provide an essential connection between their values and actions and the habitus of the ancestors with whom they closely identify. Ancestors tend to be associated with the colonization of America and the formation of the behavioural norms with which they most associate. The mythology is not new and is not unique to extremism. On the contrary, the accompanying narrative can be located within the national habitus and of which the Far Right are the most virulent supporters. The colonial roots of the American character and the enduring legacy of violence are explored by Slotkin (1973: 5), who suggested that,

> The first colonists saw in America an opportunity to regenerate their fortunes, their spirits, and the power of their church and nation; but the means to that regeneration ultimately became the means of violence, and the myth of regeneration through violence became the metaphor of the American experience.

## Controlling the violence valve[16]

At an immediate level, recruits share ideological commitment that provides sense of a distinctive form of We-identification and is accompanied by a concomitant shift in the We-I balance towards other group members. Although both the levels of knowledge and discursive consciousness vary considerably, individual commitment to the ideology and the group is an important step in the terrorist career. Obviously it is important that terror groups and individuals therein are expressive and participants want to invoke change, whether that is a new form of government or an increase/decrease in levels of religion, independence or revolution. This requires considerable commitment from individuals who may ultimately be contributing their lives for an ideology and/or 'the people.' Yet as I explained in earlier chapters, there is a danger that we could be sidetracked by focusing on altruism. Certainly people are committed but the ideology in isolation is unlikely to radicalise to the extent that individuals are willing to scare, harm and kill or be scared, harmed and killed on its behalf. Many new recruits lack in-depth knowledge and understanding about the discourse that they have quite literally agreed to terrorise on behalf of. People require evidence according to their level of discursive consciousness alongside agencies that provide political and social support mechanisms. Within these relations, greater collective identification with both the discourse and group contributes to the reduction in levels of I-identification and the influence of preceding forms of restraint associated with kin, friends and institutions outwith the group. Individuals are therefore in a period of transition, shifting from the restraints that allowed them to participate within civilian life to alternative restraints that both constrain and enable. Crucially many of the previous constraints remain relevant within the group and have to be integrated within the changing ideas and forms of behaviour. Greater emphasis upon social identification is accompanied by reformulation of social and self-restraints and less individual constraint. Hence the interaction of the recruit and the group within what could be described through adapting Bourdieu[17] (1993) as a 'field of terrorism' within 'fields of contention' (Crossley 2003). New recruits are heavily influenced by the levels and types of capital they possess, how they interact with the rules within the field and the struggles that are enacted. As Bourdieu (1993: 72) declares, for the field to function people must be prepared to be involved who are 'endowed with the *habitus* that implies knowledge and recognition of the immanent laws of the field, the stakes, and so on.' Within terror groups identification and internalising the laws of the field is processual, 'part of the ongoing organisation of interaction and everyday life' (Jenkins 2004: 106).

Of course terrorists' everyday lives may be different from the mainstream, particularly those living clandestinely and who, like the 'red' Italian Susanna Ronconi, report feeling happiness and excitement during group involvement.[18] Similar expressions of excitement and comradeship were also reported by Erickson (1981) as being experienced during shared risks that secret society members were exposed to. MacDonald's (1991: 212) discussion with a range of female terrorists identified that for leading figures such as the RAF's Astrid Proll involvement with the group also brought excitement. Proll explained that 'you must understand that then the most fantastic thing in the world was not to be a rock star, but a revolutionary.' Della Porta's (1992) research also into Italian 'red' groups reported upon how participants expressed feelings of excitement and happiness within dynamic, interesting periods. Others reported upon the levels of satisfaction that engagement brought and, in particular, successful attacks. One of della Porta's (1992: 283) respondents exemplified this when declaring 'the very fact of seeing that thing burning and falling down made me happy.' Hoffman (2006) discusses leading figures from a number of 'red' groups and the IRA who have referred to the senses of power and excitement that they felt when immersed within terror cells. By comparison, for those who are also interwoven within civilian communities, the normative life surrounding them could appear tedious and uninspiring.

Nevertheless there is a danger that the 'glamorous' incalculable side of terrorism can be overstated. Involvement is not all about escaping arrest, committing bombing attacks, engaging with the armed forces and hijacking planes. Much of the time is spent within daily, mundane tasks and for those 'on the run' the uncertainty and insecurity of their transient existence is experienced alongside mind numbing boredom. Identification with and within groups provides the regulatory framework to restrain individuals both when expressing their emotions during activities and the preceding periods of tedium. Behavioural parameters are established that are appropriate to revised identities, namely to undertake actions that are acceptable to the group and are unacceptable to the 'Other.' These ideas and beliefs are interwoven within the social habitus and provide shared frameworks of understanding for members. Cohesion can be constructed around the threats of danger and arrest.

Collectively groups' norms and values provide a reference point to help overcome self-restraint over the challenge to the state's monopoly of violence and taboos that exist within the wider habitus. Social rituals in the form of symbolic expression, practices and procedures are passed on within the group. These help towards the transformation of individual and collective identification. They also assist with individual commitment to the acts of violence and make withdrawal much harder. 'Living wills' recorded by intended 'Islamic' suicide bombers are an example of such a ritual. These recordings have a dual purpose. At one level they raise the awareness of the issues which have led to the attack and through this it is intended to increase support. And at the level of the individual, 'it is primarily a ceremony intended to establish an irrevocable personal commitment of the candidate to carry out the suicide attack. This ritual constitutes a point of no return' (Merari 2005: 80). For these 'living martyrs' to withdraw at this stage would cause shame and humiliation. Across groups that use suicide bombers such as the Tamil Tigers, Chechen insurgents and those related to al-Qa'ida there are a number of other supporting rituals. Until he was killed in 2009, the Tamil leader Velupillai Prabhakaran was reported to share the final meals of would-be bombers (Pratap 2001). This ritual honoured the contribution of the intended bomber and by so doing placed considerable pressure on them to commit the designated act. A number of groups also use two or more bombers. Again there are at least two reasons. At a stark level, more than one person can achieve greater devastation. At a more sophisticated level, two or more members collectively provide support and place pressure on each participant to follow through with their instructions.

Group polarisation and dynamics within can enable decisions to be 'made that are more extreme than the mean of individual members' initial positions, in the direction already favoured by that mean' (Hogg and Vaughan 2005: 342). Similar processes can be noticed at an individual level and through what Pape (2005) describes as 'de-individualization.' By this he is referring to a shift in focus towards group values that increase the likelihood that individuals will be able to overcome restraints towards self-harm and be willing to sacrifice their lives. Conversely, restraints have to be rigorously applied and adhered to between members. Goudsblom's (2001) reference to the state's 'paradox of pacification' also applies to competing groups. Just like state formation, terrorism requires pacification and the organisation of violence if groups are to be effective over the longer term. This is because, 'Organized violence is generally far more effective than unorganized violence. To be effective, however, it requires a high degree of internal pacification. Those who participate in exercising it must not fight each other' (Goudsblom 2001: 4).

The extent of the shift in attitudes will heavily depend on the social habitus and levels of attachment. As I explained above, emotional barriers are broken down through involvement with broader political movements, an incremental shift through to increasingly radical forms of political engagement and limited and/or less emotional attachment to other groups. This is easier to achieve if there is only restricted interaction between potential members and targeted peoples. For instance, in Saudi Arabia, Hegghammer (2009) comments on the social distance based upon cultural and relationship gaps between Saudis and non-Muslims. With the explicit emphasis within the Kingdom upon Saudi and Islamic superiority and restricted balanced exploration of other cultures, perceived levels of mutual interdependence and identification are limited. Partly as a consequence Saudis who have become involved with terror groups are more inclined to be willing to kill Westerners than other Muslims.

During earlier stages of the member or group's career, tensions can be noticed within processes of calculation, planning, preparation and logistical arrangements and the motivations for individual engagement that include anger, desperation, revenge and envy. In these periods of heightened emotions, there is, as Collins (2001) noted with regards to social movements, an adaptation of Durkheim's collective effervescence; the shared emotions transform individual identities into social identification. Terror groups face a dilemma as many people are recruited through their emotional reactions and relationships that pre-date the group and develop with existing members. Groups will try to utilise emotions to create and evoke mutual empathy enhancing the mobilisation of recruits and broader support. Emotions such as anger, compassion, hatred and indignation can be very effective in overcoming fears of involvement that is required in order to participate in high-risk social and political movements (Flam 2005, Goodwin *et al.* 2007). Yet if groups are to be successful, those emotions must be controlled, subservient to the collective goals that require careful, deliberated consideration of targets, methods, fatalities, media coverage and wider impact. For the successful terror group the importance of longer-term goals must be greater than that placed upon individual affective behaviour and impulses. Certainly these can be accommodated and utilised but this has to be to the benefit of the group. Members must share unifying social interdependancies which emphasises discourse over the individual. Consequently initial emotions can continue to inform behaviour and collective forms of identification but not at the expense of the strategic goals. A terrorist 'sleeper' is taught how to assimilate. For instance, al-Qa'ida operatives have reported being instructed to order food at Western restaurants, to wear Western clothes, to shave beards and drink alcohol. In order to adapt and be hidden anonymously within targeted communities, individuals must therefore be able to restrain their emotions in public and appear integrated into the society which they intend to attack.[19] Similarly, and in more dramatic settings, terrorists on their way to plant or detonate bombs and to blow up themselves or others must be able to manage and conceal their emotions; the fear, anger, excitement and so on. Otherwise, they would be more likely to arouse suspicion, the mission would fail and the perpetrator could expect arrest or death beyond that which they intended. In short, the social valves which regulate the application of violent behaviour must provide controls which restrict agressive behaviour and emotions to particular locations and activities.

Furthermore, when facing the distinct possibility of death, individuals understandably are less constrained and much more immediately reactive and aggressive through drives and impulses to the dangers of the situation. Crucially, as Elias (2000) outlined, the interplay between rationalities and emotions shifts, often in conjunction with the tensions between and within competing groups. Hence, the emotional-rationality[20] continuum will fluctuate according to perceived levels of threats from rivals and counter-terror forces and will change accordingly throughout careers within terror groups. There is a correlation therefore between heightened threats and greater likelihood of responsive violence. Similarly violent responses are much less likely when perceptions of threat and uncertainty diminish. Crenshaw (1992) explores how the demand for vengeance within groups becomes a form of justification that provides a moral claim for revenge and becomes an obligation. Because there is no precise measure on which to establish the principle of reciprocity the violence escalates; this is discussed in the following chapter. With group members bound by intense feelings of loyalty, the death or arrest of participants can further inflame the demand for retribution. During these emotive periods, terror leaders can struggle to detach themselves and calculate an instrumental response. Even if they personally wanted to postpone retaliation until they were confident that emotions were subservient to purposive rationality, to use Weber's term, their supporters and activists may well be less inclined to allow time for sober reflection.

## Leadership

In his work on processes of submission within groups Georg Simmel (1965: 97) argues that 'the subordination of a group to a single individual leads to a strong unification of the group.' At first glance this seems to be at odds with the perception of terrorists challenging the status quo and, in particular, authority. However, such a view is misleading. If terror groups are to be successful, discipline is required, decisions must be made quickly, strategies formulated and methods implemented. The organisation must be able to react promptly, occasionally immediately, to counter-terror activities. This requires the internalisation of restraint and a willingness to follow orders. Consequently leaders tend to be in positions of authority, particularly when group members have dispositions that expect strong individuals to assume control and who should be obeyed. The hierarchical structure of many groups tends to provide support for this. According to Bandura (2004: 132), 'the higher the authorities, the more legitimacy, respect and coercive power they command, the more willing people are to defer to them.' Moreover as Weber noted, charismatic leadership is more inclined to secure obedience and compliance from followers. In Chapter Three such characteristics were identified across a range of locations that have confronted terrorism and may help to explain levels of discipline and identification within groups. By comparison, the shift towards leaderless cells within *jihadi* and Far Right groups has weakened strategic coordination and means that discipline is determined by group levels of knowledge and inner dynamics. Arguably cell members lack the broader levels of understanding about movement goals and without discipline being imposed from outwith the group, attacks often lack the rigorous strategic and emotive calculations behind previous leader-led actions.

Within the establishment of outsider boundaries, inner relations and the rules for secrecy and trust, leaders are fundamental. Leadership can be integral to the appeal of the group and the framing of historical grievances and events with contemporary frustrations in order to mobilise support and attract recruits.[21] The construction of a 'culture of martyrdom' by Islamic leaders is a particularly pertinent example (Gill 2007). Reflections of terror groups are also heavily influenced by leaders and those whose effect continues to resonate within societies. This may be partly because of the impact and legacy of their actions but often is also because of their charismatic appeal.

Thus the characteristics of diverse individuals such as Andreas Baader, Osama bin Laden, Bobby Sands and Abimael Guzmán have transcended institutions, discursive divisions and generations. Gill (2007) argues that without charismatic or epistemic authority figures nor a control of social institutions, groups such as the Colombian FARC are unable to create a 'culture of martyrdom' and consequently fail in their attempts to recruit potential suicide bombers. To this list I would add the intersection between related historical forms of violence and contemporary habitus.

The composition of the hierarchy tends to be indicative of the social capital with which the group is most associated. Hence in terms of gender women are restricted to support roles within Right-Wing groups and rarely feature within leadership. By comparison, the prominent 'red' groups of the 1970s had women leaders. In some obvious ways this reflects the groups' discourses as ideas are put into practice. The Right-Wing groups tend to portray traditional, conservative ways of behaving in which women are relegated to the domestic sphere. By comparison, the emphasis upon egalitarianism is practised to a certain degree within the Left-Wing groups. However, other important components of their ideologies are only noticeable through their absence. Racial groups' emphasis on white purity is applied within recruitment across the hierarchy. The 'reds' support for the working classes and ethnic minorities, predominantly Afro-Americans in the case of Weather Underground, did not translate into their representation within the leadership. There are a number of reasons for this, not least being that ironically these groups, particularly in the United States, West Germany and Japan did not attract support from these groups (Varon 2004, Vertigans 2008).[22] Hence the white, middle-class leaders are symptomatic of the groups' failure to appeal to their intended audience and the overall lack of working-class and black members.

## Retention: Should I stay or should I go?

Group dynamics continue to evolve according to situations, personalities and longevity. Basic factors such as aging need to be considered. A member aged nineteen is extremely unlikely to hold the same interests and behavioural patterns ten, fifteen, twenty years later. This transformation of loyalties and the subservience of the individual to the collective entity contribute to a sense of belonging and strengthen commitment. As one respondent informed della Porta (2009: 82), 'I am unable to cultivate relationships outside the organization. With comrades from the organization, these are also relationships for life; they are, above all, friendships.' Groups are strengthened by these social bonds of loyalty between members and by extension to the group and discourse. For Simmel (1999), loyalty and gratitude are the two emotions which help retain interactions after initial emotions such as love and mutual sympathy have weakened or disappeared. And as Crenshaw (1992) remarks, the involvement of many participants through existing social ties further intensifies commitment to the associated group when the relationships become compartmentalised, demarcated from other associations through the demands of clandestine existence and secrecy. Hence, intense feelings of solidarity and loyalty to the group and each other have contributed to members retaining involvement; to leave would be a sense of betrayal to their comrades.

Because of these shared experiences and surrounding collective identification the costs of defection increase. This is because any members who left the group would also be leaving or abandoning their friends, and sometimes partners,[23] shared experiences and a fundamental component of who they are. Thus initially the personal may become political during formative stages and the political becomes personal within group dynamics. On the other side of this identification is the detachment from external social relations from people left behind or who detach themselves from the emergent 'radical.' In essence, the group becomes central to member retention and much less so the discourse. As the German Far Left terrorist Bommi Baumann (1981: 76) explained, 'I saw that it was going to go a hundred percent wrong ... I only participated out of solidarity.' The minimal number of defections from the German 'reds' is indicative of this (Neidhardt 1992). Similarly della Porta (1995) reports on the reluctance of Left-Wing activists to leave groups with decisions to quit often only being taken collectively when facing trial and imprisonment. However, among the same groups, the death of members on operations could cause a crisis of confidence in the appropriateness of terrorism and individual engagement (della Porta 2009). In the final chapter, the significance of these issues are explored in greater depth when we examine processes behind decisions to disengage from terror activities.

## Secrecy, mistrust and detachment

Almost inevitably the paradoxical emphasis both upon secrecy and trust creates problems within groups. Processes that are designed to secure secrecy often contribute to mistrust and in some instances paranoia, which impacts upon any calculative detached terror strategy. Therefore, as Bjørgo (2009) discusses, the lack of trust in new recruits and fear of being mistrusted amongst even longer established members promotes an atmosphere of conformity and submission to group values. Simmel's (1906: 491) study of social relations within secret societies again offers insight, for 'every quarrel within the secret society[24] brings with it the danger of betrayal, to avoid which in this case the motive of self-preservation in the individual is likely to co-operate with the motive of the self-preservation of the whole.' This allows the leadership considerable power which they are often able to implement uncritically. As a consequence, the skill and aptitudes of other members may be underutilised; a problem compounded if group leaders are ill-suited for the role.[25]

Group isolation, whether real in terms of physical separation or psychological in terms of detachment within communities to safeguard secrecy, can also seriously weaken long-term prospects. Within clandestine groups, leaders control information and contacts with external relations tends to place pressure on the relationship between leaders and led. The control of information and depth and breadth of secrets held is not shared equally across the group and hierarchical structure. Just like other forms of organisation, members' access to knowledge often equates to power. As the above point suggests, the impact of this controlled approach is heavily dependent on the quality of leadership.

Moreover, Holsti (1972) details the tensions and high levels of anxiety and fatigue that accompanies engagement with terrorism and associated threats and insecurities. This is particularly noticeable for groups who live without community support. In these environments it becomes more difficult for knowledgeable calculations to be made, impressions of the people on whom the group alleges to be fighting become blurred or distorted, the ability to assess and evaluate strategies and counter-terror approaches and adjust accordingly diminishes, levels of risk taking are heightened and there are overly optimistic estimates for the likelihood of success. Silj (1979: 115) observed in this regard that the Italian Red Brigades lost perspective after entering the underground. With little or no reliable information, they wrongly predicted the reactions of both potential supporters and enemies to their attacks, simultaneously undermining their appeal and strengthening the opposition. And as another member, Adriana Faranda informed Jamieson (1989: 268), 'we had to trust in our impressions which in fact were only the subjective impressions of others.'

Conversely, although community-based terror groups tend to be more secure, closer community relations can hinder levels of secrecy. In other words, within some communities there is greater interest in the activities of neighbours, friends and kin which can breach boundaries of secrecy. Certainly within Palestinian and Northern Irish loyalist and republican neighbourhoods, the role of significant members of terror organisations has often been known outwith the group. By comparison, participants in al-Qa'ida-related attacks have tended to locate within anonymous, transitory neighbourhoods where there is little or no interest in the lives of others. The non-descript immersion into American urban neighbours by the September 2001 bombers followed this template.

Finally, if we draw from Roth's (2003) study of peer relations within processes of female recruitment into labour movements, pre-existing friendships can be obstacles to the integration of other members and alienating to those who do not share these emotional ties. For terror groups this could be severely restrictive. Following on from the above points, inner dynamics and the people therein appear to be integral in the appeal of terrorism. If the existing members are self-contained and unwelcoming this would have an adverse impact at two levels. First, people may be less inclined to join if they do not like the other members, do not expect rewarding social relationships or anticipate problems integrating. And second, if groups are to function effectively and securely, members have to trust each other and develop cohesive bonds. Inner cliques are likely to hinder this, thereby weakening prospects of success and enhancing the likelihood of capture.

## Conclusion

Hopefully this chapter has shown that what is remarkable about group dynamics within processes of terrorism is how unremarkable so many of the interactions actually are. Just like other groups, members have to be committed to the purpose of meeting whether that is to gossip, drink coffee, eat cake or commit acts of political violence. Arguably the latter task requires greater commitment but some similar processes can be identified. Members need to be integrated, share layers of habitus, hold similar ideas, goals and morals and be committed to the dyad, triad and larger configurations. Hence feelings of commonality and collective purpose need to exist on which to build solidarity in order to achieve group goals. These shared feelings are often created within informal groups through gossip and the mutual identification of group charisma and de-identification with the 'Other.' Secrecy and trust, the intersection between group charisma and stigmatisation and minorities of the best and worst are integral to group cohesion, recruitment and retention processes. Cognitive and affective aspects are interwoven as individuals become immersed in groups for both rational and emotional reasons. The extent to which individuals become engaged is heavily influenced by their disposition, their individual biography, social structural location and the residues of historical discourse and forms of violence. After joining, expressive and instrumental reasoning is fluid and contingent with group dynamics remaining fundamental both to continuing commitment and the balance between levels of pacification and aggression.

The outcomes, rigour and intensity through which boundaries are drawn within terror groups may differ from passive movements but I argue that the processes are comparable. Obviously there are also significant differences. Cake eaters are not renowned for blowing up bakers. What remains most apparent and notorious about terrorism are the acts of violence, and it is to this sphere of activity that I now turn.

# 6 Actions, tactics and targets

## Emotions and rationale behind terror attacks

## Introduction

Impressions of terrorism are overwhelmingly dominated by group attacks, the immediate outcomes of death and destruction and the emotions they invoke. The dominance of the images surrounding terror actions have not helped inform an understanding about the reasons why the acts were committed, targets selected nor why people chose to become involved. On the contrary, I would argue pictures of body parts, scared children and mangled transportation contribute to heightened emotions which adversely impact upon levels of detached analysis within societies. It is therefore unsurprising that the explorations of journalists and academics are also influenced by widespread feelings within society, which they frequently portray. Individual and groups' underlying reasoning behind the attacks is all too often missing from overly emotive accounts that fall upon the hackneyed clichés. These revolve around 'inhuman' or 'abnormal' individual characteristics which are applied in order to explain why the attacks occurred. Thus only 'evil' or brainwashed people in groups consumed with hatred can kill innocent civilians and this becomes the prevailing explanation. Unless they accord with the clichés, individual motivations and collective purposes are rarely considered. The inevitable outcome is that the reasons why individuals and groups commit the attacks lack substantive insights. In essence, we need to know much more about the purposes of terrorism, the targeting, the chosen methods, the interweaving of emotions and rationality, and the shifts into, and spiralling of, violence.

Within this chapter terror tactics and strategies are examined in order to understand the instrumental reasoning behind attacks against designated sites and people. The focus is then extended to try to gain an appreciation for the interactions behind rationality and emotions that contribute to the selection of targets and their justification. In so doing I aim to challenge Weber's (1978: 18) argument that 'the unavoidable tendency of sociological concepts [is] to assume a rationalistic character with a belief in the predominance of rational motives.' Interweaving of the expressive and practical is also notable within individual shifts in attitudes and behaviour that enable people to commit acts of violence. After exploring examples of these transformations the impact of spirals of violence upon episodes of terrorism is discussed. The chapter concludes with a seeming paradox, namely the controlling of political violence by terror groups. Although I will be primarily focusing upon actions of the violence, it is important to stress that groups will usually have twin or triple track approaches that incorporate passive promotion and/or the provision of social services such as those provided by HAMAS and Hezbollah in the Palestinian territories and Lebanon respectively.

## Targets and types of attack

There are a range of activities that members can become involved with. These activities include financial, material and logistical support, recruitment campaigns, leadership, planning, couriering, kidnapping, arson, driving, assassination, bomb making and detonating whether remotely or strapped onto the individual. Some groups may be more associated with particular types of action. Examples of these 'trademark' acts include beheadings by Sunni Iraqi groups post American invasion, hijackings and early 1970s Palestinian groups, suicide bombings and the Tamil Tigers, hostage taking and the Shining Path, three-person scooter assassination teams and the Greek 17 November Organisation and car bombs and the IRA. As I explained in the early chapters, the association with particular methods is often a legacy of the past and this applies both within specific actions of directed violence towards others and alternative approaches adopted by the 'terrorists.' For instance, hunger strikes became well known as a tactic within Irish republican strategies alongside 'terrorism' with both being ultimately directed towards achieving independence. Yet the practice stems from the medieval period when people who were aggrieved at a neighbour would starve themselves outside their neighbours hut until the matter was resolved or they died. Ironically the practice had largely died out by the time that sectarian tensions heightened and solidified during the 1690s (Foster 1989). It was not until the writings of Yeats in the late nineteenth century that the practice was re-introduced with an explicitly political connotation. In the twentieth century and prior to the 1980/1 strikes twelve republicans had already starved to death (Arthur 1997).[1]

Across the modern history of terrorism, as Jenkins (1985: 17) outlines, tactics can largely be classified into three categories; 'Terrorists blow up things, kill people, or seize hostages. Every terrorist incident is merely a variation of these three activities.' Buildings and people are therefore central to terrorist incidents. Properties can include government buildings, military installations, transportation facilities, symbolic private property and public utilities. With the controversial partial exception of civilians, humans are usually selected according to their role, perceived allegiance or are known political figures. Thus government officials, members of royal families, soldiers, policemen, public employees, tourists, journalists, academics, foreign workers, immigrants, medical practitioners, political opponents, collaborators and complicit civilians can be attacked according to group discourse and objectives. As the Russian revolutionary Sergei Nechaev stated in 1868, 'the guiding principle [in selecting targets for terror] must be the measure of service the person's death will necessarily render to the revolutionary cause.'[2] Taber's application of Mao's tenets aptly describes the intention of many terror groups, when examining guerrillas' 'war of the flea.' 'The flea bites, hops, and bites again, nimbly avoiding the foot that would crush him. He does not seek to kill his enemy at a blow, but to bleed him and feed on him, to plague him and bedevil him, to keep him from resting and to destroy his morale.'[3]

The selection of targets and method of attack may appear callous, irrational or barbaric but are usually the outcome of careful consideration. Understandably the most devastating acts of terrorism, which are usually associated with bomb attacks, attract most attention. The emphasis on body counts contributes to the neglect of other significant methods that are adopted in part according to the group's requirements. For instance, Gupta (2008) explains how groups such as the Colombian FARC and Filipino Abu Sayyaf Group emphasise kidnapping and hostage taking. By adopting such tactics groups are able to raise essential funds either for the group or, on occasion, personal member's gain. Providing the number of kidnaps is restricted and depending on the profile of the captives, hostage taking attracts considerable publicity. The surrounding drama can be prolonged across several key stages ensuring that the group achieves regular, prominent media coverage. Crenshaw (1992) also points out that hostage taking can be motivated by groups' intentions such as the West German and Italian Far Left's use of captives to negotiate the release of imprisoned leaders.

At first glance the act of violence is a form of expression, a communicative medium. I argue that if terror attacks are to achieve their primary short-term aim of terrorising, acts of terrorism must attract widespread attention that is best achieved, outwith 'wars of attrition,' through novelty and variation. Hence an over-reliance on particular forms of action such as suicide bombing tends to lead to diminished rates of return. This is in part because media coverage diminishes with familiarity as groups that have made frequent usage of suicide bombers such as Palestinians, Tamils and Iraqi Sunnis have discovered. Groups must therefore be able to adapt and be fluid in their adoption of different techniques if they are to remain relevant. Emphasis on rational behaviour can often challenge the prevailing opinion because the targeting of 'innocent victims' in particular is contrary to normative standards and expectations. Yet terror groups do provide calculative, purposive frameworks in the Weberian sense with their actions directed towards longer-term goals. And groups can draw reference to numerous terror campaigns that contributed to the achievement of aims.[4] Of course opponents can point to the myriad of terror groups whose actions ultimately failed.

Nor do the methods remain static. Improvements in chemical storage, wider availability of resources and greater awareness of techniques have meant that risks to terrorists during the manufacture and blowing up of bombs have diminished. Obviously this does not apply to suicide bombings which tend to place the bomber under considerable risk. By comparison remote-controlled devices, including those strapped to another person, provide the detonator with greater control and security. Similarly, technological and chemical developments and increased availability can also contribute to new methods emerging. Webb and Cutter (2009) provide the example of the increased use of chemical agents by Pro Life extremists from the 1990s. Agents such as butyric acid are chosen because they cause extensive damage which creates more 'down time' for the abortion facility. Hence the contested services are further delayed until the premises are cleansed.

A multitude of physical buildings and humans can therefore be targets and are attacked through a variety of different methods. The choice of target is heavily influenced by the intended audience and whether the intention is to scare and/or attract support. Today many groups are also heavily influenced in their decision-making by the media, coverage they would receive and the impact upon profile. For terror leaders such as al-Qa'ida's Ayman al-Zawahiri, groups must adopt a twin track approach that incorporates military and media confrontations. Neither must the target be constant. Groups will often vary their selection in part to hinder prevention and detection while enhancing levels of uncertainty that pervades more public spaces. The 2003 Casablancan bombings are illustrative with five incidents in different locations such as a hotel, restaurant, club and Jewish community centre. A mixture of Jews, tourists, businessmen and secular middle class were targeted (Alonso and Rey 2007). Groups may also change targets when confronting revised forms of counter-terrorism which result in greater protection for previous locations and personnel. For instance, Speckhard and Ahkmedova (2006) explain how the nature of attacks changed following the hardening of military sites within Chechnya and growing news blackouts. Chechen groups decided that new tactics were required to maintain the confrontation with Russia and to arouse international media attention. Through spectacular attacks within Russia the Chechens were able both to terrorise Russians and overcome the media blackout which had been imposed within Chechnya.

Furthermore, the choice of target is pragmatically determined by accessibility, group capability, resources, infrastructure, location and support base. Thus groups in densely populated areas such as Baghdad can be expected to adopt different tactics and targets to terrorists operating in rural and underdeveloped regions. Although terrorism is not necessarily expensive, groups with considerable resources such as the IRA and al-Qa'ida, prior to 2002, could consider more elaborate, costly operations that involved communications, electronics, transportation, weaponry, surveillance and forgeries which in turn extends the possible range of targets. The environment, identified target and requirement for security and secrecy will also influence the amount of planning that is undertaken. Hence, the September 2001 attacks were formulated over many months while the destruction of Peruvian civilian villages, with little or no security or reliable legal procedures to pursue prosecution of the attackers, can be undertaken with limited preparation. Some groups develop diverse methods which create further confusion and insecurity amongst the targeted populations. Moreover the secrecy of those involved will also be instrumental in the decision-making. Devising precautions that will prevent detection both before and after the attacks is time consuming. Consequently suicide bombings can appeal in part because the group does not have to consider safeguarding the bombers' identities or likelihood of post-attack capture. Equally the clandestine level will also be influenced by the amount of publicity groups want to achieve for the attacks and themselves.[5]

Alongside the historical continuity of methods of attack, notably bombings, recently groups do appear to be more willing to take the risk of killing civilians and the potential impact upon their reputation. Certainly preceding generations of groups such as the IRA were willing to risk the deaths of civilians but casualties tended to be restricted.[6] Incidents, such as the Birmingham pub bombings in 1974, and attack on Le Mon restaurant in 1978, which killed 21 and 12 respectively, would accord with descriptions of more indiscriminate forms of terrorism. Crucially though, the attacks have subsequently been considered to be operations that went wrong due to problems with the phoned warnings (Bishop and Mallie 1988). Nevertheless attacks like these and similar bombings by ETA such as the killing of twelve civilians in a Madrid restaurant, indicated a loss of control and could not be justified according to the symbolic specific targeting of other attacks. Similarly Gupta (2008) reports on the IRA's adoption of 'proxy bombing' whereby individuals were forced to participate in attacks in which they died because the IRA had taken their families hostage. This method was quickly discarded when leaders realised that the nationalist community was firmly opposed to the tactic. Generally the IRA sought to control the impact of bombs upon civilians and would often withdraw from an attack if the risks to casualties were assessed to be excessive.[7] Yet this did not prevent attacks such as the above and the 1993 Shankhill bombing which killed nine civilians and the bomber.[8] Such non-symbolic incidents were often self-defeating and diminished the likelihood that the groups could claim legitimacy and thus support. In this regard it is unsurprising that nationalist groups sought, with the exception of 'collaborators,' to minimise civilian casualties especially in their own regions and neighbourhoods. ETA is a good example of this targeted restraint. Sánchez-Cuenca (2010) identifies that the average number of fatalities per fatal attack was 1.4[9] and military personnel comprised over 50 per cent of the group's killings; an approach that was heavily influenced by supporters lack of approval for indiscriminate killings and the deaths of civilians. By comparison ideological groups such as Italian fascists and cells associated with al-Qa'ida have been much more willing to kill civilians in public places such as cafes, market squares, public transport, bars and religious institutions. The Madrid bombings by the al-Qa'ida inspired group of Moroccans are an illustrative example of this rationale. Moreover the attacks were also memorable for their pragmatic, and ultimately achieved,[10] intention to transform the political agenda in Spain with the general elections only days away.

Webb and Cutter (2009) identify, with respect to American acts, shifts over targeting between 1970 and 2004. For instance, during the 1970s over 50 per cent of incidents were directed at government entities and businesses such as department stores, banks, hotels and supermarkets. Following the decline of the Far Left and rise of the pro-life groups during the 1980s the overall number of incidents dropped while the attacks against abortion and women's health clinics rose to 30 per cent of terror attacks. In the 2000s businesses, private citizens and property accounted for almost 70 per cent of targeted incidents. The overwhelming majority of recent attacks against businesses such as McDonalds' restaurants, biomedical laboratories and logging companies were committed by environmental and animal rights groups such as ALF and ELF. Today, Webb and Cutter argue, incidents in places and spaces of everyday activity such as supermarkets and banks have become increasingly within the sights of terrorists. To this can be added the examples from nationalist and discursive struggles elsewhere that have targeted bars, restaurants, cafes, hotels, marketplaces, shops and public transport. Nevertheless, although these locations may appear unique to the people involved, there is rarely anything novel about the targets within the history of terror attacks.

The shifting of terror targets is also noticeable within the change in approach that was instrumental in the emergence of al-Qa'ida and the redirection of attacks from the near to the far enemy. Burke (2006) explains how the 2001 attacks on America were partly inspired by a belief that many Muslims were united in their negative perceptions of the country. By attacking these bin Laden and the inner core believed that the latent support would become manifest within a global uprising. Hence attacking the 'far' enemy would mobilise support to an extent that was not noticeable within campaigns against 'near' enemies in the 1980s and early 1990s and which were acknowledged to have failed.

Islamic groups have also become associated with another controversial method, namely the beheading of victims. Lentini and Bakashmar (2007) draw upon the history of religious and cultural factors which provide the act with significance and enable the sword to be legitimised as a symbol of *jihad*. Khosrokhavar (2005) also identifies how cutting a throat (of a sheep) can be construed as a sacred act. By killing humans in the same way there is an argument that this is part of the militants' attempts to dehumanise the victims. There is also an argument that the perpetrators would be aware of the impact that the symbolic removal of the individual head would have upon Western sensitivities, not least through the connection with prevailing perceptions of the barbaric Arab. By drawing together these emotions, fears become exaggerated and stereotypes strengthened. Moreover Lentini and Bakashmar (2007) propose, and as I explored in earlier chapters, the prevalence of capital punishment including 'official' beheadings in place like Saudi Arabia mean that the act is culturally grounded and normalised. The terrorists are in some respects adapting state methods and retain restraints over the use of violence.

## Rationale and emotions behind terror attacks

Contrary to the prevailing impression that terrorism is adopted by blood thirsty maniacs, there are, in addition to the operational factors outlined above, numerous tactical reasons why groups choose to become politically violent and which are often underpinned by expressive reasoning. The reasoning and influences are interspersed within shifting emotions and levels of rationality that change in reaction to situations, perceived opportunities and risks, evolving short- and long-term objectives and so on. These influences may not necessarily be complementary. For example, a short-term demand for retaliation can bring about unwanted distractions and raise levels of risk of arrest or death for attacks that may be unlikely to contribute to long-term goals such as independence or a new form of government.

At the onset the decision to become a terror organisation is often indicative of the group's political weakness. Groups are weak at a number of levels. First, they lack widespread popular support. Second, and building upon this, they lack the human, territorial and/or military resources to challenge the dominant forces through more conventional forms of warfare. Third, under repressive regimes opportunities to engage within mainstream political processes can be extremely restricted and political violence may be the only form of expressing dissent. For instance, the cancellation of the general election in Algeria alongside increasingly indiscriminate government repression were instrumental in the decision to turn to political violence during the early 1990s or what Ali Jeddi, a prominent FIS figure, described as 'the option of the last resort.'[11]

Thus acts of terrorist violence have become known as 'propaganda by deed'[12] and are committed as a form of asymmetrical conflict. As Hayes and McAllister (2005: 606) explained with respect to Northern Ireland,

> the decision whether or not to use constitutional or extraconstitutional violence is less a moral one than a matter of expediency and practicality; if violence is seen to have the greatest chance of achieving the required political goals, then it will be utilized.

And as they point out, 'the message learned from Irish history is that the use of physical force does bring political gain' (ibid.: 608). Alongside this it should also be pointed out that numerous other terror campaigns have failed to bring about any significant political concessions. For the perpetrators, acts of political violence are, as Tilly (1978) argued when reproaching frustration theories, of an instrumental nature. The acts or methods are considered within a continuum towards the achievement of strategic objectives. In essence terror attacks are the means towards an end, although both the route to the end and what it will look like often lack clarity. Nevertheless terror groups will usually carefully consider the options. Limited alternative opportunities and the perceived overarching justness of their cause often result in the conclusion, against a backdrop of terrorists' historical failures, that the examples of political success are more relevant. As one Left-Wing member informed Neuburger and Valentini (1996: 148), 'We are the direct heirs of the concept that there are just and unjust wars; we had chosen our activities as the situation demanded as a just manifestation, as a just occupation and, hence, as a just war.'

Clearly targets are chosen, in part, because of their symbolic representation and their association with group objectives. Thus groups are careful to attack sites that are associated with that to which they are opposed and usually, but not always, not the people they claim to represent. Nationalist groups will therefore focus upon governing armies, security forces and 'complicit' civilians. Far Right groups target scapegoats, regional and national governments, trans-national Islamic groups attack Western institutions, locations or governments associated with Western dominance and Left Wing and environmental groups' direct actions against capitalist and related international organisations. The significance of oil installations highlights the tactical shifts. Groups such as the Colombian National Liberation Army sabotaged pipelines in order to undermine the economy and thus weaken government income, expenditure and ultimately power. Today attacks against oil installations can be noticed across energy regions for both political and criminal purposes which are often interwoven and ideologies which range from extreme Left to national and ethnic through to religion.

Reasons provided for terror attacks are also multifarious. This is partly because there are multi-layered targets even within one attack. Thus at an immediate level the victims are the obvious target. However in the overall terror strategy they are rarely the sole or even the primary target. This is usually the central authority that is held accountable. For instance, attacks against overseas tourists can be immediately interpreted, as in the instances of assaults by Islamic militants on Christian and Jewish visitors in places such as Luxor and Sharm el-Sheikh in Egypt, to be driven by sectarian hatred and anger at the exhibition of inappropriate, decadent Western behaviour. Hence the tourists are considered to be symptomatic of immorality and laxness. Yet beyond these emotive reasons, calculative intentions can also be apparent. The killings are often intended to deter subsequent international visitors which would damage the local economy, thereby reducing government income and expenditure to control the population. At one level government authority would diminish alongside the increasing dissatisfaction and anger over the declining economy which the militants hope to connect into. The actions are ultimately driven by long-term objectives, the targeting of the government through the political, economic and social consequences of the killings and ultimately the acquisition of power.

Similarly attacks in Saudi Arabia against foreign oil employees are partly driven by anger over the presence of non-Muslims on Islamic territory. The actions are also intended to scare away workers and investment, thereby weakening the oil economy and international and local perceptions about

Saudi short-term security and long-term stability. Following on from these reasons terror attacks are also designed to appeal to individuals who are attracted by the groups' potential and concomitant weakness of governments, security forces, military and international agencies. When attacking transportation terrorists create a legacy of fear and uncertainty that extends psychologically far beyond the physical damage. People become insecure, reluctant to travel and fearful of individuals who fit the caricature of a terrorist. In these regards terror groups want to 'wake up' their intended supporters to their versions of reality or as the Jewish group the Lehi (a.k.a. the 'Stern Gang') mentioned in a 1943 publicity leaflet, 'if it [acts of terrorism] also shakes the population out of its complacency, so much the better.'[13] Moreover, because acts of terrorism challenge nation-states' monopoly on violence they can lead to a loss of confidence in the capability of governments to protect their populations. With considerable irony terrorists hope that the population turns to them to provide protection.

The most controversial and divisive targets within broader movements are civilians. If groups are to successfully justify these targets, they have to make comparable connections with violence inflicted against the people they proclaim to protect. From the anarchists onwards, terror groups who target civilians have utilised the actions of governments to try to justify their decision-making and arouse support or to not significantly diminish their appeal. Such claims do not have to necessarily describe violent behaviour in the conventional sense. Kassel (2009: 242) provides an early example of extended grounds for justification when quoting the anarchist bomber Emile Henri who declared at his trial,

> Anarchists do not spare bourgeois women and children, because the wives and children of those they love are not spared either. Are not those children innocent victims who, in the slums, die slowly of anaemia because bread is scarce at home; of those women who grow pale in your workshops and wear themselves out to earn forty sous a day. ... At least have the courage of your crimes, gentlemen of the bourgeoisie, and agree that our reprisals are fully legitimate.

Over 100 years later bin Laden (2002) sought legitimacy through the same comparison when claiming 'we treat others like they treat us. Those who kill our women and our innocent, we kill their women and innocent, until they stop from doing so.' Similar examples abound within militant Muslim justifications. Imam Samudra, the mastermind of the Bali bombings, is indicative of the linkages drawn between group political violence and more specific Western policies. He referred to the mass deaths of Iraqi and Afghan civilians as a consequence of the trade embargoes, Israeli attacks on Palestinians and the post-September 2001 US actions in Afghanistan (Acharya 2006). Oliverio (1998) identifies similar processes within the formal rationalisation of conventional war between nation-states which resulted in saturation bombing during the Second World War and American war in Vietnam. The subsequent emergence of 'smart' missiles and camouflaging of civilian deaths under the euphemism 'collateral damage' has done little to confront Western government's sacrifice of the other's civilians in the name of peace and stability. In this regard terrorists challenge the prevailing view that their actions stem from individual weakness or innate evil and place the blame very firmly on the society or global forces they are confronting. Liston (1977: 28) observes that Henri's response during trial that 'there are no innocents' has resonated within terror groups ever since. In essence, anyone who votes for a government or does not vote for more acceptable alternatives or who pay taxes to governments that are considered to be spent upon death, injustice or repression can be a legitimate target. Moreover some groups are willing to sacrifice some of the people they claim to be fighting on behalf of. Targeting becomes imprecise and anyone can seemingly be justifiably killed. For instance, Zawqawi sought to explain the killing of both Western and Muslim civilians. Killing the latter was permissible when they,

> happen to be near the scenes of operations for some reason or another and it was not possible to avoid killing them and distinguish between them and the intended fighting non believers. There is no doubt that killing a Muslim soul is an evil act, but sometimes you cannot avoid this evil act when fighting a bigger evil which is giving up *jihad* altogether.[14]

For most groups these acts are part of a broader approach and other strands will also influence the selection of targets and intensity of attacks. Collectively these factors will influence the likelihood that terrorism will contribute to the achievement of overarching goals. Some groups quickly fail and disappear. Others are more prolonged but are often also inclined to be unsuccessful. Overall, groups with deep and broad interconnections with the communities on whose behalf they claim to act are more likely to achieve their goals. These groups tend to be nationalistic and emerge out of broader movements. Gupta (2008) identifies how the most successful groups were those acting against colonial powers such as the Jewish Stern and Irgun Gangs and Greek Cypriot EOKA against the British, Algerian FLN against the French and Angolan UNITA and FNLA against Portugal. Subsequent 'waves' have not been able to achieve their objectives to the same extent and have often totally failed. The most notable exception has been Hezbollah, who were instrumental in the expulsion of Israeli forces from Lebanon and also became renowned for campaigns that utilised suicide attacks.

Within studies of terrorism suicide bombers have attracted the most attention and have become a sub-discipline in their own right.[15] Consequently there is little requirement to examine the phenomena in great detail here. Instead I will try to restrict myself to a few salient points to help understand the potentially greater shift in norms and values which enables individuals to kill not only other people but themselves. As with other forms of attack, human bombs are adopted as methods for a number of reasons, or as Pape (2005) proposes, strategic, social and individual logics:

a. Humans are more effective than other forms of device. They are 'intelligent' bombs able to react flexibly to the situation, selecting the most damaging location in which to detonate or to abort if there is a grave danger both of arrest or failure to achieve casualties.
b. Moreover, they offer opportunities to attack previously unimaginable sites. The 2001 attacks on American sites are particularly pertinent examples.
c. Because of their intelligence, control and the lack of confidentiality post attack, planning, development and surveillance do not have to be as rigorous nor as costly.
d. Self-destructive acts demonstrate to the enemy, potential supporters and wider audience that the group's commitment is greater than life. Therefore being willing to make the ultimate sacrifice for the cause raises serious questions regarding how groups can be stopped if death is not a deterrent. For potential supporters the acts' symbolism usually resonates with a tradition of resistance and frames of sacrifice. These are reawakened or reinforced and heightened emotional commitment ensues.

The high profile of attacks such as those in New York, September 2001, Madrid, March 2005 and London, July 2005 by Muslims has led to the phenomena being widely associated with Islam. Yet this overlooks the activities of other religious groups such as the Hindu Tamils in Sri Lanka and Sikhs in India. Pape (2005) argues that contrary to the correlation between Islam and suicide, Muslims have low rates of suicide. This is part of a broader trend. With the exception of Sri Lanka, 'the incidence of suicide terrorism is highest where ordinary suicide rates are low' (Pape 2005: 181). Moreover the bombers are not the weak manipulated creatures who best accord with stereotypes of terrorists and underlying anomic factors, not least because individuals who are 'ordinarily' suicidal would lack the energy and commitment that planning and carrying out the attack requires. Instead of being disposed towards self-killing the perpetrators tend to be volunteers whose recruitment follows social processes, discussed in the preceding chapter, and who participate for interwoven altruistic, egotistical and in some instances fatalist reasons[16] (Sutton and Vertigans 2005). This combination of factors is reflected in the multifarious backgrounds of the self-immolators with many secular, well educated and middle class. Consequently it is a mistake to associate suicidal terrorism too closely with religion.

In another challenge to prevailing opinion, women are probably most prominent in the analysis of suicide bombers. This is partly because of the relatively high numbers of females involved.[17] From a rational perspective, numerous reasons have been provided for the participation of females. These often orientate around groups utilising the prevailing opinion that exists within societies both to commit the attacks and attract publicity.[18] For example,

1   The tendency to view women as less challenging and more passive has resulted in females being subjected to less suspicion and scrutiny. Tactically this has enabled easier access for females to reach targets compared to men. Hence the incorporation of women suicide bombers within Palestinian campaigns occurred when heightened security arrangements meant it was increasingly difficult for men to commit the same acts. They also required a shift in approach from militant religious leaders who had hitherto refused to allow women to be involved. Indeed there is some evidence to suggest that Wafa Idris committed the first attack without the formal support of a terror group. Certainly HAMAS only provided authorisation for the involvement of females retrospectively.

2   The death of female suicide bombers is also likely to arouse more media attention. Again this is because their actions challenge dominant stereotypes and are therefore more surprising and newsworthy. References will usually depict the woman's pre-attack physical appearance.

3   Women dying for the cause is thought to contribute to greater levels of sympathy.

4   Finally their actions are expected to mobilise new recruits, not least men in patriarchal societies who become 'embarrassed' by females acting on their behalf. The Egyptian daily newspaper, *Al-Sha'ab* provides an illustrative example when responding to the first female suicide bomber, Wafa Idris, in the Palestinian territories, that 'It is a woman who teaches you today a lesson in heroism, who teaches you the meaning of Jihad, and the way to die a martyr's death.'[19]

The advent of human bombs is a good example of the inter-weaving of rational and emotional factors. First and foremost the organisers view the incident within a strategic framework directed towards a pragmatic goal. In this sense, the attacks fit neatly within the strategic models for suicide bombers of researchers such as Pape (2005). The human bombs may view their actions differently. Individuals participate for a variety of reasons such as anger, revenge,[20] frustration, fatalism and religion, in particular to enhance their prospects of salvation as arguably a form of self-interest alongside the altruistic contribution to the national or ideological cause (Sutton and Vertigans 2005). Hafez (2007) draws upon this interplay when discussing the emotional narratives that are deployed by *jihadists* in Iraq within communications that are designed to mobilise support. Again distinctions in the analysis of male and female attackers are noticeable. The motivations of the latter replicate the concentration upon emotions and fatalism often proposed by terror groups and identified within studies of female terrorists generally, and if anything are probably exaggerated within many studies of suicide bombers. Instrumental components of the bombings are considered to be part of the male leaders' cost–benefit calculations.

Within the very different example of hunger strikes by terrorists, Dingley and Mollica (2007) discuss the emotive impact of the strikes and the heightened emotions leading ultimately to death. Within the campaign careful consideration was given to how to maximise the emotional appeal, the longevity of the strikes and the determination of those involved. Consequently a number of criteria were applied when examining the applications from potential volunteers. These included a preference for single men with no children (less family pressures to withdraw or conflicting interests) which was considered alongside the duration of sentence (those with only a short time remaining in prison may be less committed), prisoner's health (to avoid premature death) and strength of character (to be better able to confront the tensions and pressures that would emerge).

## Action men?

When studying individuals who commit acts of violence, with the exception of suicide bombers and some Left-Wing groups, there has been a tendency to concentrate on the roles of men. At one level this is understandable. Although the involvement of men can be overstated and the preceding examples notwithstanding, there is little doubt that more men than women are terrorists and this correlates with more men committing violent action. Moreover, when males and females are involved in the same groups, men often undertake more responsible or active roles. This can be noticeable even when females are part of prominent groups such as the Chechens who carried out high-profile actions. For instance, after taking hostages at the Dubrovka theatre female members were more likely to be stationary, sitting while guarding the captives and carried smaller pistols than the men who tended to hold the machine guns (Speckhard 2008). Alongside this, groups with more conservative views of women such as Islamist and Far Right expect females to underpin their discourse within the domestic environment, to give birth, to socialise children in an appropriate manner that accords with radical discourse ultimately resulting in recruits for the militant organisations. Women, particularly associated with militant Islam, have also been reported as volunteering to marry men who commit particular acts of *jihad*.[21] Furthermore the significance of the family in strengthening group bonds and reinforcing security against infiltration is exemplified by Islamic groups whose members have married the female relatives of other members (Abuza 2003 and Ismael 2006).

Obvious Left-Wing examples of prominent females include the Japanese Red Army's Fusako Shigenobu, Mara Cagol from the Italian Red Brigades, RAF's Ulrike Meinhof and Gudrun Esslin and Bernandine Dohrn from the Weather Underground. The leadership of all these groups incorporated relatively high levels of females across the groups' history. Following the reasoning provided for the limited representation in preceding chapters, there are a number of explanations for this including less violent layers of disposition, limited relevant networks, societal restraints and the tendency for male leaders to share prevailing views on gender roles. Ironically, in some less patriarchal societies women have been able to utilise their greater freedoms and acquired skills and ideas to challenge the sponsoring government or its successors. Hence the egalitarianism promoted within the Soviet Union contributed to greater liberation for Chechen females in comparison with many other societies at similar stages of development (Speckhard and Ahkmedova 2006). Levels of participation within society and acceptance of the public engagement of females arguably enabled women to become integral members of terror groups.

Victor (2004) proposes with respect to suicide bombings that female involvement has occurred within favourable social conditions and which reflects the above commentary. Furthermore if women are to become more involved in groups that formulate within societies in which their general participation is more restricted, then the past has to be utilised in order to provide legitimacy for their engagement. Ness (2005) argues that this applies both for secular groups such as the LTTE and religious organisations such as HAMAS and Islamic Jihad. In the case of the LTTE, female involvement was gradual, initially restricted to roles that reflected their contributions to Tamil society, namely non-combative such as nurses, administrators and cooks.[22] By utilising violent images of women within Hindu mythology the LTTE were able to both incorporate women within aggressive roles and gender equality within their discourse.[23] In some respects the contradictory tensions are epitomised in the assassination of Rajiv Gandhi by a female Tamil suicide bomber. She was able to breach security by her portrayal of a female admirer who garlanded Gandhi, 'bowed at his feet, and then detonated a bomb that killed them both' (Cunningham 2003: 180). Ness (2005) and von Knop (2007) report that the group had to continue to fit within broader parameters of gender behaviour. Therefore, although some gender distinctions were removed, others, such as the sexes being segregated in different camps, remained to accord with prevailing opinion about appropriate female behaviour. Similarly in the Palestinian territories, women who became involved tended to be classified according to their military roles with legitimacy drawn from the examples of violent female behaviour alongside the Prophet Muhammed. And in a manner that is not too dissimilar from Western media reporting, Ness (2005) reports that Palestinian groups have tended to idealise the female's individual characteristics such as their piety, beauty and brilliance. In short the women's participation was acknowledged and celebrated but in a manner which accorded with the normative values which continue to clearly demarcate gender roles across Palestinian society.

Overall, despite the different levels of involvement, men and women who do become involved in terrorism appear to share similar processes that connect experiences with deep-rooted histories of political violence and subsequent conditions that have not been conducive to the formulation of well-embedded restraints. It is therefore important to study particular instances that contribute to people deciding to actively become 'terrorists.'

## Stepped in and stepping into violence

Irrespective of gender, the dispositions of members who undertake acts of political violence must shift to accommodate the application of terrorism and overcome the inhibitions and cognitive dissonance[24] that many experience when contemplating the adoption of violence. This transition may well conflict with passive norms and values internalised at an earlier formative period. In blunt terms, the terrorist has to undertake actions which s/he considers for the greater good but which millions of people will consider bad. The actions are often based upon both Weber's ethics of conviction and responsibility, in other words absolute values and rational planning.[25] Levels of pacification will vary according to habitus. For instance, in the example of West German Far Left groups, Elias (1996) points out that breaking through the barriers against the use of physical violence is much more difficult for people of middle-class origin. This is because unlike the working classes, the middle classes did not experience relatively high levels of family violence and violence at school. The structuring and assimilation of these controls has occurred over generations. For individuals, the processes through which the restraints are accommodated within their dispositions is also considerably longer than some of their notable predecessors. During earlier periods of political violence when power and territory exchanged hands through warrior campaigns, drives and impulses were less rigorously regulated. Consequently controls were not as embedded and in some instances were actively discouraged. Hence, people shifted to violent behaviour with relative ease which was crucial if they were to be able to react aggressively to the potential threats that were rife within their lifestyles. For the West German middle classes, the process of remodelling behaviour was very different and had to overcome long-term processes of individual and inter-generational restraints. For these people violence is not a spontaneous reaction and justification is acquired through reflection or 'legitimation through a theory' (ibid.: 233). The first generation were able to accommodate the shift through the transition from sit-ins, protests and street battles into terrorism. By comparison violence was more prevalent in Italy between Right and Left Wing and the police, so that former terrorists regularly referred to the extent of violence that existed and its impact upon their own attitudes towards aggressive behaviour (Neuburger and Valentini 1996).

Apter (1997: 2) expounds upon this when declaring, 'people do not commit political violence without discourse. They need to talk themselves into it.' For Bandura (1999: 194), 'people do not ordinarily engage in harmful conduct until they have justified to themselves the morality of their actions.' Alongside discourse I would add group dynamics which were discussed in the preceding chapter. Within these dynamics it is conceivable that radicalism and even terrorism precedes the formation of discursive consciousness. For these people Crenshaw (1992: 35) explains, 'Once convinced that terrorism is intellectually justified, an individual is persuaded in retrospect that the initial use of terrorism was based on prior ideological beliefs.' I would add that although this may suggest primacy for rational motivation this is retrospective and emotions are not necessarily secondary at the time of the original decision. For intellectual terrorists, Elias reports on the feelings of heavily burdensome constraints, which facilitate the transgression of the constraints of their own conscience. Living in a perceived unbearably oppressive, restrictive and morally reprehensible society enabled individuals to shift in attitudes and work towards the destruction of these structures in order to allow people to live freely and humanely. When facing identified threats to lives, the scope to attack in the name of defence increases. Alongside these threats we need to incorporate feelings of insecurity that people experience when living in conditions that they consider to be unpredictable and threatening. As Mennell (2007: 198) explained,

> it is quite likely that the greater fears corresponding to higher levels of danger will produce in some people, or perhaps eventually all, behaviour that may be described as 'more emotional' or 'more impulsive,' in which the gradually acquired apparatus of self-constraints is undermined.

When applying this shift to contemporary terrorists it can be seen that with some exceptions, and again unlike medieval warriors, the use of violence is not expressive because the incidents are not emotionally satisfying in themselves. Instead attacks are, in the Weberian sense, largely instrumental, rationally chosen means towards identified objectives that require calculation and planning. Thus terrorists are able to overcome restraints concerning the adoption of forms of violence but in many instances retain the taboos regarding the levels of enjoyment and personal satisfaction that can be acquired from the acts. Nevertheless, alongside the calculative underpinning, we should not lose sight of the impact of emotions in contributing to the decisions to commit such acts of political violence. Moreover the level of instrumental use of violence shifts and as the double binding spirals, discussed below, indicate there are circumstances and interwoven relations in which ideas and behaviour become more fantasy orientated.

Many terrorists have reported upon the significance of particular events as triggers in their transformation into violence. Actions are considered as inevitable, a Kantian act for the sake of duty for themselves, their families, communities, nation and/or discourse. In Northern Ireland both republicans and loyalists became actively involved in terror groups after being forced to leave their homes, or feeling emotions such as anger, resentment and feelings of futility (Fairweather *et al.* 1984, MacDonald 1991, Toolis 1995). Other republican members participated in order to defend the community during periods when under threat from loyalists or following British army incursions. As IRA member Brendan Hughes explained, the actions of republican paramilitaries resulted in 'a sense of pride and a feeling that we had something to protect ourselves with. I wanted to be involved too because our whole community felt that we were under attack.'[26] Or as 'Seamus' informed Toolis (1995: 105), there was a sense of 'Let's get off our knees and do something – start fighting back.' Similar reasoning was noticeable for loyalists who were also critical of the British government. A loyalist paramilitary informed Bruce (1992: 198) 'there would be no need for the UVF if the government was doing its job properly. We had to step in to fill a vacuum. It was a matter of survival.' The violent outcomes of attacks were also instrumental. Following the IRA bombs on what became known as 'Bloody Friday,' David Ervine joined the loyalist paramilitaries after realising that one of the victims was his namesake. At this point Ervine believed that 'the best means of defence was attack.'[27] The deaths of family, friends, neighbours, people with whom individuals empathised, like the Ervine example, and children led to a sense that 'these people [the IRA] are out to slaughter us. They're going to kill us all, we're going to have to do something about this.'[28] Dynamics like these can help to explain some of the self-detrimental attacks undertaken during periods of heightened emotions. For example, Silke (2003) observes how the IRA's Shankhill Road bombing was carried out during a period of considerable loyalist attacks. Tensions were high and IRA brigades were under tremendous pressure to retaliate. Particular emphasis was placed upon the notorious UFF leader Johnny Adair. He was the intended target of the attack but escaped unharmed.[29]

The dynamics of competing groups such as 'red' and 'black' terrorists in Italy contributing to spirals of violence are explored in greater detail in the following section. One important difference to be highlighted here was the scale of the fascists' indiscriminate violence with three attacks in 1969, 1980 and 1984 killing a total of 117 people. The 1969 bomb at Piazza Fontana had a major psychological impact upon the Far Left. Jamieson (1989: 60) suggests that 'nearly all the "first generation" of Left-Wing terror members will point to December 1969 as a turning point; a decisive moment in which political commitment was made.' In West Germany, particular deaths are reported in the transition into violence. The most notable examples were Benno Ohnesborg who was killed by police during a demonstration against the visiting Shah of Iran and RAF member Holger Meins who died on hunger strike. For Speitel (1980: 41) 'the death of Holger Meins and the decision to take up arms were one and the same.' Within the American Far Right the action of the state has also been influential. Two particular examples from the 1990s are widely recorded within processes of radicalisation and which are believed to have been significant in Timothy McVeigh's decision to bomb a government building in Oklahoma.[30] In the two incidents a child and his mother were killed by federal agents and seventy-six members of a cult, including women and children, died in a fire. The Waco religious compound had been surrounded by federal agents during a standoff and the event had aroused huge publicity. Consequently the fire was shown live on television.

Despite such accounts Wieviorka (1997: 320) explains, as I explored in preceding chapters, the protagonists do not resort to terrorism in a single step.

Instead, 'the process leading to it is always chaotic, with moments of acceleration and others where it appears to have stopped, with steps backward as well as splits and ruptures within the movement concerned. It is not a linear progression ... .' At a basic level this can involve individuals initially being involved in support activities before graduating onto violent engagement. At group level there are numerous examples of perceived failures within broader movements such as the Aum Supreme Truth's democratic campaign, the civil rights movement in America and Northern Ireland and the Muslim Brotherhood across the Middle East. Individual shifts are comparable. For instance, Horgan (2009: 43) discusses increasing involvement with a Norwegian former Nazi 'Lars' who was imprisoned for bombing a mosque. Progression for Lars was 'very, very gradual. ... It starts with small things. ... We started by ... putting glue in the locks of the doors in their shop. ... [W]ell next time it's to smash something through the windows of the shop. ... Gradually you do more and more.' Moreover Horgan (2005) explains that the triggers become triggers and not isolated events and experiences if they interact with preconditions such as rapid modernisation, discrimination, inept government and foreign interference. To this I would add history and individual and social habitus.

Within processes of gradual progression, attempts at dehumanisation are prominent. Bandura (1998, 1999) describes processes of 'moral disengagement' that justify violent repertoires. The mechanisms include ethical justification, euphemistic labelling, displacement and diffusion of responsibility and comparisons with the 'Other's' transgression and the shifting of blame. For Bandura (1998: 161),

> Self-sanctions can be disengaged by reconstruing conduct as serving moral purposes, by obscuring personal agency in detrimental activities, by disregarding or misrepresenting the injurious consequences of one's actions, or by blaming and dehumanizing the victims.

Identifying the enemy with negative characteristics assists within processes that stereotype and depersonalise them. In turn depersonalising can degenerate into dehumanisation.[31] Jacobs (1997) and Bandura (1999) discuss a range of terms that are used that help to detach aggressors from taboos, and subsequently victims, such as pigs, beasts, genocidal robots, savages and gooks. These mechanisms contribute to the 'development of the capability to kill [which] is usually achieved through an evolvement process, in which recruits may not recognize the transformation they are undergoing' (Bandura 2004: 140). Within this shift there is a concomitant gradual disengagement from previous moral codes, sanctions and inhibitions. Over time, immersion within groups and engagement in activities can become routinised, enabling participants to reduce feelings of discomfort and cognitive dissonance. Strategies of counter-terrorism are crucially important in these environments. With their policies and actions subject to close scrutiny by the targeted communities, government aggression can help in the formulation and solidification of dehumanised characteristics. As Speckhard and Ahkmedova (2006: 481) remark, 'in Chechnya it may be less necessary for terrorist groups to dehumanise their victims through their ideology—at least when their targets are Russian military and police—because in many cases these targets have so often by their actions already dehumanized themselves.'

Moreover it is important to recall that these acts and phases did not happen in isolation. They occurred within environments in which uncertainty and insecurity were already prominent and for which there were historical precedents. In other words, individuals were already exposed to radical layers of habitus and, as I explained in the previous chapter, the particular incidents that led to individual decisions to become politically violent acted as triggers. It is extremely unlikely that these people would have become terrorists without the interweaving of history and habitus that helped to frame the interpretation and reaction to the precipitating factor. Consequently people become willing to use forms of political violence because of the shift in balance between individual and social regulation, the formulation of different types of restraints and the development of alternative behavioural patterns. When this is also accompanied by the limited or reduced mutual identification exemplified by processes of dehumanisation between groups, then the likelihood of individuals being willing to use violence to harm, injure, scare and kill people grows. Arguably reluctance diminishes and the willingness becomes magnified during spirals of hatred.

## Double binding spirals

Within processes of terrorism and counter-terrorism it is possible to identify what Elias (1996) referred to as double binds which contribute to violent behaviour and ideas spiralling. In this sense as Weber (1949: 57) explained when discussing the conflict of values, 'the highest ideals, which move us most forcefully, are always formed only in the struggle with other ideals which are just as sacred to others as ours are to us.' These circular processes are indicative of a loss of, or limited, control contributing to greater uncertainty, perceptions of threat and diminution of calculability. In these circumstances emotions become heightened, fears rise and reactions become more fantasy orientated and less rooted in rational calculation. Concerns about individual and group survival help to generate mutually reciprocal fears and hostilities and these emotions help to strengthen inner group commitment and consensus. Within self-escalating double bind processes mutual identification between groups reduces and each side comes to increasingly correspond to the negative image held by the opposing 'Other.' When examining the acceleration of violence in West Germany, Elias (1996: 263) argued that,

> The harder the adults – the police and the courts, but also the lawmaking parliament and the parties – struck, the more they resembled the

demonized image of an inhumane oppressive apparatus. And the more the restless young people fought – in the name of humaneness, social justice and the equality of the people – against a state they felt to be a violent regime of oppressors, the more violent and inhumane they themselves became.

Hence during the double bind process the balance between social and individual restraints further shifts and 'groups representing the state and others who feel themselves outside the state drive each other mutually into an escalation of acts of violence' (Elias 1996: 265). For terrorists these dynamics help to accelerate the transformation of social restraints away from mainstream consensual norms and values towards distinctive group ideas and forms of behaviour. The actions of the state within the double bind therefore help to provide support and justification for group reciprocation. At an emotional level Newman and Lynch (1987) have argued that this cycle of violence can be fuelled by vengeance. The code of vengeance becomes its own justification, both a moral claim and obligation that is based upon the principle of reciprocity. Within these group dynamics the death, serious injury or imprisonment of colleagues and friends becomes the basis for revenge. Again the spirals which follow initial attacks and subsequent revenge can detach members from the group's original aims and also further diminish the possibilities of compromise and reconciliation.

Spiralling violence is further exacerbated when there are opposing terror groups operating. Struggles involving terrorism are very often between terror groups and the state. In some instances though, in addition to government agencies and the trans-national targets of anarchists and Islamic militants, there are two competing groups such as pro- and anti-state groups in South America, republicans and loyalists in Northern Ireland and Left-Wing and fascist groups in Italy. In the latter example, Moss (1997) and Weinberg (1979) detail the rationale behind the groups selecting their opponents as the most frequent target for their attacks. Both extremes exaggerated the perceived threat from the other. For instance the 'reds' impressions had been influenced by the history of fascism in Italy, the fascists more indiscriminate approach to bombing and apparent complicity between the 'black' groups and the police. Nor do security services remain detached during these periods. The risks and killings they are exposed to impacts upon how the terrorists and those associated with them are viewed and treated. In Taylor's (1998: 96) study a former British soldier 'Jim' discusses the impact of his experiences in Northern Ireland,

> when you see these blokes [army colleagues] being stretchered out of flats, or dying in gutters ... it makes you bloody bitter. It makes you angry ... and it fills you with hate ... I hated the people in those areas with an intensity that used to make me feel almost physically sick when I heard them speak. (Taylor 1998: 96)

Complexities within and between groups have been further complicated in Iraq. Initially Sunni groups were attacking American forces and Shi'ites alongside al-Qa'ida in Iraq. By 2007/08 and through the Akbar awakening these allegiances had changed and the 'Sons of Iraq' targeted al-Qa'ida-related groups. There are a number of reasons for this shift including community concern over the attempts by al-Qa'ida to impose their literalist religious interpretations upon the population and repulsion over their gratuitous kill-ings. At one level this revulsion could be surprising. Political and sectarian violence in Iraq was prominent under Saddam and following the consistency of my argument we would expect these to have permeated the habitus. To some extent this is true and helps to explain the quick adaptation of violent methods by Sunnis post-2003 invasion. Equally though, because the Sunnis were largely considered to be supporters of Saddam, they were less exposed to the imposition of violence. Moreover Saddam's violence was often regiona-lised and directed at particular denominations, namely Shi'ites and Kurds. Saddam's tactics also incorporated more covert methods which meant that the application of violence was more selective, imposed within government buildings and out of sight of the majority of the Sunni population. Conse-quently despite decades of political violence across Iraq the Sunnis could still be repulsed by the indiscriminate, brutal killings that were committed by their 'allies.'

Within 'triple binds,' groups such as the IRA and Italian Red Brigades and Prima Linea had to develop aggressive and defensive approaches. They must confront and confound government counter-terror strategies and rival terror tactics. Consequently the legal and illegal threat they faced was magnified more than if the opponents were restricted to counter-terror forces. The dual threat can be seen to have further fuelled levels of fear and insecurity and strengthened group allegiance and solidarities. In such situations, particularly when interwoven with common historical memories, the fear of the rival 'Other' becomes exaggerated. Against a backdrop of a perceived growing threat from other terror groups, emotions become further heightened and support grows to protect, defend and attack in order to safeguard individuals, the group and ultimately the community. 'The Troubles' in Northern Ireland are illustrative of this dynamic. Particular controversial incidents and policies were often accompanied by the mobilisation of members for both republicans and loyalists. For example, in the early 1970s when British army tactics began to seriously infringe upon nationalists while the community was also being attacked by loyalists, recruitment rose markedly to the IRA. And when the republican threat was considered to be increasing, in part through growing membership, loyalists also experienced a surge in recruitment (Taylor 1998, 2000). The reciprocity in recruitment and attacks is exemplified by a member of the UVF, Eddie Kinnear, who declared that at the most emotive periods he believed that 'whenever they [the IRA] blow up a location in the Shankhill [Protestant area], killing one or two people, I would want to blow up some-where in the Falls [Catholic area] killing double.'[32] In a similar vein, John

White, former UFF member, suggested that he was motivated to 'let the IRA know that if they gave us victims, then we in turn would give them victims ....'[33]

When opposing groups commit attacks against rivals some of the same processes that are applied against governments to isolate, dehumanise and justify are noticeable. For instance, Hafez (2007) explores some of the attempts by Sunni groups in post-2003 Iraq to justify attacks against Shi'ites. According to groups such as Ansar al-Sunna Army, in addition to being servants to occupying forces, Shi'a militias torture, abuse, humiliate and kill Sunni civilians. In this light Sunni attacks are construed as being in defence of the community or revenge for fallen civilians. Similarly Devji (2005) examines increasing hostility towards Shi'ites in Pakistan which he argues has become incorporated within the global landscape of *jihad*. The nature of the violence has shifted, for Devji, away from the traditional political rationality that related to particular persons, places and events. Today sectarian violence is indiscriminate and organised to confront Shi'a facets of similarity and which are considered to compete with Sunnism rather than fundamental differences between the sectarian denominations. However, there is a danger that even within these dynamics excessive violence will damage the image and capabilities of groups. In Northern Ireland, for instance, Nelson (1982: 54) discusses the loyalist UVF's 'particularly savage rampages' in the mid 1970s. A vicious circle ensued as 'straight militarist' members became disillusioned and left and 'hard men' moved in. Strategic leadership and group discipline deteriorated and the key objectives for the group's formation, namely the defence of Ulster, became blurred as racketeering activities became dominant and feuds with other loyalist groups escalated. When groups become less concerned about the communities they proclaim to be protecting and hence more detached, there is less restraint upon the use of violence.

Conversely, the impact of triggers is variable even within the same context. Particular killings are often instrumental in an individual's immersion as noticed within spirals of violence in Northern Ireland, especially during times of seemingly intractable tensions, heightened emotions and demands for vengeance. Since the peace process, attacks have continued but they are often isolated acts that are no longer part of concerted campaigns. Instead of violence, fear and insecurities permeating the social habitus, peace and hope have become dominant. Consequently terror activities have not reignited emotions to heightened levels that would have led to growing support for the armed return of paramilitaries. This is not to say that political violence will not return to Northern Ireland. Instead certain preconditions such as limited political representation, segregation and restricted employment prospects continue to exist which can interact with triggers. Thus the likelihood of terrorism returning is heavily determined by the presence and interactions of triggers and preconditions. In Northern Ireland I would argue that the preconditions for violence have not entirely disappeared from the habitus and suggest that the ongoing low-level paramilitary tensions are indicative of this.

## Controlled political violence

Today the prevailing belief of terrorists as unrestrained mass murderers may be understandable but lacks a grasp of the difficult balance that terror groups seek to attain between terrorising, appeal and revulsion. Similarly counter-terror strategies should strive for a balance between security and repression, not least because provocation is another intended outcome from terror attacks; the extent of which is difficult to judge for both the terrorist and counter-terrorist. Aylindi's (2008: 913) observation for nineteenth-century Anarchist and government strategies applies to subsequent generations,

> The trick for the Anarchist attackers seeking to increase the movement's recognition and ultimately representation, was to accurately assess the public's anger and frustration and design powerful—but not *too* powerful—attacks. The countering forces had to assess the public's outrage at the attacks and design appropriate—firm, but not too firm—responses.

Although attacks by Timothy McVeigh and groups such as the Aum Supreme Truth and al-Qa'ida deliberately sought to maximise fatalities, this does not mean that groups operate without restraint. Emotions such as anger can be instrumental within recruitment processes and encouraging activism both to social movements and terror groups. Nevertheless, as I explored in the previous chapter, group security and prospects would be severely threatened if emotions were unrestrained. Consequently, leaders have yet another difficult balance to achieve, namely to encourage emotions in the recruitment and retention of members but within controlled behavioural parameters. In other words, there are limits both to the extent of killings that groups will be willing to commit and the challenging nature of the methods they select. A former member of Prima Linea illuminates upon this when declaring that 'it was only permissible to kill certain persons in accordance with particular rules.'[34] Rules and methods obviously differ according to group, discursive consciousness and forms of justification. For example, one of the most notorious forms of behaviour associated with terror groups has been beheadings in Iraq. Beheadings quickly gained notoriety and certainly were instrumental in rising perceptions of Abu Musab al-Zarqawi as a lead figure within *jihadis* (Brisard 2005). In this regard the tactic successfully generated high levels of fear and shock value. Yet al-Qa'ida's inner core expressed huge concerns about the gratuitous use of violence and the negative impact it was having upon potential Muslim support.[35] Therefore, although those involved are often willing to commit acts of murder they have to be mindful both of the need to terrorise and to attract support. The latter will only be possible providing the targets are considered to be legitimate and the methods appropriate. And because potential supporters have not assimilated the same ideas and forms of behaviour as the terrorists, there are clear thresholds beyond which they will be repulsed and likely to detach from the use of such forms of political violence.

## Conclusion

The selection of targets and methods of attacks are influenced by a multitude of factors, expressive and purposive, contemporary and historical. Terror actions are the most obvious and immediate method of communication that the asymmetrical groups possess. Yet although the overarching aim is to terrorise identified audiences through their acts, groups have boundaries which they do not want to cross. In other words they do not want to terrorise too many people with excessive or unnecessary numbers of fatalities. What constitutes the requisite number or appropriate victims varies according to discursive consciousness and the past and present legitimacy for attacks and scapegoating. Certainly the nature of historical and contemporary relationships with the targeted 'Other' will significantly influence both the extent to which violence can be used and how widely it can be applied. Groups and communities subjected to government repression or the imposition of brutal foreign forces can find support for asymmetrical violence and recruits willing to commit attacks more easily than groups with recourse to alternative means of protest and who lack residues from a violent past. For violence to be adopted as an appropriate method by individuals and groups requires calculative consideration based upon factors such as the successes or otherwise of other groups and an estimate of what constitutes an acceptable level of violence against an emotional backdrop. In essence, the violent actions are constituted by rational and affective components which provide the purpose and expressive feelings behind the decisions to commit acts of terrorism. Individuals are best able to negotiate this shift through gradual immersion in radicalisation in figurations which provide historical and contemporary legitimacy for the use of political violence. This enables them to conclude that terrorism is the only solution both for the group and themselves.

The attacks are the means towards particular ends that are often based upon affective values; the interplay between emotions and rationality continues to shift throughout group and individual careers and which impact upon the extent and nature of attacks. Often the extent to which leaders can attempt detached, instrumental diagnosis will be heavily influenced by perceived levels of risk to themselves, identified 'communities' and discourse. Simplistically, the lower the risk the higher levels of calculation. Yet low level risks maybe desirable in enhancing detached reasoning but would also indicate a lack of government retaliation. In turn this could suggest that the government was close to defeat or had yet to be provoked to retaliate. In the latter instance, government attacks are very often a pre-requisite for any group wanting to mobilise enough opposition to have a probability of victory. At some point therefore leaders would have to anticipate planning and executing actions in environments which are not conducive to careful consideration. Conversely within double and triple binding spirals of hatred, levels of insecurities, fear and demands for vengeance rise. During these heightened periods of feelings, objective calculation of methods, targets and outcomes and the controlling of violence within demarcated zones becomes increasingly difficult. Instead groups' approaches are more reactive, responding to perceived threats from governments and opposing groups and demands for revenge which become increasingly prominent. Within these dynamics, governments and other groups react accordingly and levels of attack and counter-attack spiral.

This is one of the reasons why overly aggressive acts of counter-terrorism can have the opposite impact from that intended; rather than destroying terror groups, government actions contribute to a strengthening of their support and justification for terror attacks. As I explain in the following chapter on the end of terror careers, if disengagement from terror groups is to be successfully encouraged, counter-terror approaches have to be multi-layered. In short, purposive and affective reasons have to be provided in order for terrorists to leave terrorism.

# 7   The End Game

## Stopping and leaving terrorism

### Introduction

Within sociological studies of groups considerably greater emphasis is placed upon the processes behind why people join rather than why they leave.[1] The literature on socialisation exemplifies this. Fuchs Ebaugh (1988: 181) observes that related studies have 'de-emphasized the issue of disengagement and placed emphasis primarily on the new role that one is acquiring.' There is little indication of much subsequent progress. This is also true for studies of religious and social movements,[2] and neglect is particularly noticeable within the mass of literature dedicated to terrorism. At a number of levels this is surprising. That groups' end is hardly astounding. On average groups have a short life expectancy,[3] but this should not detract from their significance during spans of operations nor the manner of their demise. By neglecting this final stage in the careers of groups and individuals, academics, policy makers and counter-terror specialists are missing an excellent opportunity to understand why terrorism ends. And if we are able to gain greater insights into this phase, we become more knowledgeable about both how to encourage members to leave and to stop terror groups. Consequently for the purposes of counter-terrorism, learning why groups end or disband and people stop behaving politically violently is as important as discovering why they initially became terrorists. The extent to which the counter-terrorists are aware of this is open to question. Arguably studies of terrorism have replicated this neglect. Hence there is considerable scope to enhance levels of knowledge and understanding about this crucial final phase.

The end game for terrorists and counter-terrorists can be considered to incorporate the phases which contribute to groups no longer being committed to political violence, either voluntarily, through force or by incarceration. At an individual level I am referring to processes in which members leave groups, again either through their own volition or against their wishes. In this chapter I explore both the deliberate counter-terror strategies that are designed to defeat terrorism and the dynamics within groups and out-with that contribute to collective and individual decisions to step away from political violence. Although there is a relative dearth of analysis about this phase, there is an argument that the studies which have explored the reasons why groups end and members leave can be very much considered to be a case of quality over quantity; an observation which has not always been raised within the field. The relative lack of attention placed upon this final stage is also noticeable in studies of other social units, although again there are illuminating studies that can be drawn upon. For instance, Bjørgo and Horgan (2009: 8) draw upon the literature on gangs, which identifies 'the shorter the time they had stayed in the gang, the more easily they adapted to an ordinary lifestyle.' From these studies it is possible to draw parallels with earlier phases in the careers of members not least the challenge to the assumption that changes to values must precede individual and group shifts to and from violent behaviour. Just as with the joining and forming stages, as Horgan (2009a and 2009b) notes, there are complexities and differences in individual and group exit strategies. In other words there is no single pathway in or out of terrorism.

When discussing disengagement it is important to clarify what is being discussed. Although the terms are often applied interchangeably, disengagement is not the same as de-radicalisation. Horgan (2009b) explains that psychological disengagement can include disillusionment with the ideology, members, strategy or failure and burnout and changing, conflicting personal priorities. Physical disengagement incorporates voluntary and involuntary exit from the movement or from terrorist related activities to other subversive, non-violent roles. Processes involved within individual disengagement differ from the group dynamics. Although there is an obvious impact upon members, group disengagement tends to mean that the organisation abandons terrorism. Individuals are part of this disengagement but their departures from political violence can also incorporate decisions to leave when groups remain committed to terrorism (Bjørgo and Horgan 2009). Consequently I want to explore the reasoning behind the groups ending and people voluntarily exiting. Individuals can leave groups and retain extremist ideologies. In essence they can still want fundamental changes within societies or global relations and in this sense continue to be radical. However, they are no longer willing to commit acts of violence towards this end, thereby disengaging without de-radicalising. Consequently the assumption that behaviour follows ideas is as over-generalised for the end phase as it is for the beginning. Of course it is possible for individuals to leave groups in part because their views are less extreme and they are less committed to the use of violence.

## Individual disengagement

When seeking to explain why people choose to depart from groups a useful starting point is to return to the reasons why they joined and remained. Hence grievances, events and social dynamics that were instrumental in the earlier stages in the terrorist career can be re-examined. In other words, does commitment continue to be legitimised by experiences, discursive consciousness and social relationships? If these reasons were at least partly addressed by, for example, government concessions such as electoral politics in South America, then members may consider that this justifies a shift away from violence. Alternatively the lack of progress, the rigidity of governments, effectiveness of counter-terrorism and failure to mobilise broader support can contribute to feelings of futility, self-doubt and personal shortcomings. Individual emotions can therefore be instrumental. Sociologists of emotions such as Hothschild (1979, 1983) have noted how feelings more generally have to be managed to try to minimise distress, discomfort, emotional exhaustion, burnout and withdrawal. Normative emotional boundaries are deeply embedded within the social figurations which will vary according to composition, habitus and purpose. Within social movements Flam (2005) draws upon organisational sociology when arguing that activists require re-charging opportunities. Within terror groups problems in managing feelings can be magnified and emotional releases out of the group gain even greater significance. Yet the centrality of the group and social demarcations that often accompany engagement can severely restrict or prevent this.

Other members may become frustrated through the apparent futility of their commitment and seemingly endless engagement with no visible signs of instrumental progress. Facing what appear to be insurmountable odds and hostility from intended supporters, members can decide that the group has unrealistic expectations because power is not going to be achieved through violence. Individual costs or risks of engagement interwoven with methods of repression can also contribute to participation within political violence considered to be too costly (Tilly 1978). One cost can be detachment from the communities that groups claim to represent. As Demant and de Graaf (2010) comment with respect to South Moluccan radicals in the Netherlands during the 1970s, the decline and withdrawal of tacit and covert support of relatives and friends can also contribute to members seriously questioning the purpose of their actions.

The realities of life within cults and terror groups is often, Wright (1991) and Horgan (2009b) argue respectively, hugely discrepant against preconceived fantasies. Wright (1991: 132) suggests that,

> Idealized notions of the relationship lead to unrealistic goals and expectations. The star-crossed lover and the zealous convert anticipate remaining on an emotional high, blinding them to the difficulties that inevitably accompany intensive commitment and adjustment to a more demanding and regulated life. Entry into the new social unit requires adjusting to a changed identity, new roles and responsibilities, and less personal freedom (in exchange for the benefits of dyadic/group intimacy).

This is also notable for individuals who are partly attracted to terrorism by idealistic images of romanticised excitement, or as a loyalist informed Crawford (2003: 193), 'the other reason I joined up was out of sheer boredom, there was nothing else to do.' When experiencing frequent prolonged bouts of inactivity and tedium, original motivations quickly dissipate and need replacing if the individual wants to remain. In these settings, the mundane takes on greater significance than one might anticipate against the perceived backdrop of excitement and risk. Patrizio Peci, from the Italian Red Brigades, discusses his disillusionment following his first meeting with his superior, Fiore. After Fiore,

> wolfed down his food ... suddenly he took off his shoes. ... There was a horrible stench. But the worst was yet to come. He took off his socks as well; he grabbed the bread knife ... and began to pry off the filth from between his toes with the point of the knife. Zap! And off came the filth from between two toes. ... What kind of manners are these? I said nothing and I tried to minimize things in my mind. 'They are just little things, nothing', I thought, but I was worried. 'If everybody behaves like this, how will I be able to live among them?[4]

Of course it would be as facetious to draw the conclusion that the bread knife was responsible for people disengaging as it would to suggest that counter-terrorists concentrate on arousing tensions over etiquette. Nevertheless this kind of experience highlights that triggers are also instrumental in decisions to leave groups and may not immediately fit within the perceptions of the discursive precipitating factors that contribute to the end of membership. The mundane can be a significant trigger but needless to say the departure of people is instigated by much more than table manners. There maybe particular incidents; the arrest of a colleague, failure of attacks, the realisation that violence was not leading to the goals,[5] impact of counter-terrorism,[6] denunciation of the group by their intended support, which invoke the process of leaving or may be the immediate cause of disengagement if the member had already been considering leaving. Conversely the excessive use of violence, particularly against civilians, can prove a tipping point. Horgan (2009b: 23) reports on examples of such attacks, the manner in which other members could discuss killing people and the resultant distance between initial romantic ideals and the stark reality. For instance, with his commitment already waning, the decision to inform for Sean O'Callaghan, a former IRA commander, followed the killing of a female police officer and in particular a colleague implying that he hoped she was pregnant and then 'we might get two for the price of one.'

Government interventions can also feed into this decision-making process such as the Italian policy of repentance during the 1980s which provided 'the extension of leniency in return for disassociation' (Weinberg and Eubank 1987: 129). The success of the policy can be measured by 389 terrorists repenting by 1989. Nevertheless, the introduction of the policy cannot be examined in isolation. It was partly effective because at the time the failure to mobilise popular support and the realisation that the predictions about the demise of the Italian government were somewhat premature led to numerous members re-evaluating their commitment. This approach allowed the terror- ists an easier exit route and triggered or possibly accelerated the disengagement process. Consequently, the significance of precipitation factors in disengage- ment depend on whether they connect with existing emotions and rationality such as levels of gratification, group dynamics, the appeal of alternative peers and family members and levels of security, fear and shame.

The extent to which the individual identifies with historical connections and group objectives is also instrumental in members departing. Neither indivi- dual nor group ideas and behaviour remain static and it is by no means cer- tain that they will both shift in the same direction. Although history could be considered to remain static, shifting contemporary experiences and relations can contribute to the past, and the legacy of violence, being re-evaluated. In this regard Richardson *et al.*'s (1986) justificatory or excusatory account can be extended to incorporate what Demant and de Graaf (2010: 411) refer to as 'neutralizers.' Their role is to,

> counteract or undermine existing legends and serve to neutralize the injustice frames that legitimize radical ideology. They could include public apologies for police excesses ... , sanctioning of police officers involved in these excesses, dialogue sessions with the radicals' con- stituencies, or other statements by government representatives, aimed at neutralizing a politicized and polarized atmosphere.

On the other side of the counter-terror neutralisers is the challenge to the radical discourse, the battle over ideas. This has to go beyond name calling and include rigorous debate between members and respected figures and in which interpretations of integral concepts in the use of violence are discussed and challenged. For instance, credible Islamists have engaged within de-radi- calisation programmes in Egypt, Indonesia, Saudi Arabia and Yemen (Boucek 2009, Gunaratna and bin Ali 2009, Horgan and Braddock 2010, ICG 2007). The Islamists' discussions do not necessarily conform to government inten- tions. On the contrary they may raise comments that are distinctly unappeal- ing to Western governments. For instance, Ali Imron, who was sentenced to a life in prison for his involvement in the Bali bombings, does not challenge the justification for *jihad* in order to implement the Shari'ah in Indonesia and to attack America for its unjust dominance and collaboration with Israel. Hence in principle the targets in the Bali bombings were legitimate. Nevertheless the attacks were strategically flawed because no consideration was allocated to whether they would have the support of the Muslim community. In short they did not consider the costs and benefits of the attacks and were ill-prepared for dealing with the aftermath.[7] The longer-term solution is therefore to work with communities in order to encourage greater levels of religiosity. Because of the militants' credentials, including time in Afghanistan and the nature of their arguments, they have a credibility that is beyond more passive, pro-government alternatives. On a cautionary note there is an argument that in the longer-term this approach is ultimately suspending and even strengthening the problem with the militants returning to violence if they determine there is greater community support and potential for such actions.

Alongside the disengaging issues within the group we also need to explore the potential appeal of life 'outside.' A life without the constant fear of arrest, imprisonment or death has obvious attractions. Similarly Horgan (2009b) refers to instances where both male and female terrorists want to start families. Groups tend to forbid personal relationships, often insisting on separating pre-existing couples because they are considered to weaken emotional commitment to the cause and risk-taking on its behalf. In this regard they share Simmel's (1950) observation that in a dyadic involvement, one relationship is intensified at the expense of others. Consequently members must exit from groups if they are to be able to start families of their own. Nevertheless for many terrorists identification is closely bound within the processes of terrorism and group relations. These extend beyond discursive consciousness and can include social arrangements such as the example of Jemaah Islamiyah where members ate, played volleyball and did business together (ICG 2007). Yet these relations can also provide the basis for withdrawal. Studies of social movements have identified that the departure of a close friend also weakens the likelihood of continued participation (McAdam 1986). There are grounds to suggest the disengagement of friends from terror groups would also influence other members to leave. Moreover there is an obvious strategic downside to the tendency towards social isolation. For instance, Silj (1979) explains with regard to the Italian Red Brigades, members living in the underground often become isolated from relevant audiences and there is a greater tendency to misperceive what is happening 'out there.' In the Italian example this is exemplified by the unfounded expectation that in 1971 the government was on the verge of collapse. Yet even during these periods and across terror groups, to give up on terrorism is not an easy option. For Post (2005: 462), leaving groups 'would be to lose their very reason for being.'

Studies of religious cults discovered that the extraction of individuals by relatives was partly dependent upon the nature of relationships within the group. In essence the tighter the emotional bonds between members the more difficult it was for relatives to successfully encourage individual departure (Richardson *et al.* 1986). The likelihood of a person being willing to leave was also affected by what Richardson *et al.* (1986: 110) refer to as 'a justificatory or excusatory account.' They propound that members, relatives and significant others must develop an account which explains why individuals joined the group in the first place. If the member is to leave the group then the account must not deride or mock the individual's decision. Instead it is important that 'an account must be negotiated that is acceptable to all concerned' (ibid.). As Fuchs Ebaugh (1988) notes with regard to role exits, generally it is not only the leaver who has to adjust; significant others may also have to accommodate changes. In the instance of terrorists I would add counter-terrorists to the list of those formulating accounts. The emphasis upon negotiation has to accommodate the initial engagement and help to provide an insight into the dynamics of life outside the group.

In order to enhance the appeal of life outside terrorism, governments and other interested parties could therefore seek to provide alternative ideas and forms of behaviour. Within contemporary approaches there has been growing emphasis placed upon the maintenance of social relationships. For instance, the Indonesian government's prison programme included paying relatives' expenses to enable visits to detainees and encouraging the strengthening of relations with civilians which included marriages in custody. Economic concerns and employment prospects are also considered. To help improve prisoner opportunities a number of *jihadis* have been able to take advantage of long distance learning and some support for domestic matters and business loans have been provided (ICG 2007). Similar arrangements have been introduced in Colombia. Crucially though, Porch and Rasmussen (2008) comment that the Colombian government lacks the resources to re-educate and find jobs for the unexpectedly large number of militants requesting demobilisation. Consequently the programme has not been implemented fully.

Because of the significance of groups like Jemaah Islamiyah and the social frameworks they provide, there is no guarantee that prisoners' possible gratitude for government financial contributions to their families will overcome the appeal of the group. Hence the additional offer of business support may help the prisoner consider a positive future out of the group. Although there is a lack of detailed information about recidivism, Saudi officials have claimed that their more extensive rehabilitation programme that incorporates employment, transportation, funds and accommodation has successfully rehabilitated between 80 and 90 per cent.[8] This emphasis upon materialism could be considered to be a re-working of rational choice for the end game with the emotional attachments and feelings of being wanted submerged under pragmatism. Many people did not join groups for reasons that accorded neatly with rational choice and this will also apply for many members disengaging, although not necessarily the same people. In other words people may become members for very different reasons to those they leave for. For instance, amidst the seemingly successful Saudi rehabilitation programme consideration has to be allotted to the ways in which this interacts with familial relations and habitus. Boucek (2009) explains how the Ministry of the Interior extends the responsibility for the released offender's behaviour across the family network.[9] By connecting with traditional Saudi norms and values such as social responsibility, honour and family hierarchies, the approach to rehabilitation guarantees considerable interest in the individual which provides social restraints alongside legal restrictions. Moreover prisoner reintegration programmes have long been established in Saudi Arabia which enables government officials to learn from and adapt existing programmes. Just as the history of violence influences behaviour, a history of rehabilitation should also enhance the prospects of disengagement because the possibility is embedded within the social habitus and has been accepted. In essence there are multiple past and present precedents for members who wish to leave groups.

The impact of disengagement will also vary at least in part according to individual and social habitus, the nature of experiences and events during the terror career and social relations within the group and out-with. Richardson *et al*.'s (1986) study of disaffiliation from religious movements identifies that the psychological impact of leaving communal groups is greater than for looser forms of organisation. This would seem to apply to individuals leaving nationalist terror groups whose disengagement may well result in the end of relationships with family and friends. Obviously this only applies during periods of violence. During peace processes, such as in Northern Ireland, disengagement is broadly accepted and accommodated within shifting relationships and activities. Furthermore ontological security is better managed if disengagement is part of a group withdrawal and/or gradual transition. Just as the shift from non-violent to violent ideas and behaviour can easily result in cognitive dissonance, the reverse can also be applied. Disengaged individuals have to accommodate their involvement with violence after deciding that it is no longer appropriate. The extent to which they are able to come to terms with this will again be influenced by multiple factors including their roles in attacks, outcomes in terms of death and serious injury, reasoning for disengagement, habitus before, during and after engagement and the degree to which the individual is threatened or attracted by, and ultimately integrated within, 'civilian' life.

All the points in this section may well imply that disengagement is a matter of personal agency, determined by members reacting to group dynamics, discursive consciousness and shifting external relations. The reality is somewhat different because groups want to retain members in order to maintain numerical strength, knowledge, experience and skills. Moreover, members leaving raises obvious yet fundamental questions: why does the person want to leave? Is the problem down to the individual or the group? What would be the impact of their departure? Can they be trusted after leaving? And how will their disengagement be considered within the group, intended supporters and counter-terror agencies? Answers to these questions vary across and within groups and have contributed to groups having different policies for members wishing to disengage. For instance a former leader of the Northern Irish loyalist UDA declared that during the 'war' 'once you're committed, once you take that oath, you're there until obviously, you're dead, or you've been released on special grounds, which is very rare.' When asked to explain the basis of the 'special grounds' he replied 'if someone had found God' and 'also the fact that the older the member … you just let him go.'[10] Aging does seem to be a factor within some groups. Rashwan (2009) explains how the lengthy sentences imposed upon Gama'a al-Islamiyya members meant that the leaders aged in prison and over time transformed from zealous youth to more tempered and better informed middle age. By comparison within

Scandinavian Far Right groups, Bjørgo (2009: 38) explains that by around the age of 30, members feel they are getting too old. 'They no longer have the same need for excitement; they may have less energy, and want to calm down.' Furthermore 'their authority and prestige may also be challenged by rebellious teenage members, who may even see them as representative of their parents' generation.' Yet despite the tensions that can arise Bjørgo adds that remaining members can consider departure to be personal betrayal. Hence there can be considerable risks involved in leaving groups and considerable cognitive dissonance as the individual's ideas, behaviour and relationships shift against a backdrop of threats and insecurity.

## Group dynamics in the end game

Arguably outside relationships, interconnected social capital and potentially transferable skills such as capacity building, communication and logistical techniques have to appeal more than those within the group and help the transformation to 'civilian' life. When groups, largely national and ethnic, are interconnected within communities, there can be less incentive to disengage. Hence the interweaving of friends, childhood acquaintances, family members and community figures within and across groups and the broader movement provides an important support base for individuals. These relations help to confirm the legitimacy and popularity of their commitment and actions. Nevertheless community support cannot be taken for granted and can weaken or even backlash if terror actions cause revulsion,[11] groups become detached from community perceptions or are not receptive to shifting conditions, values and expectations. Nor can groups complacently accept that the lifespan of the broader movements with which they interconnect will be endless. Tarrow and Tilly have both outlined how movements lose momentum or relevance as opportunity structures are restrained, issues become incorporated within mainstream politics and the rallying call loses resonance. And as former members of the Red Brigades informed della Porta (2009), there can be a growing sense of the bonds of solidarity weakening through arrests, prison sentences and diminished credibility of the revolutionary programme.

Jones and Libicki (2008: 81) argue that groups have specific political purposes and choose strategies that are intended to best advance them.

> Consequently, they are influenced by cost-benefit calculations. Resorting to terrorism has benefits if groups can successfully achieve their goals. But is also has costs. Terrorists are constantly on the run because government security forces are trying to capture or kill them. Terrorism provokes repression that some organizations believe they cannot survive.

In these settings 'non violent approaches may become plausible alternatives' (ibid.). Disengagement can also be the outcome of calculative, prolonged analysis at both group and individual levels. Again though, these rational assessments are interwoven with emotions such as fear and uncertainty related to the constant threat of arrest or death.

Just like in other forms of groups leaders must seek to accommodate people with different expectations, provide frames for ontological security. As Debray (1967) commented with regard to revolutionary movements, address members' drift, overcoming the practical difficulties of maintaining a daily sense of focus. New members have to be integrated, and their involvement and the departure through arrest and so on of old participants contribute to different dynamics. With the new relationships comes the risk that remaining members may feel estranged or less committed to the additional members. This is particularly true following a surge in membership as Klandersman (1994) and Wallis (1977) showed for the Dutch peace movement and Scientology respectively. Members will have different views and requirements about how they should be managed, the tactics that are being adopted, feasibility of particular actions and are aggrieved that some individuals are receiving preferential treatment unlike themselves who are undertaking the cold, dirty and dangerous tasks. The strategic approach of groups must therefore aim to reconcile the potentially different expectations of supporters and members while maintaining bonds, motivation and commitment. The former will often be less committed to the use of violence and the latter will be more inclined to argue for greater damage and destruction, particularly within spirals of hatred. Moreover within groups members must accept the requirement for acts of violence. Achieving a consensus on what is justifiable is more problematic. Some members struggle to adjust to the repercussions of their involvement in terror attacks and the injuries and fatalities that ensue (Gupta 2008). When terror actions are considered to be either unnecessarily cautious or destructive individuals may decide to form or join other groups with a less restrained strategic approach to fatalities. Alternatively they could become dissonant and repulsed by the deaths their group has caused.

The outcome of the difficulties in managing members' different interests and expectations, as with other forms of religious, social and political organisations, is that terror groups are prone to internal disputes over principles, strategies, tactics and ethics (Smelser 2007). These can often become personalised around individual characteristics. During long periods of boredom, intense self and group criticism has been observed, most notably within the 'red' organisations and in particular, the somewhat ironically titled, United Red Army in Japan.[12] Factionalism is not unusual in these environments and boundaries quickly formulate and solidify. The splintering into rival groups (Jones and Libicki 2008) can become almost inevitable with the newly created units sharing beliefs and forms of behaviour that are more reflective of the members' habitus, at least initially. This is not necessarily fatal. For instance, Benfold (1993) has claimed with respect to social movements that accompanying problems can be at least partially offset by the greater coherence within the different, newly independent factions. Nevertheless the groups have to overcome the split of support and membership, diminished capabilities and accompanying tensions with the rival group/s with whom they compete for appeal and resources. For smaller groups that are further splintered questions must often be confronted about the feasibility of continuing. There will often be a point at which members will decide to join larger groups with greater capabilities and longer-term sustainability.

Similarly individuals can be de-motivated by the style of leadership, quality of managerial decisions or accepting orders from people who in other walks of life may be their social equivalent if not inferior. Such differences and personal foibles within groups have to be resolved if the group is to continue, be effective and prevent members leaving. On the other hand, leaders may decide that problems associated with particular members justifies their involuntary disengagement and they leave the group, not always vertically. Conversely the death, arrest or imprisonment of leaders, particularly when charismatic, can result in the group's disbandment or severely weakens their capabilities resulting in defeat (Gupta 2008). Succession is also problematic when leaders such as the LTTE's Prabhakaran, PKK's Ocalan and Guzman from the Shining Path become such integral figures and the focal point of power that potential successors are undermined, restricted or even destroyed. Neuburger and Valentini (1996) explain how groups with leaders who are pivotal figures have less cohesive relations between members. Consequently when groups lose 'stellar' leaders they are often fragmented because of a lack of sufficient resources and cohesion. By comparison, Sageman (2008) explains how leaderless movements face very different problems. Although the lack of leadership restricts counter surveillance it also hinders a lack of consensus and collective ability to compromise. An unfounded argument could therefore be raised that leaderless cells can be less inclined to negotiate and thus are more inclined to end in violent defeat, ignominious arrest and imprisonment.

Following on from the counter-terror section, approaches such as that employed by the Colombian authorities towards collective disengagement can be productive. Group leaders may feel they have little option but to collectively disengage and return to civilian life after renouncing the use of violence, if not necessarily their radical ideals. The likelihood of groups being willing to negotiate and compromise is also influenced by preceding events, external sponsorship which may be based upon particular conditions or funding,[13] the acts and policies of their opponents and the extent of members' sacrifices which are often measured in fatalities. Deaths of members which connected into prevailing impressions of martyrdom make negotiation over 'non-negotiable' demands extremely difficult. To some extent this is the position of Palestinian groups, HAMAS and Islamic Jihad. HAMAS has declared 'the blood of our members will not be wasted on the negotiation table' and, echoing the dynamics of spirals of violence, are apparent within statements such as 'blood demands blood.'[14] In these environments groups can be restricted by the level of sacrifices and rigidly oppose any attempts to compromise upon that which martyrs died for. By comparison, the globalisation of culture which provides shared music, literature and sporting allegiances, (pre-2008) economic opportunities that transcend sectarian boundaries (Kerr 1996), 'battle' fatigue across engaged groups and communities and diminishing British support provided a backdrop for paramilitaries in Northern Ireland to commence the peace process, in part because violent strategies were increasingly losing support (Taylor 1998, Vertigans 2008). Both republicans and loyalists, nationalist and unionist communities were willing to negotiate because they believed that the 'realities on the ground' had shifted sufficiently for compromises to be accommodated. Moreover, as Bjørgo and Horgan (2009) point out, groups are more inclined to negotiate when they consider that outright victory is unlikely. This stage is, for Art and Richardson (2006), the optimum at which to grant members an amnesty thereby providing members with a less humiliating way out of a losing situation. In the Netherlands disengagement was further enabled by the limited prosecutions, continuing non-violent radical outlets and the opportunity for members to 'slide back into "normal life"' (de Graaf and Malkki 2010: 634).

## Counter-terror approaches to ending it all

Consideration of government attempts to prevent and defeat terrorism tends to be dominated by particular visible actions. The interpretation of these acts is very often heavily influenced by the extent to which viewers connect counter-terrorism as a necessary reaction to terrorism or whether counter-terrorism is an extension of a repressive and/or discriminatory regime. Irrespective of individual opinions, all are to some degree influenced by the emotions that attempts at the forcible ending of terrorism arouse. The tendency to concentrate on more visible actions such as high profile, media covered arrests and the 'targeted' bombing of properties where terror suspects are believed to be located contributes to partial portrayals. In this regard, the sensationalist coverage and accompanying heightened emotions are comparable with the emphasis placed upon attacks within terrorism. The outcome is the same, namely all too often the coverage is narrow and driven by ideological and ethical attachments. Counter-terror approaches are therefore readily generalised as the appropriate use of force or excessive and unprovoked aggression with dissent tending to formulate around whether the attacks can be ethically and politically justified. Without wishing to engage with the ethical debate there are numerous examples where the over-concentration on violent counter-terror tactics has failed and in the process terror groups have been strengthened (Jones and Libicki 2008, Horgan 2009b).

Just as with terrorism, the concentration on the violent strands within counter-terrorism hinders attempts to understand the ways in which non aggressive tactics connect with groups and encourage disengagement. Today counter-terrorism which emphasises aggression is widely associated with the Bush Administration's 'war on terror,' not least because of the title adopted for what is in essence a counter-terror strategy. Within the administration,

Donald Rumsfeld has attained the position of prominent 'folk devil,' an easy target for liberals for the worse excesses within the 'war.' However, there is some evidence to suggest that he was conscious of the requirement to avoid an overly military stance and in particular was concerned about the application of the word 'war.' Feith (2008) argues that like many of his critics, Rumsfeld believed that the title overemphasised the significance of the military at the expense of the multi-dimensions. This is largely borne out by experiences elsewhere. At the very least, covert police and intelligence services alongside legal measures are required in order to identify leaders, funding, main nodes of contact, logistical support and criminal activities. For a more rounded strategy a 'softer' approach should also be considered which aims at dialogue, reconciliation and negotiation.

Just as terror tactics have to evolve, counter-terrorism must also take into consideration events and shifting levels of risk, fear, insecurity and demands for retaliation. Lessons can be learnt from apparent counter-terror successes and concomitant terror failures. In this regard De Graaf and Malkki's (2010: 623) study of the Dutch Left Wing organisation Red Youth (RY) is illustrative, not least because the group's fate 'seems in many ways a counter-terrorist's dream,' although I hasten to add that I am not proposing this example for a universal template. What works in counter-terrorism varies according to the multiple factors identified repetitively throughout this book; an observation evidenced by the more aggressive and successful approach adopted by the Dutch against South Moluccan radicals. The RY study explores the interactive impact of levels of political inclusion, counter-terror strategy and culture. A former member, Lucïen van Hoesel draws upon these factors when comparing the Dutch experiences with those of comparable West German groups when stating,

> If you situated my case in Germany, I would have been dead, received a life sentence, or I would still have been a fugitive. ... In the Netherlands, you get so much leeway that the motivation to act falls apart. ... The liberal climate in the Netherlands put a stop to terrorism, whereas in Germany, reactionary forces artificially sustained terrorism for ten years.[15]

Some support for this argument can conversely be found within a case study of the most militant RY faction that operated in Eindhoven between 1969 and 1972. During this period Eindhoven was the part of the Netherlands in which police brutality was more noticeable and there was evidence of spiralling levels of heightened emotions and aggression. Nonetheless van Hoesel's comparison is somewhat simplified. De Graaf and Malkki (2010: 624) extend the analysis to argue that the '"success" of countermeasures resulted not only from wise decisions and their skilful implementation, but partly from failures to take action.' Moreover, through contact with the West German RAF, the Dutch group gained deterrent glimpses into the risks, uncertainties and precautions that dominated their careers underground. The arrest and widespread detention of RAF members was also informative, leading to RY members drawing the fatalistic conclusion that if the more professional German group was failing there was little likelihood that they would succeed.

By comparison with the Dutch government approach to the RY, when undertaken in isolation there is little likelihood of state-sponsored aggression being successful, certainly over the longer term. Military aggression and repression can only contain while there is political will and military might. Jones and Libicki's (2008: xiii) study of terror groups between 1968 and 2006 concluded that 'military force has rarely been the primary reason for the end of terrorist groups' and was only responsible for 7 per cent of the endings of terror groups. Even when allowing for the increasingly sophisticated, precise modern weaponry, the scale of their capabilities means, Jones and Libicki argue, that they are much more effective when confronting large insurgent groups. These opponents may utilise terror tactics but overall their approach conforms more within the conventions of warfare. Consequently government weapons that are designed predominantly to be applied against opposing armies are well suited for the confrontation. They are less well suited when confronting dispersed, clandestine enemies. And when applied against such foes indiscriminate force often results in the death of civilians, an upsurge of anger against the counter-terrorists, legitimisation of terrorist discourse and behaviour and the mobilisation of new recruits. This compares with the Dutch approach which did not include new counter-terror legislation. Instead the Prime Minister Biesheuvel declared that 'an open society should not be afflicted' by counter-terrorism measures.[16] Such an approach meant that it was very difficult to convict RY members. Only a handful were ever sentenced for terror activities and those that were received relatively short spells of imprisonment.[17] The state provided little or no evidence that would enable its actions to be widely portrayed as authoritarian. Both the lack of high-profile prosecution cases and repressive measures meant that the RY were not provided with opportunities for awareness raising and mobilising support. Alongside this 'repressive tolerance'[18] the government were able to convince politicians and the media that the Netherlands was not facing an RAF style group. Therefore extensive counter-terrorism was not necessary and would be self-defeating. Again there was an element of fortune to this. For example, De Graaf and Malkki (2010) argue that the clashes between the police and RY members did not produce any fatalities which would have heightened emotions and probably levels of retaliatory aggression. Certainly this is correct, but to this could be added that the Dutch reciprocal counter-terror and terror approaches significantly reduced the likelihood of fatalities.

A different argument can be put forward against the use of repression. In Egypt since the 1980s, Peru from the 1990s and Russia in the nineteenth century, repressive measures against Islamic Jihad and al'Gama'a al-Islamiyya, Shining Path and the anarchist Narodnaya Volya respectively proved effective in the short term. However, if the political restraints were to weaken without having being internalised during the preceding period, or the reasons why people join groups are addressed or become superfluous, then violence as a form of asymmetrical political challenge could be anticipated. The massive uprisings in Russia during the early part of the twentieth century are indicative of the failure of such an approach over the longer term. Similarly the Egyptian approach prior to 2011 proved relatively successful in terms of security within the nation-state and has been extended to confront the ideological challenge (Gunaratna and bin Ali 2009).[19] Nevertheless many of the causes for radicalisation remain, and it is no coincidence that Egyptian Islamic militants have been instrumental in the shift of targeting from the near (in this instance the Egyptian government) to the far (Western) enemies. Yet despite this, governments often rely predominantly on a physical approach. In this regard parallels can be drawn with the dynamics between nation-states during the descent into war and the interweaving of rationality and emotions. Elias (2010: 119) explores this when declaring that,

> in this constellation of powers there are so many possibilities of a rash transition, driven by wishful or fearful images, from cold to hot war, that the hope that human reason will sooner or later hold in check the immense pressure towards war of such a constellation seems to me quite illusionary.

This is fuelled by a

> tradition of humanity to resolve group conflicts by force of arms, and how little are the leading people of the leading states able to escape the power of this tradition, the compulsion of the institutions and habitual actions which this tradition has created. (Elias 2010: 126)

The use of violence within strategies of counter-terrorism could be classified within this tradition, as a struggle over state formation and ultimately survival. Crucially this is a tradition for which there seems to be popular public support, not least of course because populations share social habitus in which this use of aggression is normalised.

Hence, although people may be comforted by the thought that their governments act following calculative and detached consideration, in reality, their actions are also heavily influenced by the social habitus and the history and prevalence of violent ideas and forms of behaviour. Arguably these are instrumental in determining reactions to acts of terrorism, public requirements and political decision-making. I am not arguing that counter-terrorism is overwhelmingly determined by emotions. My main point here is that feelings influence counter-terrorism. These can sometimes be hidden by the nature of the adopted strategies. Again, just like acts of terrorism, the immediate outcomes of counter-terrorism can dominate perceptions of the processes that led to the overt actions. Thus arrests of suspects can reinforce perceptions of a wider threat, identification of the 'other' which is extended across the associated ethnic or religious group and conversely for those who are adversely affected provide evidence for a discriminatory, unjust and brutal nature of the regime (Vertigans 2010b).

Building upon this, governments must also consider levels of threat and new areas of tension that their rhetoric, policies and actions create. By reducing the threat level Gordon and Arian (2001) argue that the decision-making of governments and populations alike become less emotive and instead both emotions and 'logic' have a role to play. They go on to declare that although this relationship appears so obvious there are innumerable examples of policy makers seemingly thinking the opposite and using threats to try end conflicts. The outcome has often been the escalation of violence. A number of examples are provided such as the Israeli intention to bomb Lebanon in order to stop attacks on Israel. Instead attacks continued with the aims reinforced by the hardening of Lebanese attitudes against Israel. In a non-violent example, international opposition to the Right-Wing Austrian leader leader Jörg Heider resulted in support for him growing in reaction to the confrontational stance of other nations. These are classic examples of the reinforcement of collective consciousness when the group, prominent leaders or habitus is perceived to be under attack whether oral or physical.

It is against this backdrop that counter-terrorism strategies are formed and which can consist of multiple levels which differ in levels of aggression, visibility and impact. Counter-terrorism will often intend to pre-empt attacks. Tactics adopted to prevent acts of terrorism include arresting, imprisoning or in some countries killing (potential) terrorists and enhancing security arrangements which reduce the likelihood of terror successes. Surveillance, government undercover agents and the use of informers play a prominent feature once it becomes apparent that groups or movements have the capability to threaten. In the United States for example, Hewitt (2003) details how FBI investigations of Right-Wing extremists increased four-fold in the aftermath of the Oklahoma bombing and multiple arrests followed. Because of the relatively small size of most terror groups such actions often have immediate impact upon their effectiveness, particularly if the leaders are 'taken out' of action. The response of the American Far Right is also indicative of changes in the structure of terror groups around the world that consider themselves under threat of physical attack and penetration from within. In these situations groups will often adopt cell-like arrangements, minimising contact with the broader movement, leaders and other cells. This approach may enhance cell security in the short term but, as I argued in the preceding chapter, it is often detrimental to the longer-term goals of the movement.

At a pragmatic level MacGinty (2010) notes with regards to counter-insurgency that campaigns can be too successful. In essence the defeated foes will have to negotiate, compromise and engage in political discussion. To do so requires leaders who represent the support base and who can meet to discuss the options and consult supporters. An over-vigorous counter-terror campaign can hinder this. At an extreme level the eradication of group leaders prevents meaningful discussion and new leaders lack appropriate credentials and authority with which to accept the terms of their defeat. Therefore the capabilities to reach an agreement which incorporates and integrates militants and supporters and addresses grievance is less likely and the continuation of, or return to, political violence remains possible.

Rather than wait until they face terror attacks, governments also develop pre-emptive measures. The application of the legal framework is often integral to this, with anti-terror laws providing the basis for removing many suspects from society. Moreover the potential risks to life, livelihood and freedom can act as a deterrent to potential members who may be considering joining. At the other end of the terror career, the enforcement of anti-terror laws or their possible negotiation in return for cooperation can influence decisions to remain within or to depart from groups. The underpinning of terrorism through criminal activities provides a further opportunity to severely, potentially fatally, confront group capabilities (Hamm 2007). Groups rely upon criminalising activities in order to function. Consequently through intelligence and legislation, policing services can prevent methods for income generation such as fund raising and recruitment alongside existing illegal means such as credit card fraud and money laundering. Through the targeting of financial sources, policing can at the very least restrict group activities and opportunities for expansion; factors which can ultimately result in the defeat or disbandment of the group.

Finally, there is growing awareness about government programmes of demobilisation and rehabilitation which seek to have a direct impact on individual disengagement if not de-radicalisation. For instance, Horgan and Braddock (2010) discuss Colombian initiatives that were largely designed to facilitate demobilisation at group levels rather than at individuals who tended to leave for more idiosyncratic purposes such as fear of excessive punishment and disillusionment with leadership. Evidently when violence ends without the physical defeat of the terrorists it is advocated that members should be unarmed. Otherwise there is a distinct possibility that they become members of what Mulaj (2010) describes as violent non-state actors who are serious threats to security. Consequently Mulaj stresses the importance of disarmament, demobilisation and reintegration (DDR) programmes which assist in the transition to peace. As part of these programmes a number of violent actors such as the IRA in Northern Ireland and the Colombian April 19 Movement become incorporated within democratic and consensual politics. The transition to non-violent means can, as Jones and Libicki (2008) observe, also be instigated by government concessions and/or growing political activism among the targeted supporters. There are a number of reasons why this can occur including the distinct and relatively narrow strategic goals that ultimately prove negotiable. By comparison, more discursive organisations tend to have broader ambiguous goals which create problems. These include a lack of clarity about what precisely is being demanded, and in most instances the huge trans-national transformations which would be required to accord with what was apparent about the ideology such as the end of capitalism, the removal or eradication of non-whites or establishment of one global Muslim nation. Jones and Libicki (2008: 21) explain that 'terrorism may persist in a country precisely because the goals that the government and the terrorist group are pursuing are so far apart.'

Despite notable successes after DDR has been implemented to secure peace and stability to societies torn apart by civil war, Bjørgo and Horgan (2009) expose the relative lack of application within counter-terror strategies. This may well be indicative of the very different perceptions that are held about civil war and terrorism, both causes and solutions. Civil wars appear to have a credibility in terms of justification and rationale that is rarely attributed to terrorist forms of political violence. Arguably DDR programmes are also considerably easier when the transition occurs following victory and the formation of the designated nation-state such as Israel. Within the independent nation the Irgun and Stern Group disengaged and many members became influential politicians including most notably Prime Ministers Begin and Shamir. This transition can be compared with that of the PLO into the Palestinian Authority and in which the shift from terrorism to state sponsored violence was much less distinctive. By comparison with post-independent Israel's formation of an independent coherent armed force the PA's military capabilities are severely restricted. Hence when groups such as HAMAS and Islamic Jihad were gaining prominence, in part through the use of terrorism, and the peace process broke down, the military options available to the PA to challenge Israel were limited and the prevailing stance of an asymmetrical conflict resumed. The anticipated success of DDR programmes will therefore be influenced by numerous factors. One of the most significant influences upon the likelihood of individuals being willing to be rehabilitated is the closeness of bonds out of the terror group.

A final challenging question to ask in this section would be, how can we address or undermine the popular issues that terror groups utilise to arouse and maintain members? In short, because of the nature of the issues such as the overthrow of capitalism and opposition to events and policies in other countries such as the 'red' groups opposition to the American war against Vietnam, this may prove unrealistic. Nevertheless it is instructive to examine the rhetoric of groups associated with al-Qa'ida over recent years to evaluate the feasibility of resolving some of their primary concerns. Many of the issues raised within *jihadi* publications orientate around Western forces in Afghanistan, Iraq, Saudi Arabia and the Palestinian situation. The question can therefore be raised, would al-Qa'ida related groups disband if these issues were addressed, the West withdrew and Palestinians gained independence? The withdrawal of American forces from Saudi Arabia and the British from Iraq did not noticeably alter the intensity of anti-American and anti-British sentiments nor deter subsequent plotters from undertaking attacks. Instead attention concentrated on other locations and it is difficult to argue that the removal of Western forces from Iraq and Afghanistan would contribute to significant global disengagement. Nevertheless this would lead to further shifting of attention, possibly towards Central Asia and maybe the re-examination of the relationships between the 'near' and 'far' enemies. The Palestinian-Israeli situation is more complicated, but Sageman's (2008) observation requires acknowledgement. He noted that the first two waves of global Islamist terrorism occurred during periods when there was hope that the end to the conflict was imminent. Overall I am inclined to argue that the unlikely resolution of these issues would not end *jihadi* terrorism. The relevance and legitimacy of militant discourse would however be weakened and could be anticipated to be less appealing to potential recruits.

## Conclusion: Softly softly does it?

Government attempts to defeat terrorism are most widely associated with physical confrontation, legal measures and repression. When applied in isolation this approach will either fail by legitimising and invoking greater opposition or may succeed in the short term by repressing violence. Yet unless the causes for the emergence of terrorism are addressed or undermined, the threat of political violence remains and is likely to re-appear once conditions permit. Contrary to the tendency to concentrate on the violent contest counter-terror strategies do indeed often involve numerous, over-lapping methods. Hence there is a strong argument that 'hard' approaches should be accompanied by a 'softer' touch that incorporates communication, consultation and compromise. However, as Demant and de Graaf (2010) explain, the likely success of the 'softer' approach will be heavily determined by the extent to which the terrorists are supported and expectations of victory or defeat. Groups have to be willing to enter discussions and this will require certain conditions and expectations. There is, for example, less incentive for groups and their supporters who anticipate achieving their aims through political violence than those who consider the strategy to be failing.

In some ways, reasons why people voluntarily leave terror groups can reflect or be an inversion of the factors behind their initial involvement. Pathways out of terrorism can be as complicated, gradual and variable as the inwards routes. Moreover there are, Gupta (2008) remarks, a number of different combinations and pathways that result in the end of terrorism. Ideas, perceptions and/or forms of behaviour have to shift. In-depth understanding regarding how and why these happen, immersed in gradual and relatively rapid processes and with different triggers and outcomes has yet to be confidently established. Nevertheless it is possible to draw together some common strands such as factors that contribute towards negative emotions like defeatism and disillusionment and/or positive feelings such as a desire for a family, security and stability. There are some similarities between and within groups in the shifting processes and pathways out of groups. These can include the layers of habitus shared with other group members becoming less fundamental and no longer providing the synergy for individual and collective identification. Instead alternative ideas, relationships and forms of behaviour become integral in the individual disposition. To achieve this, members must re-cross the boundary that separates violence from normative behaviour.

Crossing the boundary to non-violence may appear easy according to normative standards. Terrorism is widely held to be wrong. Hence leaving it behind should be easy. Instead the transition is potentially daunting and unappealing. The group and possibly wider movement has provided the primary basis of identification, for ideas, forms of behaviour and restraint. Individuals must also accommodate the displacement of their main 'We' image for collective emotional attachment. Mennell (1994) and Elias (1996) explain that for the last century or two this has usually been the nation-state. Levels of attachment fluctuate during times of crisis and danger. I would argue that for members opposed to the nation-state, the group becomes the focal 'We' image with allegiances strengthened because of the insecurities and threatened environments in which the groups operate. Leaving these loyalties, support and control mechanisms and interrelationships behind can lead both to huge voids within individual lives that would appear empty and transform behavioural boundaries that require considerable adjustment. Understandably former terrorists can experience cognitive dissonance as their ideas, behaviours and relationships adjust to the new way of life. Wright's (1991) comparative analogy between new religious cults and divorce is in this regard also applicable for former terrorists. Of particular relevance is his discovery that the initial period of separation is the most difficult as 'defectors' struggle to come to terms with fundamentally reorganising their lives and making the necessary adjustment.

> Restablization was enhanced by the identification and affiliation with other social groups and networks, providing a reformulation and identity and worldview. Disorientation, moodiness, loneliness and general disorganization abated as new friends, reinvigorated family ties and a redefinition of self crystallized. (Wright 1991: 140)

DDR programmes that anticipate this are more likely to be attractive to wavering yet apprehensive members.

When considering disengagement, the appeal of 'civilian life', the nature of their existing relationships out-with the group, anticipated amnesty, punishment and social reception will be examined by members. Consequently if counter-terror approaches want to enhance rates of withdrawal they have to consider individual expectations, livelihoods, legal penalties and whether 'repentance' will incorporate the renouncement of political violence or must include a distancing from radical ideas. The two may appear synonymous, but are not, and the insistence on both can significantly reduce possibilities of either. Horgan (2009b) explains that disengagement is not always accompanied by a de-radicalising of ideas. For these individuals Barrett and Bokhari (2009: 175) suggest there is often a need for 'the creation of space and opportunity to vent frustration outside terrorism.' Clearly appropriate political and civic channels for debate and engagement would help to incorporate reformed terrorists within the mainstream providing both the incentive to stop the commitment to political violence and to hinder any subsequent return.

If former members are to be integrated within societies that they formerly challenged, levels of hatred and suspicion that they held, and were held about them, have to subside. Resentments have to dissipate, heightened emotions diminish and levels of empathy, moderation and cooperation rise. As Elias (2010) commented with regard to the Cold War enemies, this can only occur within less adversarial stances with more moderated language that seeks to replace hatred, bitterness and hostility with tolerance. Instead DDR programmes have to look to accommodate former terrorists in ways that are acceptable both to the individuals and enough of the rest of their respective societies to make the process feasible. Nevertheless this is still a lengthy process, exemplified by the continuing rumbling of political violence in Northern Ireland. Arguably the transition away from political violence can only become embedded and robust within secure and confident environments. This will depend heavily on the history and habitus of political violence and the nature and implementation of the DDR programmes. Consequently, there are no grounds to declare with any confidence what the optimum length of time is before the risk of asymmetrical political violence disappears from particular societies. The continuing threat within the United States by American 'patriots' is perhaps the best example of the complications and contradictions to be found within even the most modern of nation-states.

Finally, while it is easy to criticise governments' counter-terror strategies, it also has to be acknowledged that defeating terror groups without mobilising greater opposition and encouraging individuals to disengage is a hugely complex, often contradictory process. What works for one individual or group may fail for another. Moreover the transfer of a successful strategy in one location to another is destined to be unsuccessful unless it can be adapted to meet the local variations and foibles. Nevertheless, despite the complications and inconsistencies lessons can be learnt from other counter-terror approaches and from preceding attempts that have both failed and succeeded. The end of terrorism can be brought forward just as the beginning can be postponed or prevented. Although we still lack considerable knowledge about the processes and why particular programmes work with certain groups and members and not others, there are signs of progress. If the tentative figures of rehabilitation coming from Saudi Arabia are an accurate reflection of the effectiveness of their approach, then it will provide an important indicator for governments that are willing to commit the resources and political authority to integrating hard and soft approaches; the military and the community; the stick and the carrot.

# 8 Conclusion

## From beginning to end

### Introduction

When considering the vast amounts of money and media coverage, blunt and complicated counter-terror strategies and burgeoning academic, publishing and security related industries, the extent to which our knowledge and understanding about processes of terrorism has developed over the last 100 years could be viewed as disappointing. Sensationalist reporting, excessive government reactions and inflated feelings of fear and insecurity continue to surround outbursts of these forms of political violence obstructing both detached academic analysis and counter-terrorism. Too often explanations hint at determinism or rely on prevailing caricatures which hinder attempts at understanding. This is further obstructed by the accompanying denunciations of terrorists within emotive and provocative discourse which inflame feelings and hinders calculative reactions. It does enable images of terrorists as evil, sullen, weak and brainwashed to be conjured up. Unless we are able to reconcile that those people who choose to destroy, maim and kill can also be charming, engaging, likeable individuals the appeal of terrorism and terrorists will not be fully grasped. Somewhat immodestly this book is partly designed to contribute towards a more detached perspective with which to consider and confront terrorism.

Throughout the preceding chapters I have, to varying degrees, been working towards this. I have also been confronting two diametrically opposed spectrums which I argue are obstructing our ability to grasp the multifarious facets within processes of terrorism. Across one spectrum are varying levels of instrumental materialism with motivations ranging from leaving behind abject poverty to career enhancement. In essence, individuals become terrorists in order to improve their personal income and/or relative wealth. This compares with the rival spectrum which positions and interweaves emotions, weak personalities and gender, individual engagement as the consequence of feelings and/or manipulation. If we are to crudely summarise the two approaches then members become terrorists either because they want to improve their prospects or they are disillusioned with what life has to offer them. Evidently these are factors. Nevertheless they are over-applied, not least in the crude implicit demarcations which classify men as rational terrorists while women are driven by their emotions. In this final chapter I seek to draw together the apparent dichotomies within terrorism that have been noticeable throughout this book. Hence the rational and emotional, the past and the present, constraints and violence, secrecy and trust are intertwined within social processes and embedded within a sociological framework. The chapter concludes with an indication about what the sociology of terrorism may contribute within a multi-disciplinary study.

## Pre-roots and predispositions

One of the primary aims of this book is to overcome the tendency to examine terror attacks and the emotions that ensue in isolation. Acts of political violence should be embedded within long- and short-term processes and not demarcated as a detached event that encompasses, and is restricted by, the attack and its aftermath. By comparison, groups describe their bombings, hijackings, assassinations and so on as a 'means to an end.' They are also 'means' with elongated beginnings which often predate the engagement of the bomb-maker, hijacker and assassin. If we push the boundaries of exploration backwards in time we can incorporate not only the commencement of individual engagement, the formation of the group, the emergence and fissures within the wider movement and trace preceding ideas and types of behaviour that continue to reside within individual and social habitus. By mapping locations where terrorism emerges, the nationalities and ethnic groups involved with historical events and subsequent levels of state controlled violence and concomitant individual restraints, a pattern starts to emerge. In short, strategies of terrorism are more likely to be formulated where violent ideas and forms of behaviour continue to reside. I am not declaring that violence is necessarily rife in these environments. Instead I am proposing that the possibility of political violence is just that, a possibility. The extent to which possibility will become probability and eventuality will be dependent upon how people think, feel and act. If the pacification of behaviour, norms and values occurs uninterrupted across generations I would anticipate social constraints of political violence to be normative, robust and uncritically internalised. This is not to say that these people would never challenge the nation-state through group terrorism that emerges out of a wider social movement.[1] It is to say that in places like Britain the emergence of prominent terror groups would be heavily dependent upon massive transformations such as devastating natural disasters, environmental catastrophe, and unprecedented modern economic or political collapse.[2] These events would have to trigger such high levels of fear and uncertainty that people overcame generations of constraints in order to become politically violent. Nevertheless it is not impossible. Constraints may take generations to become fully and uncritically internalised. Consequently counter-terror strategies must be embedded within longer term processes of pacification if the underpinning restraints are to be internalised uncritically. Alternatively, restraints can be rapidly weakened and overcome when circumstances change severely. Becoming politically violent on behalf of the state would be cognitively easier. For instance, images and narrative of world wars, colonialism and collective self regard and source of pride, albeit one that is unravelling,[3] continue to permeate the British national layer of the social habitus and are a source for mobilisation if required. Pride can therefore help inform conformity to the state's monopoly of violence. Conversely, in nation-states with well-publicised stained recent histories, acquiescence to the national collective identification is considerably weaker. Indeed as Elias (1996) points out, the past for many post-1945 Germans was a source of shame and stigmatisation. Thus instead of providing a source of restraint, the past was the basis on which Far Left groups challenged the nation-state.

By building upon this point it can be argued that countries and regions with weaker social and individual restraints and a history of political violence are potentially more vulnerable to terrorism, not least because as Gupta (2008: 204) explains, 'the roots of most conflicts can be traced to the distant past.' In this regard the histories of countries as diverse as the United States, Colombia, Ireland and Saudi Arabia are illustrative. I argue that the legacy of political violence in the past remains in the present partly because processes of pacification have been incomplete, often taking place during times of perceived threats and uncertainty. Hence in regions, if not all of the countries, political pacification has not become normative. Burke (2006: 234–35) elaborates upon this when discussing radicalisation of Iraqi Sunnis post American invasion,

> What was noticeable a year after the invasion was a hardening in the general atmosphere. The exposure to constant risk was steadily brutalizing people, forcing them back into themselves. Thirty years of brutal dictatorial rule had already embedded violence as a natural part of everyday life and behaviour. The chaos of the new Iraq merely reinforced the tendency. As in Afghanistan and parts of Pakistan, the smallest dispute escalated rapidly.

Nor is 'We' identification uncritically shared with the nation-state and national consciousness. On the contrary, discursive consciousness is often at odds with the nation-state, connecting into conflicting ideas that can be traced to the past. For instance, the American Far Right tends to literally draw upon Christian scriptures and narrative from the exploits and doctrine of founding fathers both in their diagnosis of what is wrong with the country and the cure. Similarly militants in Saudi Arabia interpret Islamic discourse and apply their understanding of the actions and traditions associated with the Prophet Muhammad and a number of subsequent significant figures within a critical appraisal of the kingdom and proposed alternatives. In Mennell's application of the work of Norbert Elias to the United States, he suggests that higher rates of affective and impulsive violence are indicative of both less effective 'muting of drives' than exist in comparable parts of Europe and relative weakness of federal control. Although the formation and development of Saudi Arabia is obviously very different it is possible to identify some similar characteristics, not least the tensions between individual and social constraints. That both countries also impose the death penalty in regions vulnerable to terrorism connects into these processes. Following on from my line of argument, state sponsored violence against civilians is entwined within retributive and gun orientated cultures that reinforce the view that killing people can be acceptable and provides a clear barrier to levels of pacification. In essence, ambiguity surrounds violence and killing that does not exist in societies with more advanced levels of pacification. The shift into political violence is therefore likely to be less ontologically challenging in the United States and Saudi Arabia than in places such as Sweden, the Netherlands and the UK. The histories of Colombia and Ireland (and post partition the North) are somewhat different. Both have been littered with sporadic and prolonged bursts of violence within spirals of hatred against one or more 'other.' Heightened emotions and omnipresent feelings of insecurity and fear have prevented the pacification of aggressive norms, values and forms of behaviour. Again there are historical precedents and political inspirations on which terror groups draw.

Such processes are not necessarily bound within geographic regions. Habitus can be trans-national. Migrants migrate and initially share dispositions both with other travellers and those left behind. Over time individual habitus will transform to accommodate the surrounding layers of social habitus and recent experiences. For many migrants these experiences will include discrimination, racism, antagonism, threats and stress. In other words, the new locations have considerable risks and insecurities and contribute to a greater We identification around that which is under threat, namely ethnicity and religion. Both the aggression and reaction permeate the habitus solidifying negative perceptions of the 'other' while strengthening collective consciousness. If we apply this observation to Pakistani migration to the UK we can begin to develop a deeper understanding both about the militancy of some second and third generation migrants and trajectories into terrorism by the few. The weakness of the Pakistani state and the multiple problems since partition has meant that periods of political stability and uninterrupted processes of pacification have been notable for largely being absent. Certainly some of the individual constraints of original migrants would not have been deeply embedded and the experiences of subsequent generations within Britain alongside the ongoing problems within Pakistan and neighbouring Afghanistan have also hindered the uncritical internalisation of political restraints for many. Furthermore, these examples also highlight that contrary to popular opinion, terrorism is not restricted to authoritarian regimes; indeed in the short term, excessive repression can curtail terrorism. In countries such as Northern Ireland, Britain, America, Italy and West Germany multi-party parliamentary arrangements were in place and periodically are so in Pakistan. Yet the functioning of these democracies did, and does, not accord with particular individual and group personality structures. Instead people involved consider that their views are not accommodated meaningfully within parliamentary politics and challenge the legitimacy of governments including their monopolies of violence.

Conversely when there is a history of restraint this can restrict the levels of aggression both by terror groups and counter-terrorism. For instance, de Graaf and Malkki (2010) discuss how pluralism and consensus were recurrent features within Dutch political life. When confronted by radical groups in the 1970s the Dutch went to greater lengths to avoid confrontation and were distinctly uneasy about the use of police violence. In this regard the neglected Dutch Provo Movement of the mid 1960s were instrumental. Provo used provocative 'pranks' and 'happenings' to confront political and social indifference and to arouse police over reaction.[4] And because the society had not polarised along deep ideological divides like the Left and Right in West Germany and Italy and without their recent histories of authoritarian regimes, the Netherlands' inclusive and consensual approach weakened the conditions in which the Far Left Red Youth may have flourished. Moreover the same dynamics meant that Red Youth were more constrained when adopting violent tactics and engaged in much lower level attacks in comparison with groups in the other countries. The recent rise of the Far Right is probably an indicator of changing dynamics in the Netherlands which are contributing to deeper, more antagonistic cleavages and are threatening some of the well-established internalised behavioural and discursive constraints.

In the more recent history of societies affected by terrorism we can point to groups emerging out of broader movements. These include religious resurgences, student, nationalist, human rights and discursive organisations. Movements provide opportunities for values and social networks to be strengthened. They can also fracture around levels of activism, with tensions forming over the likelihood of success surrounding passive actions. Terror groups tend to break-away not least because they consider that non aggressive approaches such as democratic participation, civil society, demonstrations and protests have failed. Political violence becomes the chosen mechanism with which to achieve long-term goals through short-term intentions such as provoking the government, arousing popular support and awakening the nation. At this point I should again reiterate that I am not proposing that terrorism is the inevitable consequence of the legacy of political violence in conditions that do not encourage deep-rooted processes of internalised controls. The ideas that encourage the adoption or resumption of political aggression must resonate with potential members. Precipitating events and triggers which interact with the habitus and vestiges of violence must also be considered. The interaction frequently provides the impetus for groups to form and for people to become actively involved.

## Becoming a terrorist

If we examine the processes within the earlier stages in decision-making, then the likelihood of commencing a terrorist career is heavily influenced by shifting, or otherwise, individual identification and collective consciousness. In other words, levels of loyalties and personal restraints must shift through the perceived legitimacy of leadership and group dynamics that appeal to, and incorporate, individuals if they are to recruit new members. This is rarely an overnight experience. Instead there are multiple pathways and interacting triggers. Peer relations are an integral part, with prominent cells such as those living in Hamburg who went on to commit the 2001 attacks on America, the Bali and London bombers, the West German RAF, the Japanese Red Army and The Order or Silent Brotherhood in the United States. Taylor and Quayle (1994: 21) have argued that such social dynamics can 'result in a diffusion of responsibility for violence, weakening moral prohibitions against the use of violence.' People are extremely unlikely to join groups that are composed of members that they do not like, who share collective identity that is considered distasteful or whose discourse does not connect with experiences. Inversely the appeal of groups and, in particular, shared norms, values, affection and collective consciousness that results in adhesive social bonds is instrumental within recruitment processes, retention and the end phase. Arguably, pathways into terrorism that emerge from broader movements and are accompanied by friends will help stabilise ontological security. The potential magnitude of these steps should therefore not be dismissed. Individuals are choosing to leave behind physically, and/or psychologically, family members and some close peers when they become perpetrators of violence. In many instances, this will challenge normative precepts, although it should be added that terrorists have also been exposed to environments that endorse, at least implicitly, political violence. These tensions have to be managed and overcome and group relations are integral to this process. Yet although peer dynamics are fundamental to the processes of engagement they do not feature within popular portrayals, in part because these are underpinned by the assumption that ideas precede behaviour. Both Horgan (2005) and Sageman (2008) challenge this. Horgan (2005: 138) explains that 'for the individual terrorist increasing psychological investment, or the process of becoming a more committed member, is shaped most remarkably through engagement in terrorist activities.' Therefore terrorists 'have to be trained both in terms of what they do (the mechanics of the trade as it were) and in terms of how they make sense of what they do (ideological formation)' (Taylor and Horgan 2006: 595).

Groups, or to be more precise their leaders, will also make decisions about potential recruits as only the most desperate of organisations will not employ a recruitment policy. Decision-making will be influenced by a number of criteria such as knowledge, enthusiasm, communication skills, IT aptitude, ability under pressure, reliability and trustworthiness. Hence the potential member's capital will heavily determine their appeal to the organisation and the requisite networks which would provide the necessary support and evidence on behalf of their application to join. In short, to use Bourdieu's classifications, the person's pre-terror social, cultural and often economic capital will be heavily instrumental in whether the person wants to join and whether the group wants them. Consequently pragmatic and discursive socialising experiences influence the likelihood of individuals becoming terrorists. Alongside peers, agents include significant others such as parents and siblings and generalised others such as the media and education. Particular agents, symbols and frames of reference will contribute to layers of radicalisation. Examples include portrayals of the Jewish 'other' throughout the Palestinian territories and disproportionate media coverage about black rapists, murderers and drug addicts which connect into racialist perceptions about the 'threats' to white American communities. Once the initial steps into groups are taken, and for groups with longevity, violence can become widely dispersed, routine, normative behaviour that becomes embedded within dispositions with reduced constraints on active involvement. Individuals who are recruited at this stage may experience various emotions and hold different reasons for engagement. Moreover, because the moral, ethical and political dilemmas concerning the adaptation of violence have already been resolved, at least to the satisfaction of the founding members, the duration of subsequent individual shifts into terrorism may be condensed. In turn the more rapid transformation into political violence may contribute to newer recruits experiencing greater ontological insecurity.

Within groups, a combination of emotive factors and purpose and value rationality such as intensified commitment and loyalties to other members, camaraderie, pride, enjoyment, status, honour, financial rewards and identification, are integral to individual decision-making about remaining or leaving. The emotional emphasis often incorporates and plays upon gender stereotypes with female involvement viewed as very distinctive in terms of emotions and motivations. Yet as Nacos (2005: 436) explains,

> there is no evidence that male and female terrorists are fundamentally different in terms of their recruitment, motivation, ideological fervour, and brutality—just as there is no evidence that male and female politicians have fundamentally different motivations for seeking political office and abilities in different policy areas. Yet, the media's treatment of female terrorists is consistent with the patterns of societal gender stereotypes in *general* and of gender biases in the news coverage of female politicians in particular.

The classification of females as passive and hence less capable with little or no motivation to be terrorists provides organisations with opportunities. Nacos explains that terror groups are able to utilise the prevailing gender prejudices that exist within societies and employ women terrorists who are less likely to be identified than the male facing counter-terror strategies.

If we extend the criticisms of gender representations across studies of terrorism more generally, then neither 'feminine' emotions nor 'masculine' rational explanations can account for engagement. Again insights can be gained from processes within other types of groups such as cults and social movements and the transformation of values, feelings and actions that can result in heightened emotions and activism. These can be coordinated and channelled in particular strategic directions. Shared group norms, ritualised ties and feelings heightened by perceptions of threats and prevailing risks provide a basis for unity and are instrumental in the formation and reinforcement of collective identification. The emphasis upon trust and secrecy further strengthens these bonds but at a cost, namely looser associations with broader support and populations which can result in detachment from popular ideas and values and weaker levels of empathy. Moreover the tensions between secrecy, operating publicly and requiring enough information about members for a foundation of trust must be managed. Without sharing these allegiances and intimacies and internalising or retaining core beliefs it would be extremely difficult for individuals to retain membership. In-group solidarity is reinforced around gossip, common history, traits and behaviour that is entwined within collective charisma, esteem and oppositional stigma. Despite the selected similarities only being applicable for the 'minority of the best,' they come to symbolise the group's superiority. The reverse of these enhanced group loyalties is the reinforcement of comparative differences with outsiders. These groups are often stigmatised according to perceived differences which are based upon the exaggerated behaviour of the 'minority of the worst.' This minority become the stereotypical representatives of the 'other.'

## Constraining violence

Processes of stereotyping assist in the mechanisms of moral disengagement through which terror groups target and attack individuals. The selection of targets and methods, through which to attack, are often the result of careful consideration that connects into areas of expertise, historical legacies, likelihood of success, possibilities for escape and resources, intended outcome, depth of broader support and credibility of sources for justification. These are decisions which challenge the popular perception of the bloodthirsty maniac and epitomise the overemphasis upon emotions within the analysis of attacks. Consequently the necessity for the management of emotions within terror groups is overlooked. For the purposes of recruitment and retention, emotions such as anger, revenge and hope are certainly utilised. When planning and undertaking attacks the extent to which these emotions can be managed will be instrumental in the likelihood of success. In other words, emotions can hinder calculative planning resulting in self-damaging outcomes while bombers who are expressing feelings such as anger and hatred, either orally or physically, will arouse suspicion and probably arrest. Hence emotions have to be both sufficiently detached to allow the shift into politically violent behaviour and controlled to allow that behaviour to be optimised as a means to the end. Nevertheless, when groups are immersed within spirals of hatred alongside rival groups and/or government security forces this becomes difficult to

implement. When members experience fear, insecurity and demands for retaliation, detached approaches are hindered and leaders can lose sight of the
broader, longer term objectives in the haste to secure or appease support.

Along with the neglect of emotions the rational attention upon tactics and
calculations risks overstating the intentional nature of terror groups. In reality
groups form, people participate and attain popularity in part due to considerable elements of mis/fortune and a high degree of connection with time
and place.[5] Within social relations, levels of discrimination and degrees of
hostility that individuals encounter, through their association with a collective
identification, can contribute to that allegiance being strengthened. Today this
is noticeable within Muslim reactions to Islamophobia and the zoning of the
'war on terror' (Vertigans 2010b). Yet as Chapter Six discusses, these unintentional outcomes from governments' perspectives are very much intended
by terror groups, indeed provoking excessive, indiscriminate retaliation is
instrumental to their actions. Nevertheless government actions also incorporate considerable unintentional consequences that the militants have not considered and which work to their advantage. The Saudi government's
promotion and financial and logistical support of more radical forms of Islam
within and out-with the Kingdom, outlined in the previous chapter, is a very
good example of this.

## Staying violent

The lifespan of groups is to some degree influenced by support levels both
within groups and broader societies. Thus, groups like the Provisional IRA
were able to operate and retain members across three decades in part because
of the extent to which they were supported and protected by the communities
in which they were embedded, and which were largely impenetrable to British
government counter-terror measures. By comparison today, the support for
the Real IRA and Continuity IRA is considerably weaker, severely restricting
appeal and capabilities. Hence although attacks have continued since the
onset of the peace process, they are often isolated acts that are no longer part
of concerted campaigns. And instead of violence, fear and insecurities permeating
the social habitus, peace and hope have become prominent. Consequently
terror activities have not reignited emotions to heightened levels that would
have led to growing support for the armed return of paramilitaries. This is not
to say that political violence will not return to Northern Ireland. Both triggers
and preconditions remain to some extent. Moreover Hayes and McAllister
(2005) note how a significant minority continue to be sympathetic towards the
aims of the republican movement and violence as the means to achieve them,
not least as so many people have been directly touched by the use of political
violence. Thus the likelihood of terrorism returning is heavily determined by
the presence and interactions of triggers and preconditions.

There is also a requirement to look beyond the discursive surface because
there are often other less obvious factors that contribute to group dynamics

and radicalisation and which may need to be addressed if members are to remain committed to non violence. Northern Ireland is again a useful example. At one level violence has been embedded within habitus for generations and arguably centuries. I explain above that the eradication of violence can only occur within secure, stable environments, and even then this is a lengthy process. The onus is therefore on creating such an environment, which is a huge task even for social constructionists. The peace process has begun the shifting of norms, values and behaviours but the residues of violence remain. This is in part because of the policy-driven concentration upon sectarianism. The emphasis on sectarian divisions has been at the expense of important differences within the communities. Graham (2004: 490) explains how the Protestant working class is divided between 'a relatively contented embourgeoised majority and a socially excluded *lumpenproletariat* living in marginalized, polarized housing estates festooned with ethnic territorial markers.' In these localities the impact of globalisation and multiculturalism is less noticeable. Graham (ibid.) points out such processes can be overtly and violently resisted, exemplified by the escalating number of attacks carried out by UVF members against ethnic minorities in 2003–4. Instead of shifting their identification outwards, loyalists continue to look inwards. Lacking contemporary positive sources of consciousness, members are united by historical events and distrust and hatred of an increasing mix of political elites and communal 'others.'

## Ending terrorism

If we follow on from the declaration that pathways into terrorism are deep rooted, convoluted and complex then attempts at prevention, and ending, of terrorism will have to consider the myriad of processes involved. These include methods and tactics such as disengagement programmes and potential roles for former terrorists, constriction of money suppliers, targeting of criminal activities, careful selection of counter-terror personnel, sensitive implementation of the rule of law, retention of moral and ethical principles and the application of the military hardware. These are to some extent determined within a complex interplay between national habitus, political agendas, international relations, the nature of the threat, pre-existing levels of controls, the spiralling of emotions and feelings of insecurity. Alongside the more visible militarism there must be an acknowledgement that social relationships within groups are a significant component of being a terrorist. Hence perceptions of life outside the group should be considered. By this I mean terrorists, and by extension counter-terrorists, will think about whether social relations out-with the group appear attractive. Are there alternative political organisations that offer meaningful solutions? Are there cultural resources with appeal or do these elements contribute to high levels of anger, fear, uncertainty, hatred and shame? Focusing on what is wrong with terrorism is inadequate. Instead a comprehensive approach should be formulated that focuses not only upon negatives about the groups but negative perceptions within groups about external social relations and activities. Similarly an acknowledgement of the appeal of the terror group would help in the construction of appealing alternatives that exist beyond the social entity.

## Studying sociologically: Backwards and forwards

Following on from my earlier points, it will be apparent that I think there are a number of generic weaknesses within studies of terrorism. I want to explicitly confront these in this section. To start with, academic musings about terrorism all too often share the failings of media and political commentators that are heavily influenced by personal and public ethical frameworks and the emotional dispositions to which they are exposed. Without acknowledging these influences and their impact, attempts to understand terrorism are doomed and will remain fixated on the act and the demonisation of those responsible. The processes that led to the act will be as neglected as the processes that caused the demonisers to demonise.

Across the different phases of terror careers, there is a distinct lack of empirical fieldwork and a tendency to over-generalise based upon small samples that fail to acknowledge diversity within and between groups and localities (Horgan 2005, 2009). In parts of the world where terror groups operate that do not explicitly threaten the West or related interests, such as Central Africa and South America, these problems are magnified. Conversely there has been a huge growth in the publication of terrorist (auto) biographies which can provide invaluable insights into experiences and processes, providing they are subjected to critical analysis. By comparison the vast increase in government counter-terror related costs and the passing of extensive legislation which has created new terror crimes and punishments have not largely been accompanied by access to those arrested and imprisoned. Consequently there are vast numbers of people who are classified as terrorists by national governments and about whom we know little or nothing. Without a greater sharing of information and opportunities to speak to terrorists, academics find their knowledge, understanding and contributions restricted. Ultimately the denial of access is indicative of government dismissals of the potential role of academics within approaches to end terrorism. Yet academic methods are essential if counter-terror strategies are to be more informed, incisive, constructive and relevant to the targeted groups. Today this neglect is most noticeable at the final stage of disengagement. Bjørgo and Horgan (2009) comment upon the lack of data which hinders attempts to evaluate the effectiveness of programmes designed to facilitate people leaving terror groups. And of course, comparative analysis between different approaches is even more difficult with problems over limited information compounded by different definitions and collation methods.

Based upon this it is perhaps understandable that comparative analysis of different groups is underdeveloped. The tendency to demarcate and isolate according to religious or secular, ethnic or ideological, Left Wing or Right Wing, pro state or nationalist epitomises this. I am not declaring that these distinctions are unimportant; they clearly are, not least for the people involved. Today the most notable distinction is drawn around religion and it has even been awarded its own wave following on from anarchist, colonial and 'New Left.' Religious groups are the most notorious and seemingly one of the easiest to demarcate. Theological interpretations can incorporate different value systems that contribute to the justification and acclaimed legitimacy of attacks. The moral frameworks of groups associated with al-Qa'ida and the Aum Supreme Truth can therefore provide the basis for unrestrained attacks which result in numbers of fatalities that have hitherto been unknown in the modern era. Yet social processes, ideas and activities transcend these divisions and classifications contain elements of others. For instance, in the Palestinian territories, Hamas could easily be classified as nationalist, ethnic or religious, al-Qa'ida adopts tactics and rhetoric from the nineteenth-century anarchists, groups in Northern Ireland interweave sectarianism with ethno-nationalism and the Aum Supreme Truth and the Red Army Faction members were highly educated and from overwhelmingly middle-class backgrounds. We should not lose sight of the fact that secular groups also have moral frameworks upon which they draw to justify and legitimise their killings.

In this book I do little to address or help to develop a number of these issues. This should not detract from the importance of developing these areas. Sociology should be positioned within the evolving approach. The problem however, and this is a weakness both within studies of terrorism and sociology, is that the latter is badly under-prepared to be constructively involved. I argue that the neglect of terrorism by sociologists and the concomitant hole within our understanding of terrorism is a fundamental weakness for the subject. The absence of sociological contributions is indicative of the discipline's relocations post 1945 and the detachment from politically violent forms of behaviour. By comparison, after futilely chasing the definitive terror personality, psychology has made massive strides in helping our understanding of pathways into and increasingly out of terrorism.

There is much that sociologists can learn from psychologists in terms of detachment, fieldwork and the positioning of processes within terror careers. The surge of psychological contributions has however created an imbalance within studies of terrorism; namely, there is considerable emphasis upon individual interactions and experiences which intersect with studies from political science and associated formations, policies and discourse. Hence the inter-disciplinary approach to terrorism is frontloaded because the broader social processes that position the individual and groups within broader movements and intertwine contemporary and historical forms of radical ideas and violent behaviour are neglected. In other words the inattention of sociology has meant that the terror backdrop is largely missing. A staged play without a scenic backdrop usually results in partial impressions as audiences struggle to situate the words and actions. Without the sociological backdrop terror groups can appear to have lost their moorings, detached from the very processes that were instrumental in their creation. I am therefore arguing that terrorism is rooted in broader social processes and activities and these have to be drawn into the sub-discipline. This can be best achieved through sociological concepts, epistemological tools and ways of thinking that complement and supplement psychological, political and economic contributions. An immediate stumbling block is the shallow depth of sociological studies of terrorism which is more of a gaping hole than a rich seam on which to mine. Nevertheless sociology more generally does have much to offer, commencing with strands which incorporate some similar processes such as studies of gangs, criminal behaviour, cults and social movements. Through sociological contributions we can gain greater knowledge about fundamental challenges such as why terrorism occurs in places with histories of political violence, the intersection between triggers and habitus, the impact of repressive and liberating regimes, the social failures of democracy, the creation and reinforcement of stereotypes, the interweaving of emotions and rationality, socialising processes and group dynamics throughout terror careers. Moreover, sociology can better inform counter-terror strategies, illuminating the broader social processes, exploring the construction and application of terrorism as a risk concept by media commentators and political legislators, and emotions such as fear and insecurity which impact upon reactive approaches and ultimately contribute to spiralling of hatreds and self-defeating policies and actions.

The opportunities for academic insights are nevertheless not without limit. Horgan (2009) identifies, for instance, that we cannot precisely predict the likelihood that a person or 'type of person' will become a terrorist. Nevertheless we can identify what he refers to as predisposing risk factors such as temporary emotional state, permanent individual factors, dissatisfaction about current political or social activity, personal agency, identification with victims, expectation of rewards and social ties. Alongside these could be added more explicitly sociological and historical factors such as politically violent discourse and behaviour in the past, the formulation of rules, subsequent levels of social constraints, periods of uncertainty and risk, levels of mutual identification and interdependencies, the internalisation of self discipline and contemporary habitus. Furthermore, sociological perspectives can help in plans for reconciliation with particular emphasis placed upon the oft neglected requirement to acknowledge that well-established hostilities are not inherently eradicated with the declaration of peace or the ending of terror groups. Instead reciprocal psychological barriers that have formulated around the 'other' and spirals of antagonisms need to be knocked down gradually and replaced with normative, robust values and restraints and non threatening interactions. This can only occur under a stable monopoly of violence and within secure spaces of mutual interaction, chains of interdependencies and ambivalence of interests accompanying moderating institutions and leaders that challenge, and ultimately overwhelm, established, disparaging stereotypes.[6] Finally, as part of a softer counter-terror approach, sociology can help to acknowledge shifting forms of collective identification and to highlight the appeal of the group out-with terrorism. The dynamics of civilian life can help individuals make the transition from terrorist to pacifist. Consequently I am drawn to conclude that attempts towards a more holistic, cross disciplinary approach will always be incomplete without sociological insights. At a time when the role and value of sociology is open to questions concerning financial feasibility and societal relevance, there is certainly scope for sociologists to contribute to enhancing levels of knowledge and understanding about the processes of terrorism, and how such acts of political violence can be prevented.

# Glossary

**Al-Aqsa Brigade**: Palestinian terror group which is very closely associated with the Fatah Party, the more secular and dominant political party in the West Bank. The group emerged during the second *intifada*.

**Al-Qa'ida**: 'The base.' Has been transformed since its early roots in the Afghan war against the Soviet Union into an international organisation which targeted the 'Far enemy.' Osama bin Laden was the prominent figure. Today it is more accurately described as a loose association of militant Muslims who connect into the ideas and actions of al-Qa'ida.

**Aryan Nations**: A racialist group established in the mid 1970s by Richard Butler that integrates racism and Christian Identity philosophy.

**Aum Supreme Truth**: 'Aum Shinrikyō.' Japanese religious cult led by Shoko Asahara which was responsible for the 1995 sarin attack on the Tokyo underground.

**Bhindranwale Tiger Force of Khalistan**: Sikh separatist movement which emerged in Punjab, India, in the early 1980s.

**Black Widows**: Term originally coined by Russian media for Chechen women involved in terror attacks against Russian targets. They are commonly associated with suicide bombings and unfounded claims that the women are relatives of men killed by Russian forces.

**Christian Identity**: Adaptation by American racialists of Anglo-Israelism. Emphasis is placed upon Aryans as the chosen people and the United States as the 'promised land.'

**Dar al-Harb**: 'House of war.'

**Dar al-Islam**: 'House of Islam.'

**Dar al-Kufr**: 'Land of impiety.' The opposite of dar al-Islam.

**Deobandi**: Muslim conservative movement which originated in the nineteenth century on the Indian subcontinent. Strongly associated with militant madrassas.

**ETA**: 'Euzkadi Ta Azkatasuna' (Basque Homeland (or Fatherland) and Freedom). Basque separatist group from north-east Spain and south-west France. Emerged in 1959.

**FARC**: 'Fuerzas Armadas Revolucionarias de Colombia' (Revolutionary armed Forces of Colombia). Marxist guerrilla army largely based in the south-east of the country. Has been active in terror activities since the early 1960s.

**Fatwa**: Religious legal edict based on Islamic holy texts.

**Front Line**: 'Prima Linea.' Left-Wing Italian terror group that was active between 1976 and 1980.

**HAMAS**: 'Enthusiasm' or 'zeal' and is also the acronym for *Harawat al-Muqawama al-'Islamiyya* (the Islamic Resistance Movement). Palestinian Islamic terror group which formed in the 1980s with strong links to the Muslim Brotherhood. Terror activities are usually undertaken by the group's military wing, the al-Qassam Brigades.

**Hezbollah**: 'Party of God,' prominent in Lebanon since 1962. Best known for terror activities particularly during 1980s and early 1990s. Today it is both a political and paramilitary organisation.

**Imam**: 'Leader' (of the prayers) of the Muslim community. Shi'a Muslims believe that the term refers to the Prophet's descendants, who are the true Muslim leaders.

**INLA**: Irish National Liberation Army. A republican paramilitary group that split from the IRA in 1974/5.

**Intifada**: 'Uprising.' The term is best known for the Palestine uprisings in 1987 and 2000.

**IRA**: Irish Republican Army. Republican group originally formed to achieve independence from Britain and then, following the partition of Ireland into the north and south, sought to bring about unification through political violence.

**Irgun**: Jewish terror group that was active in Palestine in order to achieve an independent nation-state.

**Japanese Red Army**: New Left terror group led by Shigenobu Fusako. After leaving Japan the group was based in Lebanon and became involved in Arab armed struggle against Israel. Disbanded in 2001.

**Jihad**: 'Struggle,' 'effort' or 'striving.' There are two forms. In the greater Jihad individuals strive to improve their own religiosity and in the lesser Jihad, struggle by military means, often referred to as Holy War.

**2 June Movement**: West German New Left group led by Bommi Baumann. Formed in 1971 and disbanded in the 1980s.

**Laskar Jihad**: Indonesian group that emerged in 2000 to wage 'holy war,' particularly against Christians.

**LTTE**: Liberation Tigers of Tamil Ealam: Tamil separatist organisation based in Sri Lanka. Formed in 1970s.

**LVF**: Loyalist Volunteer Force. Northern Irish loyalist paramilitary group formed in 1996 by members of the UDA and UVF who were disaffected with the peace ceasefire. Prominent leader was Billy 'King Rat' Wright who was killed in 1997.

**Mano Blanco**: 'White hand.' A Right-Wing anti-communist group which formed in the 1960s in Guatemala.

**Militias**: Organised groups of armed citizens. They are notable within numerous American states and are associated with the Patriot movement.

**Montoneros**: Organisation that emerged in Argentina during the 1970s which incorporated radical Catholicism and populist nationalism.

**NICRA**: Northern Ireland Civil Rights Association that was inspired during the 1960s by other civil rights groups, particularly in America.

**Official IRA**: Name given to the more ideological component of the IRA when the organisation split into two groups at the onset of 'The Troubles' in 1970. The 'Officials' concentrated more upon Marxist ideology than the Provisional IRA who quickly attained dominance within republican circles.

**Order, The**: American neo-Nazi group formed by Robert Mathews in 1983 and who committed terror attacks. Also known as the Silent Brotherhood.

**Palestinian Islamic Jihad**: Islamic terror group formed out of the Muslim Brotherhood in 1980 and remains more detached from mainstream politics than other Palestinian terror groups.

**Provisional IRA**: Irish Republican Army or paramilitary group that is also known as 'the Provos' who were the dominant republican group from 1970 to the 1990s. Formed out of the 1970 split in the IRA.

**Qu'ran**: 'Recitation.' The sacred book of Islam.

**Red Army Faction**: West German New Left terror group that operated during 1970s and 1980s. Also known as the Baader-Meinhof gang after two of the leading members, Andreas Baader and Ulrike Meinhof, died in prison.

**Red Brigades**: New Left terror groups that were prominent in Italy during the 1970s and 1980s.

**Revolutionary Organisation of 17 November**: Greek Marxist group named after the date of a student uprising which occurred in 1973. The group formed two years later.

**Salafist**: Originally a movement founded in the late nineteenth century that revered the 'pious ancestors.' From the 1970s it has been associated with conservative Islam in the Arabian peninsula.

**Sendero Luminoso**: 'Shining Path.' Peruvian Marxist-Maoist organisation formed in 1969–70.

**Shari'ah**: Divinely sanctioned Islamic law.

**Shi'a**: Islamic 'denomination' that emerged during conflict over the succession to the Prophet Muhammed. Followers are called shi'ites and are estimated to constitute 10–15 per cent of Muslims. Numerically the shi'ites are dominant in Azerbaijan, Iran and Iraq.

**Sinn Féin**: Meaning 'We Ourselves,' founded in 1905. Political Party and wing of the Provisional IRA. First became internationally prominent during 1916 Easter Rising.

**SLA**: Symbionese Liberation Army. A Left-Wing terror group that operated in America between 1973 and 1975.

**Stern Gang**: Jewish terror group operating in Palestine prior to formation of Israel.

**Sunni**: 'Tradition,' often referred to as orthodox Islam. The dominant 'denomination' within Islam following the conflict over succession to Muhammed which led to the emergence of sunnis and shi'ites. Followers are estimated at between 85 and 90 per cent of Muslims.

**Tupamaros**: Uruguayan Marxist organisation which largely operated as urban terrorists.

**UDA**: Ulster Defence Association. Northern Irish paramilitary loyalist group which formed in the late 1960s. Initially sought to bring together the different defence associations that had formed during the onset of 'The Troubles.'

**UFF**: Ulster Freedom Fighters. Formed out of the UDA's military wing in 1973.

**Ulema**: A man of learning who is a Muslim religious figure.

**Ummah**: Islamic nation or community of believers.

**UVF**: Ulster Volunteer Force. Previous incarnation was led by Edward Carson pre-First World War to defend the union. In 1966 the Northern Irish paramilitary loyalist group formed with the same name.

**Wahhabism**: Conservative doctrine associated with followers of ibn Abdul al-Wahhab (1703–87). Today the doctrine is official ideology of the state of Saudi Arabia.

**Weather Underground**: American New Left Wing militants that formed in 1970 out of the Students for a Democratic Society and disbanded during the 1980s. Previously known as The Weathermen.

# Notes

## Introduction

1 Equally as Alexander (2002) remarked with respect to al-Qa'ida-related groups, and which can be applied to numerous examples over the last 40 years, the increase in the quantity of publications has not necessarily been accompanied by a similar enhancement in quality.

## 1 Peoples, places and processes

1 Oliverio (1998) and Oliverio and Lauderdale (2005) provide illuminating explanations for shifting parameters.
2 Again this is a short summary. In addition to the preceding references further details can be found in Gill (2007), Long (1990), Sageman (2004, 2008), Silke (2003) and Victoroff (2005).
3 In his sample Sageman also identifies seven per cent who were brought up as Christians.
4 The emphasis upon authoritarian personalities has a clear link with Adorno *et al.*'s (1950) study.
5 For instance Kassel (2009: 246) quotes an article from 1902 in which a terrorist assassin is described as a 'poor wretch' and 'through such men, semi-insane ideas work out an insane propaganda of the deed.' By the standards of contemporary newspaper coverage, the editorial is almost admirably restrained.
6 This is epitomised by a convicted republican who informed Taylor (2000: 8) that 'an IRA man's normal just like everyone else.' When Taylor replied that normal people did not kill other people the republican responded that this was because they did not live in Northern Ireland.
7 Speckhard and Ahkmedova (2006) acknowledge that traumatic experiences are also instrumental in men joining groups in Chechnya.
8 Again this is noticeable within the treatment of groups even more challenging than terrorists to popular sentiments such as paedophiles. For instance, the recent conviction of Vanessa George in the UK was framed in such a way that her involvement could only be understood in terms of being manipulated by men.
9 When gaining prominence, Sjoberg and Gentry (2007) observe that the members are invariably classified by their sex as 'women or female' terrorists in a manner that is never applied to men. Of course I have arguably replicated this here albeit with the defence it was for illustrative purposes. Boyle (2005) identified similar processes in the coverage of 'female' criminals in press reports.
10 Female LTTE members have been widely reported to be motivated to join as a consequence of being raped by peace keepers or Sri Lankan military forces (Cunningham 2003). Rape becomes both a motivation for women to join and for the terror groups to justify their involvement, often in suicide missions.

11 Studies of female suicide terrorists, particularly in the Palestinian territories tend to provide examples of these experiences (Bloom 2004, Dworkin 2002 and Victor 2004).

12 Women who do act violently are often portrayed to be more fanatical and aggressive than men. Antolin's research into female members of ETA is typical. The women are described as 'more cold-blooded and more lethal than men because they have to prove their worth' (cited in Nacos 2005: 444). Such perceptions have been shared by security forces. MacDonald (1991) reports on the West German counter-terror unit who were commanded to 'shoot the women first' because they were considered to be more ruthless and aggressive than men.

13 Gilbert (2002) and Ristock (2002) explore the myths that surround violent women and lesbianism. Moreover parallels can be drawn between terrorists and other notorious females such as the 'Moors Murderer' Myra Hindley whose sexual relations with women in prison were the subject of considerable media speculation (Boyle 2005).

14 Morgan's (2001) account of the 'Demon Lover' is probably the best known explanation for women in patriarchy who, she argues, commit acts of political violence because they are sexual slaves and victims.

15 There are a number of studies which analyse the sexualised reporting of female terrorists such as Brunner (2005), Issacharoff (2006) and Nacos (2005: 436) who describe references to manicures, smile, hair styles, make-up, clothing and beauty. Nacos argues that these reflect 'patterns of societal gender stereotypes.' Today, almost 40 years after her actions, it is still possible to read contemporary references to the original 'glamour girl of international terrorism' Leila Khaled.

16 The portrayal of Fusako Shigenobu is particularly unsympathetic, combining references both to her sexuality and 'cold-blooded' aggression. Farrell (1990: 105) for instance describes reports of her as a 'fanatical, attractive, dark-haired woman ... who cared little about human life' and was 'coolly sending lovers and husbands to their deaths.'

17 Comparisons are undertaken by Brunner (2005) and Issacharoff (2006). Nevertheless, as Ness (2005) argues, there is still a tendency for the Middle Eastern media to associate the women with idealised female qualities.

18 Data is reported in Nacos (2005).

19 I explore the wider impact of the 'war on terror' in much greater depth in Vertigans (2010b).

20 One of the issues raised by Sageman (2008: 102) in a manner that would find support across the Right-Wing spectrum is that welfare payments 'remove the urgency to find regular work and allow some of the leisure time to become full-time Islamist terror "wannabes" ... .'

21 Fiorillo (1979: 265) offers a somewhat unfounded claim for Italian terrorism seemingly based upon 'commonsense' that 'it is well known how unemployment breeds an inborn stimulus, also irrational, towards violence.'

22 An alternative, yet potentially complementary approach is Bandura's social learning theory. In the Palestinian territories individuals 'learn' through observing political violence and the symbolic representations which they then imitate. The standard criticism of all theories can be applied to social learning theory, namely as Taylor and Quayle (1994) commented, the account can only explain why the minority became terrorists and not why the majority did not.

23 Although, as Hafez (2004) and Rashid (2002) report, government repression has been influential in a number of locations including Egypt, Algeria and Central Asia.

24 Further details can be found in Crenshaw (1990) and Vertigans (2008).

25 Malešević (2010) proposes that the emergence of the pacifist themes pointed to the importance of Marx, Weber and Durkheim because their research interests were complementary. By comparison other significant sociological contributors from

preceding eras such as Gumplowicz, Oppenheimer, Ratzenhofer and Alexander Rustow, whose research interests did not accord with the change in sociological direction became marginalised as the 'holy trinity' acquired enhanced prominence that they did not attain when alive.

26 Sageman (2008) explains that some of the marriages were between members and relatives of other members. In so doing, group bonds were tightened through kinship. There is also evidence of some terrorists becoming married in order to merge more effectively within the communities they relocated to.

27 Bakker's (2006) analysis of European *jihadis* was less supportive of Sageman's 'married mujahedin.'

28 Example is reported in Sjoberg and Gentry (2007: 123).

29 Although many members have been married and had children including most notoriously RAF's Ulrike Meinhof and Gudrun Esslin, who both left their children when going underground. Thus they not only challenged the perception of women as passive but also their 'natural' role as mothers.

30 Within studies of social movements young people are also identified as being more inclined to activism partly because they are available, willing to take risks, earlier links have been weakened and individuals are less conditioned about new social ties (della Porta and Diani 1999).

31 The slight exception to this is when terrorists are considered to have manipulated individuals through these other roles. In this regard the love life of 'playboy' terrorists such as Ilich Ramirez Sanchez (Carlos the Jackal) and individuals who are believed to have 'duped' their lovers to become involved in terror activities has attracted considerable media coverage.

32 This is indicative of the tendency to neglect the long-term and figuration-specific construction of rationality and the inter-relationship with social, political and economic changes and shifts between affective and reality-orientated demands discussed by Elias, particularly (2000) and (2005).

## 2 History: the legacy of political violence

1 Ironically within contemporary Northern Ireland, loyalists have been more inclined to express allegiance with Israel while republicans support the Palestinians.

2 Numerous texts explore the historical evolution of terrorism including Burleigh (2008), Law (2009), Laqueur (1977) and Sinclair (2003).

3 At a more pragmatic level, groups also acquire information about weapons and tactics from earlier or well-established contemporary terrorists.

4 Hewitt (2003) reports that since 1954 to before the September 2001 attacks, there had been in excess of 3,000 terrorist incidents and over 700 related fatalities within the United States and Costa Rica.

5 Hunter is quoted in Trautmann (1980: viii).

6 Kaplan (2007) adds a fifth wave, 'The New Tribalism,' which includes what he refers to as anomalous movements. In comparison with the groups under investigation in this book, the fifth wave consists of more explicit guerrillas and militia type organisations. To reiterate, the focus of this book is upon groups which are more narrowly defined as 'terrorist' because of the form of political violence with which they are most closely associated.

7 Pearse is quoted in Fitzpatrick (1992: 198).

8 The Express is quoted in Kee (1995: 178).

9 The Aum Supreme Truth attained notoriety following the 1995 sarin gas attack on the Tokyo underground.

10 Van Krieken (1998) points out that Elias placed historical analysis and social development at the cornerstone of his sociological approach at a time when sociologists were distancing themselves from history.

11  There are numerous exceptions to this in particular world-system theorists, Weberians and figurational sociologists, see for example Mennell (2007), Moore (1966), Skocpol (1979, 1984), Wallerstein (1974, 1980, 1989) and Wouters (2007).

12  Of course entwining past and present in order to justify violence is not restricted to terror groups. Governments have also applied the trajectories of justification. The most notorious example of the twentieth century is the Nazi narrative that established a long history of national subjugation by foreign enemies, in particular, Jews, communists and allied occupiers (Weaver 1997).

13  This is not to state that the historical narrative is unfounded. As Khalilov (2003: 410) commented, between 'the late 18th Century and 1944, not a single decade passed without Russian or Soviet authorities committing massacres in Chechnya.'

14  Many of these events are also captured in songs and poems of the period.

15  In the Declaration the British government was to support the establishment of a Jewish national homeland in Palestine. However, the British had also offered to support Arab claims for post First World War independence if they fought against the Ottomans. A third proposal, the 1916 Syke-Picot agreement which was decided between Britain and France was to dismember the Ottoman territories. Under this agreement Palestine would be placed under British control.

16  Qasim is quoted in Allen (2006: 207).

17  The first Saudi state ended in 1818 with the victory of Egyptian forces on behalf of the Ottoman Empire.

18  Wahhab's *jihad* was however largely against corruption (Hodgson 1974).

19  Shank is cited in Croft (2006).

20  Although loyalists are of the Protestant denomination, it would be misleading to assume that the conflict in Northern Ireland was religious in nature, a sort of Holy War. Religion is not the cause of the 'Troubles.' Nevertheless religion became immersed within national, largely secular ideologies. Coulter (1999: 58) comments that 'it has exercised a palpable influence. Religious beliefs and practice within the six counties [Northern Ireland] have served to promote those secular identities and disputes that form the basis of the "Northern Ireland problem."'

21  The Battle of the Somme has been particularly integral within collective memories. Graham (2004) discusses how the UVF claimed ownership of the Somme, making explicit links between the fallen in the Somme and the UVF's dead. Within the rhetoric of resistance, the Somme became a central icon.

22  Kee (1995) notes that the higher figure is grossly exaggerated, exceeding the total number of Protestants in Ireland at that time.

23  There are two forms of *jihad* which translates as struggle or striving. The greater *jihad* refers to individual striving to improve their religiosity. The lesser *jihad* is widely interpreted in the West as Holy War. The mainstream Islamic meaning tends to emphasise war in the pursuit of territory or defensive war when the religion or way of life is threatened. Of course 'defensive' is much open to interpretation and has been applied by some Muslim terrorists to include women and children as legitimate Western targets.

24  Lapidus (2002) argues that during this period a Middle Eastern Islamic civilisation was formed.

25  Bonner (2006) also explores the evolution of *jihad* and discusses distinctions between recent terrorist usage and earlier applications.

26  Tone belonged to the United Irishmen and, highlighting the movement's early cross sectarian ambition, was a Protestant.

27  For instance, at the commencement of the Easter Rising, Padraig Pearse declared in the proclamation read from the steps of the Dublin Post Office that there had been six times in the past 300 years when the Irish people had taken up arms in order to attain freedom and national sovereignty.

28 It is possible to extend the scope of duration of Irish history. Foster (1992) discusses how Brian Boru's confrontation with Norsemen in 1014 had become incorporated within the narrative of an Irish Gaelic identity by the early nineteenth century.
29 In the following chapters I shall also argue that this is because of the different dynamics of opposition and resultant spirals of hatred which existed in Italy.
30 Parallels can be drawn with the cross-fertilisation between Muslim ideologues and movements such as the Arabian Wahhibism and Indian sub-continent Deobandis which shared uncompromising and puritanical approaches.
31 Quoted in Akbar (2004: 138).
32 These are in Mecca and Medina and stem from the time of Muhammed, although strictly speaking the Meccan Kaaba was significant beforehand.
33 Sánchez is discussed in Waldmann (2007).

## 3 Habitus: terrorism and violent dispositions

1 Yet it would be a mistake to consider violence to permeate throughout all Somali interactions. Alongside a backdrop of southern state lawlessness, informal mechanisms and systems of governance have (re-)emerged to varying degrees, imposing forms of regulation and achieving revised levels of security. Security is most prominent in nomadic areas where traditional regulatory arrangements and structures have been less adversely affected by colonialism and subsequent Somali governments. Radical Islamic groups are also providing forms of constraint (Menkhaus 2003, 2004, Møller 2009, Vertigans 2010a).
2 I am arguing that habits are a component of habitus; the two are not synonymous.
3 Elias' application also has components that could be refined. First, Van Krieken (1998) notes the inconsistency in which the durability of habitus in changing social conditions is discussed. In particular, he asks would a different habitus rapidly follow on from social transformations or would there be a possible 'lag' whereby the social changes moved ahead of the psychological structure? Second, Crossley's (2003) observation that Bourdieu tends to neglect wider preconditions for protest and movement formation such as political opportunities, resources and mobilisation networks can also be applied to Elias. Third, in comparison to Bourdieu, Elias tends to be vague regarding the mechanics of habitus; indeed arguably he generally under-utilised the concept. For instance, the processes through which agents were provided with practical consciousness that is integral for social reproduction are underdeveloped. By comparison Bourdieu details how individuals experience habitus phenomenologically as 'second nature' (point developed in discussion with Chris Thorpe). Nevertheless Elias' less mechanical and more fluid approach allows for different layers within national and transnational consciousness that both integrate and detach terrorists from broader social relations which Bourdieu's greater emphasis upon the socio-economic location hinders.
4 With this observation Bourdieu seems to be at least implicitly undermining Crossley's (2003) critical remark that he neglects the possibility of habitus falling out of alignment.
5 Substantial funding from within the kingdom has been, and continues to be, received by radical Islamic groups within Afghanistan.
6 Palgrave is cited in Allen (2006: 235).
7 Degregori (1997) traces the rejection of the West and the appropriation of Western instruments of domination to the sixteenth century.
8 Almana (1982: 241) declares that in establishing the modern judicial framework, King Ibn Saud referred to the saying of the Prophet Muhammed that 'harsh punishments are often necessary for the protection of the innocent.' Forceful remedies were to be the solution to lawlessness.

9 Hewitt (2003) details the range of groups that have undertaken terror attacks in America. These include white and black racists, Islamic militants, communists, neo-Nazis, militant Jews, anti-abortionists and Puerto Rican secessionists.

10 There are also grounds for supposition that the gun has quickly attained tremendous symbolism within black 'ghetto' culture but for more contemporary factors such as popular culture, diminished opportunities and shifting social and self-restraints (Wacquant 2004).

11 Further details can be found in Mennell (2007), Nisbett and Cohen (1996) and Wyatt-Brown (1982).

12 The roots for white supremacy can be located within the culture of the early European settlers and given legal emphasis through legislation such as the Naturalization Act, 1790. The Act included the requirement for being white within the criteria for citizenship and contributed towards a racial character within reformulated nationalism (Johnson and Frombgen 2009).

13 Mennell (2007) describes the extent of the support. Such was the backlash against the possible abolition that politicians formed policy to accord with the vocal, vociferous opposition.

14 There are a number of factors which can help to explain the limited focus on Saudi targets including the longevity and charisma of the Saud ruling family, relative wealth, cooptation and rehabilitation of rivals and militants, incorporation of religious leaders, traditional familial relations and tribal crosscutting loyalties which weaken other alliances. Hegghammer (2009) details how the militants' initial emphasis was on the 'Crusaders.' The government through its security services only became targeted when they were seen to be intervening on behalf of the West. For groups associated with al-Qa'ida this may be part of a two-stage approach; namely to mobilise the population against the crusaders before overthrowing the regime.

15 Collins is cited in Kiberd (1992: 231).

16 For instance, none of their respondents proudly acknowledged their son or daughter to be a martyr. This is in marked contrast to the territories where Palestinian expressions of pride and even 'celebrations' have been well-documented.

17 These sentiments can be found within publications across the Far Right. Eric Rudolph (2005), an anti-abortion bomber, provides an illustrative reflection upon the immorality of abortion which he connects to other forms of immorality. 'Thousands of years of moral progress were sacrificed upon the altar of selfishness and materialism. A new barbarism, a culture of death has now taken root in America.' The act of abortion is 'the vomitorium of modernity helping the hedonistic partiers disgorge the unwanted consequences of their sexual license.'

18 A similar correlation can be made between Reagan's approach to abortion and associated violence. Blanchard and Prewitt (1993) point to the more aggressive stance against family planning and abortion by the Reagan administration compared to the previous Carter government. Anti-abortion violence dramatically increased. For the authors this was evidence that Reagan tacitly approved the tactics. However, Hewitt (2003) challenges the data and argues that the violence remained after Reagan's departure and even increased. Moreover, the murders committed by anti-abortionists were during Clinton's Presidency, who was much more pro-choice. Despite appearing contradictory, it is conceivable that both explanations offer important insights. Reagan did contribute towards a more politicised form of anti-abortionism and supporters could easily have mis/understood his actions and rhetorics to be complicitly supportive. By comparison, under Clinton, conservative morality was felt to be threatened and some of the abortion restrictions imposed under Reagan and George Bush were lifted, which anti-abortionists viewed as threatening to their beliefs.

19 The perceived threat from the nearest theological rival partly helps to explain the brutality of attacks against Shi'ites by militants. For Devji (2005) the growing

similarity between radical Sunnis and Shi'ites and competition over ideas and behaviour is contributing to more indiscriminate attacks by the former on the latter.

20 General Zia ul Haq governed from 1977 until his death in 1988.

21 Parallels can be drawn with the surge of lynching that occurred in the southern states following the civil war and fears of greater black political and economic participation (Lane 1997, Mennell 2007). For Mennell (2007: 147) the decline of lynching and vigilantism is indicative of 'the taming of warriors' that signified the extension and greater efficiency of state monopoly of violence and greater trust of the government. Arguably the former is proving more effective in restraining the Far Right than feelings of trust which are seriously lacking.

22 Nevertheless, despite the younger spread of members, it is important to acknowledge that membership of terror groups is not necessarily 'ageist.' A cursory glance at the leadership of leading terror groups such as al-Qa'ida, Aum Supreme Truth and IRA indicate that experience is also highly regarded at senior levels. And while Elias develops upon the youth of the West German Red Army Faction he fails to acknowledge that both Horst Mahler and Ulrike Meinhof were well into their 30s when they became involved.

23 Akbar mentions that the *jihad* was against Richard II but his rule was two hundred years later.

24 The perpetrators of terrorism within Guatamala and Chile have been somewhat different. Levenson (2003) points out with regards to the former that 93 per cent of the acts of violence and terror that resulted in the deaths of 200,000 between 1962 and 1996 were attributed to the state. At the time, the political system was nominally based upon the Western democratic model. Similarly Chile under Pinochet reacted during periods of fear over a potential coup within spiralling levels of hatred and insecurity and persecuted and assassinated opposition groups and personnel (Zárate 2003).

25 Egypt has regularly encountered terrorism. The most prominent surge in radicalisation arguably occurred when President Sadat lessened social restraints upon political activism. After failing to deliver promises that contributed to opposition being further radicalised, he was assassinated by militants who had formed and acted within the looser frameworks of restraint. Both China and Russia have largely encountered secessionist groups that share considerable similarities with other struggles for independence.

26 An observation that appeared to have bypassed the American administration whose perception that democracy would be the panacea to problems within the Middle East generally and Iraq in particular has been proved to be fatally naïve.

27 For anyone wondering about the extent to which the situation in Northern Ireland contradicts this statement, the short answer is that it does not. Northern Ireland is not part of Britain (it is part of the UK) and the island's colonial status meant that it was not part of the longer term processes of attunement. Moreover, following partition subsequent levels of established security and mutual interdependence have remained low which has prevented closer alignment between parliamentary and personality structures.

## 4 Becoming a 'terrorist': processes into groups

1 Bourdieu did not refer to radical habitus, not least as he considered the socioeconomic location of the group to be integral to the type of habitus. Radical political discursive practice would therefore stem from the group's social position.

2 Parallels can be drawn within religious movements where Wallis (1984) identified an inner core of committed devotees and a larger group who were less involved.

The extent of their engagement was heavily influenced by the depth of individual conviction in the religious message.

3 An additional reason drawn from social movement studies by Gupta (2008) relates to the 'free riders.' These individuals share group goals but for largely 'selfish reasons' are unwilling to actively participate.

4 Crossley applies Bourdieu's concept of field and which is defined by Bourdieu (1993: 72) as 'a structured space of positions (or posts) whose properties depend on their position within these spaces and which can be analysed independently of the characteristics (which are partly determined by them).'

5 Further details can be found in Lumley (1990), Pisano (1979),Varon (2004) and Vertigans (2008, 2009).

6 Fioroni is in discussion with Neuburger and Valentini (1996: 147).

7 All these emotions have been expressed by members of a number of terror groups such as the IRA (Adams 1996, Fairweather *et al.* 1984, MacDonald 1991, Taylor 1998 and Toolis 1995). By comparison loyalist and South American pro government groups are more associated with protecting the status quo against change.

8 In this regard the emphasis within Islam upon the duty of all Muslims to help those less fortunate extends beyond social services and charity when interwoven within processes of radicalisation. Help can then be interpreted to be part of political violence that is designed to free those who are living under foreign invaders, 'godless' regimes and so on.

9 For example, Timothy McVeigh, the Oklahoma bomber declared 'I did not do it for personal gain … I did it for the larger good' (quoted in Michel and Herbeck 2001: 382).

10 As one Palestinian terrorist informs Post, Sprinzak and Denny (2003: 178) '[r]ecruits were treated with great respect. A youngster who belonged to HAMAS or Fatah was regarded more highly than one who didn't belong to a group, and got better treatment than unaffiliated kids.' Studies that identify the other emotions are too numerous to mention here and include many of the sources listed in these footnotes. Further examples are also provided in the trigger section.

11 Many terrorists have described feelings of excitement which engagement brought. Beg and Bokhari (2009) and Elias (1996) discuss individuals who report seeking excitement through the engagement with terror activities. Hoffman (2006) mentions that Mickey Collins (IRA), Silke Maier-Witt (RAF) and Susanna Ronconi (Red Brigades) have all described the sense of excitement. On the reverse of the same coin, Crawford (2003: 193) reports his discussion with 'Combatant A' who stated 'the other reason I joined up was out of sheer boredom, there was nothing else to do. A lot of my friends joined for that reason as well, simply because it gave them something to do.'

12 Morgan (2001) provides one of the best known accounts of female terrorists who are considered to be attracted to terrorism by love for particular men. As I mentioned in earlier chapters the emphasis on these, usually unfounded, types of feelings diminishes the intentions and contributions of females.

13 Studies such as Bloom (2003) and Victor (2004) of the Palestinian territories and Tamils in Sri Lanka will often report upon the sexual humiliations or dishonour of women which contribute to their engagement.

14 Revenge tends to be prominent in numerous studies of Chechen 'Black Widows.' Sjoberg and Gentry (2007) argue that the application of the term 'Black Widows' by the Russian government conveys a racialised and monstrous image of the women. This is not to declare that revenge is not a mobilising factor. As Kimhi and Even (2004), Silke (2003) and Speckhard and Akhmedova (2006) discovered, it is for both males and females.

15 Rape is provided as a reason when committed by both opposing security personnel and the terror groups. Reports that tend to claim that women were raped,

blackmailed, kidnapped or drugged tend to originate with the rival government or media sources. There have been some reports of such abuses by terror groups that seem convincing, particularly by LTTE and PKK, but generally most of the commentary lacks substantiation and does not correlate with female narratives (Sjoberg and Gentry 2007, Speckhard and Akhmedova 2006, von Knop 2007).

16 Speckhard (2008) does argue that women face some increased psychological vulnerabilities such as greater incidence of traumatic stress, depression, blocked roles and may be more reactive to the loss of familial and intimate relationships.

17 Sageman (2007) suggests that contrary to the popular perception of the mobilising effect of humiliation, individuals who experience the related shame are more inclined to passivity. However, if the humiliation is experienced vicariously, individuals can be motivated through anger to act on behalf of family, friends and others who share discursive consciousness.

18 Della Porta's (1995) study of the Italian Red Brigades discovered that the recruiter was not a stranger to the recruit in around 88 per cent of instances.

19 Concerns over the relationship between religious schools and extremism are not restricted to the contemporary era. For instance, the emergence of the Deobandi madrassas in the nineteenth century with their uncompromising and rigorous Islamic applications, frequent denunciation of Shi'ism, Hinduism and Christianity and enhanced emphasis upon *jihad* as a central pillar of faith caused tremendous consternation amongst the other religious denominations, more moderate Sunnis and the British colonialists (Allen 2006).

20 The principles behind many of the schools can be traced to the Deobandi institutions that formed from 1866 onwards. Early schools sought to attract students including the poor and uneducated and appealed to parents partly because they offered free learning, food and lodgings. With children living in the madrassas throughout their childhood, the religious teachers became highly influential in the development of psyches. To some extent this remains true for today.

21 It should also be pointed out that although the burqa and other forms of 'Islamic' clothing such as the veil are considered restrictive and symbolic of patriarchy within the West many females consciously chose to wear such items. Indeed for some converts the clothes seem to be part of the attraction to the new religion (Ahmed 1992, Zubaida 2000).

22 Nevertheless it must be stressed that considerable conflict remains within Islam over the accuracy of the interpretations which is often overlooked within the West.

23 This is reflected in the speed and relative ease through which terrorists such as Andreas Baader, Ulrike Meinhof, Abu Nidal, Carlos the Jackal and Osama bin Laden became internationally prominent.

24 Further details can be found in Diani (1995), Flam (2005), Lofland and Stark (1965), McAdam (1986), Snow *et al.* (1980) and Stark and Bainbridge (1980).

25 Russo was interviewed by Neuburger and Valentini (1996: 120).

26 Studies of recruitment into cults have also identified the prominence of geographically mobile individuals, often students who had recently left home and had yet to establish new rewarding social relationships (Stark and Bainbridge 1980).

27 Within studies of social movements, militant members have also referred to the sense of family they gain from the movement and the substitution for other forms of social life (Klandermans 2007).

28 Within the Palestinian territories widespread expressions of familial pride and celebrations that often involve the distribution of drinks and sweets have been noticeable following terror activities especially martyrdom.

29 Post *et al.* (2003) also argue that the material assistance provided to the families of perpetrators of armed attacks strengthened popular support.

30 Quote is from a former IRA member who was interviewed by Horgan (2009: 82).

31 Further details about these processes within Northern Ireland can be found in Bruce (1992), Crawford (2003), Fairweather *et al.* (1984), Taylor (1998, 2000) and Taylor and Quayle (1994).

32 Merkl (1986) discusses the neo-Nazis.

33 Further details can be found in Allen (2006), Alonso and Rey (2007), Kepel (2004a, 2004b), Niblock (2006), Steinberg (2006) and Vertigans (2009).

34 Niblock (2006) argues that the terror problems of the late 1990s and particularly post-September 2001 have their roots in the policy decisions such as these from 20 years previously.

35 Morocco is an illustrative example of a country permitting greater Wahhab inspired religiosity and which has also experienced a rise in religious extremism. Terror groups have formed out of the radical movement, most notably committing attacks in Casablanca in 2003 and Madrid in 2004. With hindsight there were clear warnings about the radical trajectory. For instance, prior to the bombings there had been a gradual increase in anti-feelings against tourists, Jews and moderate or non-practising Muslims which was to find expression in personal attacks. By 2002, 166 had been killed in this type of assault. Moreover, alongside internal actions, growing numbers of Moroccans were travelling to conflict zones in Afghanistan, Bosnia, Chechnya and Indonesia.

36 In essence, capital for Bourdieu is resources through which groups gain and maintain power and status. He argued that habitus is composed of capital and which impacts upon individual dispositions. In his framework there are four principal, interrelated forms of capital; economic, social, cultural and symbolic.

37 Within Bourdieu's (1996) typology the disposition to enter particular fields is largely structurally conditioned and rarely reflected upon at a discursive level. I would argue that discursive reflection is more prominent within processes into terrorism.

38 The concept of social capital is most associated with the work of Bourdieu (1984, 1986), Coleman (1994), Field (2008) and Putnam (2000). Each takes a different stance on what the concept actually means. All agree with the emphasis upon social relationships and which can be considered a resource to individuals or groups.

39 For instance, von Knop (2007) examines the correlation between surges of female recruits to the LTTE and the preceding loss of male members.

40 Elias (1996: 233), when discussing RAF, argues that it was more difficult for professionals from middle class backgrounds to transgress social and personal self-constraint taboos against the use of violence than in 'working class families in which physical threats against the weak are the order of the day.' Weaker restraints are likely to mean less reluctance to use violence, although I would argue that it is by no means inevitable that aggressors within family settings will make the transition to political violence. Similarly, those members of the middle classes who did become politically aggressive would not necessarily be inclined to become violent within cultural and social settings.

41 Although I am not arguing that the transition is not difficult for individuals, as Maikovich (2005) argued the extent of dissonance people experience diminishes according to the width of the social support networks. I would add that the depth of these ties is just as important if not more so in providing more robust ontological security.

## 5  Group dynamics: trust, secrets, ties

1 Furthermore, Long (1990) points out that anyone wanting to achieve terrorist goals can rarely expect that these would be possible if they were operating in isolation.

2 Ronconi is discussed in Neuburger and Valentini (1996).

3 'Ken,' a Northern Irish loyalist, was interviewed by Crawford (2003: 70).
4 Further details can be found in Bruce (1992), Coogan (1995) and McDonald and Cusack (2005).
5 The Weather Underground were also known as The Weather. Initially they were called the Weathermen until it was realised that the name was symptomatic of the processes of social exclusion they aimed to eradicate.
6 Faranda is cited in Jamieson (1989: 267–68).
7 Castells (1997) has made similar points regarding the imposition of collective identity by outsiders and which leads to the strengthening of collective consciousness around these demarcations and the development of oppositional dynamics. This is not to declare that this is a simple self-fulfilling prophecy. Einwohner (2002) details how the animal rights movement reacted to identity attacks by 'identity disconfirmation' and 'identity recasting.' Through internal reaction to the criticism the movement's identity was renegotiated.
8 The authors acknowledge that this example can be applied in larger-scale, more tense and virulent examples. Further discussion and a more extensive application can be found in Sutton and Vertigans (2005).
9 In Elias and Scotson's original study, gossip is used by the established group to blame the outsiders while praising their own community. Although the role of gossip has not been well documented within terror groups there are indications that it can fulfil similar functions to discourse in blaming the other, solidifying group ties and providing informal mechanisms of social control within close knit groups. However, because of the lack of, or limited, interaction between established governments and outsider terrorists gossip does not feature in their exchanges. Instead within these relations, as Sutton and Vertigans (2005) explain, ideologies and ideological beliefs tend to fulfil a similar function, in identifying both superior and inferior characteristics according to minorities of the best and worst.
10 Levels of detachment tend to be less for members who are part of nationalist groups that are broadly supported by communities and who share feelings of injustice, anger at armed government intrusions, air raids and suffocating repression. Ideological groups such as RAF and groups associated with al-Qa'ida tend to be more cognitively and emotionally separate from the people they claim to support.
11 Giddens (1990) points out that trust has been too associated with instrumental calculation and explanations need to take 'leaps of faith' that cannot be incorporated within rational choice contributions. Incorporating feelings within and towards the group and members helps to acknowledge the intersection between the cognitive and affective.
12 Although the concentric circles that Simmel (1906) described within secret societies are less noticeable within terror groups, especially the 'self-starters,' there are definitely elements where some new recruits cross from outer to inner circles following a period of testing, an apprenticeship in which the individual proves the capabilities and concomitant trustworthiness.
13 Lewis (2007) details an example from the PKK where a female member was executed in front of others after declining a suicide mission. Staging the killing in front of other members was clearly designed both to punish the individual and act as a warning to anyone else who may consider refusing to carry out an attack.
14 Jacoby (2008) mentions how the US army has also sought to overcome hierarchical divisions through the introduction of smaller, decentralised units consisting of companies of 'buddies' and which has intensified group identity.
15 Nazi groups in Germany also continue to meet in types of location first associated with the emergence of the Reich, namely beer halls.
16 The concept of violence valve stems from discussions with Cas Wouters and my original intention to apply his research on informalisation (Wouters 1977, 1986, 2004, 2007).

17 Bourdieu (1993: 72) defines a field 'as structured spaces of positions (or posts) whose properties depend on their position within these spaces and which can be analysed independently of the characteristics of their occupants (who are partly determined by them).'

18 Ronconi was interviewed by MacDonald (1991).

19 Examples provided in Jessee (2006).

20 I am not suggesting that emotions are inherently irrational or that rationality and affective experiences are incompatible. On the contrary, expressive and instrumental forms of action combine both the emotional and rational (Eyerman 2005).

21 This also applies to social and new religious movements.

22 One of the most pertinent reasons for the failure was that the 'red' discourse was not legitimised by the perceptions and experiences of the working classes and ethnic minorities (Vertigans 2008).

23 For instance, there were numerous romantic attachments within the 'red' groups.

24 Simmel (1906) defined secret societies as an interactional unit characterized in its totality by the fact that reciprocal relations among its members are governed by the protective function of secrecy.

25 When comparing the quality of leadership in Northern Ireland, republicans tend to be viewed more favourably. Bruce (1992) argues that the IRA has been able to recruit across socio-economic groups while the loyalists were competing with state institutions with similar aims and greater remuneration and security. Crawford (2003) added that the loyalist suspicion of people outwith their working class communities also resulted in a reluctance to recruit members from the middle classes. Moreover, during the 1970s when membership became a serious commitment, the initial batch of full-time loyalist leaders tended to be appointed from those who were available. Thus unemployed members were able to commit full-time to leadership. Participants who had civilian employment and often held transferable skills did not have the scope to become involved in the groups on a more extensive basis. The problems with appointments such as these are then often compounded because it can be difficult to remove leaders once in post for some of the reasons discussed in the leadership, mistrust and detachment sections.

## 6 Emotions and rationale behind terror attacks

1 By comparison, as Dingley and Mollica (2007) document, loyalist attempts at a prisoner hunger strike failed to attract more than one volunteer and there was no outside support. For Dingley and Mollica this was because the greater emphasis upon personal salvation within Northern Ireland Protestantism and restricted perceptions of communal sacrifice and emotions meant that hunger strikes could not attain support.

2 Nechaev is cited in Garrison (2004: 264).

3 Taber is cited in Stout (2009: 881) who also points out that Salafi *jihadist* strategies explicitly reference Taber's contributions.

4 Oft quoted examples include Irgun and Hezbollah attacks which were instrumental in the British leaving Palestine and the creation of the state of Israel and withdrawal of American, French and Israeli military forces from Lebanon respectively.

5 Not all groups claim responsibility for their actions, pre-September 2001 al-Qa'ida being a prime example.

6 This is the impression that the IRA liked to portray. Nevertheless as Neumann (2005) explains, during the 1980s 25–40 per cent of IRA victims were civilians and in the early 1990s and the period of heightened sectarian reciprocal violence this rose to nearly 60 per cent.

7 Silke (2003) reports that between 50 and 90 per cent of planned attacks were abandoned or postponed for different reasons.

8 Following such devastating outcomes Silke (2003) suggests that the IRA would hold enquiries to discover what went wrong in order to ensure it did not occur again.

9 The Provisional IRA had a rate of 1.3 per fatal attack.

10 The bombings are widely believed to have contributed to the defeat of the government which had committed Spanish troops to the post-Iraq invasion and the election of a new government who campaigned for the armed forces withdrawal.

11 Jeddi is cited in Hafez (2003: 81).

12 There is some debate as to whether the expression was first introduced by the Russian anarchist Peter Kropotkin or the Italian anarchists Malatesta, Cafiero and Covelli.

13 The Lehi are cited in Townshend (2002: 89).

14 Zawqawi is cited in Ayers (2008: 867).

15 For further details see Ayers (2008), Bloom (2004), Gambetta (2005), Gupta and Mundra (2005), Hafez (2007), Khosrokhavar (2005), Kimhi and Even (2004), Lewis (2007), Pape (2005), Pedahzur (2006), Silke (2006) and Sutton and Vertigans (2005, chapter three).

16 A sense of fatalism has been particularly noticeable within the Palestinian territories.

17 Schweitzer (2006) details that female bombers have comprised around 40 per cent of attackers in Turkey and 20 to 25 per cent of those in Sri Lanka. Von Knop (2007) suggests that the figures are two thirds and one third respectively and 43 per cent in Chechnya. Between 1985 and 2006 the overall percentage of females committing suicide attacks was nearly 15 percent. This level of participation is not replicated within leadership positions where women are seriously underrepresented.

18 Detailed explorations of the reasons can be found in Bloom (2005), Cunningham (2003), Gunawardena (2006), Schweitzer (2006), Sjoberg and Gentry (2007), Speckhard (2008) and Victor (2004).

19 Quote is included in Cunningham (2003: 183).

20 Silke (2008) reviews analysis of the goals of revenge which include righting self-perceived wrongs, restoring individual self-worth and deterring future injustice. Thus attacks can act to prevent subsequent injustice and to strengthen collective identification and group charisma.

21 Details are discussed in Blee (2005), Speckhard (2008), Vertigans (2008) and von Knop (2007).

22 Jacques and Taylor's (2009) review of female terrorism and Whaley-Eager's (2008) study of the Algerian independence group FLN also discovered a progression of roles which women can hold.

23 Von Knop (2007) argues that the number of female participants increased markedly after 1990 following the significant loss of male members.

24 Crenshaw (1992: 35) explains that individuals are able to achieve cognitive consistency by absorbing 'only information that supports their beliefs, and' neglecting, 'to reconsider decisions once they have been reached.' Cognition is also protected by the culture of conformity that tends to exist within groups which can severely restrict critical analysis and reflection upon core beliefs and actions.

25 Weber's (1978) ethical ideal types considered 'conviction' to be based around absolutes or ultimate values which required unconditional and uncompromised commitment. The ethic of responsibility was about the pursuit of clear objectives based upon instrumental rational planning and the calculation of costs and benefits.

26 Hughes is cited in Taylor (1998: 74).

27 Ervine is cited in Taylor (2000: 109).

28 Loyalist 'Billy' in conversation with Crawford (2003: 81).

29 Silke (2003) points out that the attack led the security services to appreciate that the chances of peace were hindered by the presence of Adair on the streets. Consequently they focused on collating the evidence which led to his imprisonment shortly afterwards.

30 Further details can be found in Barkun (1997), Berlot and Lyons (2000), Dees (1996), Dobratz and Shanks-Meile (2000), Karl (1995), Levitas (2002) and Michel and Herbeck (2001).

31 Similar processes can be noticed within conventional armies as Grossman's (1996: 252) 'boot-camp deification of killing' highlights. Another comparison can be drawn with the dehumanising mechanisms employed by the Nazis against Jews during the Holocaust. The degradation of the victims enabled the executioners and guards to be less overwhelmed by distress (Levi 1987).

32 Kinnear is cited in Taylor (2000: 91).

33 White is cited in Crawford (2003: 91).

34 The member is cited in Neuburger and Valentini (1996: 121).

35 Ayman al-Zawahiri, the then deputy of al-Qa'ida is believed to have written to Zawqawi explaining the detrimental impact of the killings.

## 7  End Game: stopping and leaving terrorism

1 Fillieule (discussed in della Porta 2009) has identified important exceptions including families and employment.

2 Studies of disengagement within social movements include Klandersman (2003) and religious movements (Robertson 1978).

3 Gupta (2008) reports that nearly 90 per cent of groups disappear within a few years of formation.

4 Peci is cited in Horgan (2009: 31–32).

5 Demant and de Graaf (2010: 415) quote a Moluccan respondent in the Netherlands who argues that disengagement followed the group realising that 'if we gun everyone down … that doesn't work. So we stopped. We changed strategy.'

6 Demant and de Graaf (2010: 415) cite another respondent who claimed 'we can't be butchered like that anymore.'

7 Reported in International Crisis Group (ICG) (2007).

8 Discussed in Horgan and Braddock (2010).

9 In one example discussed by Boucek (2009), three family members must guarantee the return of detainees if they are to be released to attend family events such as weddings and funerals. No prisoner had absconded under this arrangement.

10 Quotes are from a meeting between 'Doug' and Horgan (2009: 106–7).

11 Cronin (2009) discusses examples from Northern Irish republicans, Palestinian PFLP-GC, Spanish ETA and Sikh separatists in India whose actions have all undermined community support which arguably they never fully recovered.

12 Group and self-criticism within the United Red Army degenerated into purges, torture and twelve deaths.

13 The end of sponsorship by the United States and Soviet Union during the Cold War and exercises of war by proxy had a huge impact on the activities of groups in South America and Africa in particular.

14 Cited in Oliver and Steinberg (2005: 92–93).

15 Van Hoesel is cited in de Graaf and Malkki (2010: 624).

16 Biesheuvel is cited in de Graaf and Malkki (2010: 632).

17 De Graaf and Malkki (2010) point out that the police did seek to increase arrest and conviction rates but ultimately failed because of the lack of evidence within the existing legal framework.

18 The original Dutch word was 'gedogen' which Cas Wouters informs me does not neatly translate into English. Repressive tolerance was partly adopted as the translation due to Marcuse's influence. Wouters suggests that 'controlled allowing' would be more accurate and helps to explain the emphasis on mutual respect.

19 Postscript: The 2011 upsurge against Mubarek indicates that his regime failed to accommodate the population sufficiently. The over reliance or 'security arrangements' and limited social incorporation meant that the regime was vulnerable once security weakened.

**8 Conclusion**

1 This is distinct from the 'lone wolves' who have emerged out of the Far Right such as David Copeland 'the nail bomber' who targeted a pub in London's gay district, killing three people in 1999. There are some similarities, with Copeland emerging out of the broader racist and homophobic movement. Nevertheless as I explained in the Introduction, individuals acting in isolation are not within the parameters of this study.
2 I am not arguing that no terror groups have emerged. On the contrary there have been numerous 'low-level' organisations such as the Animal Liberation Front (ALF). However based upon the nature of their tactics, targets and demands, these groups have not been included within the framework of this book.
3 Elias (1996: 280) suggests that with the series of shocks to British perceptions of superiority 'the protective covering of civilization seems to be coming loose.' Although the cloak remains in place there is little doubt that British national identity is being weakened as emphasised by the political debate around what it means to be British. Moreover Elias' tendency to apply British and English national identities interchangeably hides the impact of rising levels of Scottish and Welsh nationalism and the dilemma of 'British' Unionists in Northern Ireland which is part of the United Kingdom and not Great Britain.
4 Relevance of Provo movement pointed over to me by Cas Wouters.
5 As one former member of the IRA explained when asked why he became involved, 'I think it was just honestly, time and place to a large extent' (Horgan 2009: 79).
6 These processes are adapted and applied from Elias (1996 and 2000).

# Bibliography

Abdallah, A. (2006) 'Egypt'. In Faath, S. (ed.) *Anti-Americanism in the Islamic World,* London: C. Hurst & Co.

Abu-Amr, Z. (1994) *Islamic Fundamentalism in the West Bank and Gaza,* Bloomington: Indiana University Press.

Abuza, Z. (2003) *Militant Islam in Southeast Asia: Crucible of Terror,* Boulder, CO: Lynne Riener Publishers.

Acharya, A. (2006) 'The Bali Bombings: Impact on Indonesia and Southeast Asia', *Center for Eurasian Policy Occasional Research Paper, Series II (Islamism in Southeast Asia)* No. 2.

Adams, G. (1996) *Before the Dawn: An Autobiography,* London: Heinemann.

Admon, Y. (2007) 'Saudis criticize their School Curricula – Again', *Middle East Media Research Institute,* (Inquiry and Analysis No. 325). Available at http://memri.org/bin/articles.cgi?Page=archives& Area = ia& ID = IA32507.

Adorno, T.W. Frenkel-Brunswik, D., Levinson, D. and Sandford, R. (1950) *The Authoritarian Personality,* New York: Harper and Brothers.

Ahmed, A. (2004) *Resistance and Control in Pakistan,* New York: Routledge.

Ahmed, L. (1992) *Women and Gender in Islam: Historical Roots of a Modern Debate,* New Haven and London: Yale University Press.

Akbar, M. (2004) *The Shade of Swords: Jihad and the conflict between Islam and Christianity,* London: Routledge.

Al-Berry, K. (2005) 'Inside the Yearnings of a Potential Suicide Bomber', *The Observer,* 24 July.

Alexander, Y. (2002) 'September 11: US Reactions and responses', Paper presented at the *ESRC Conference of the St Andrews/Southampton Research Project on the Domestic Management of Terrorist Attacks,* 19–20 September.

Allen, C. (2006) *God's Terrorists: The Wahhabi cult and the hidden roots of modern Jihad,* London: Little Brown.

Almana, M. (1982) *Arabia Unified: A portrait of Ibn Saud,* London: Hutchinson Benham.

Alonso, R. and Rey, M. (2007) 'The Evolution of Jihadist Terrorism in Morocco', *Terrorism and Political Violence,* 19(4): 571–92.

Apter, D. (1997) 'Political Violence in Analytical Perspective'. In Apter, D. (ed.) *The Legitimization of Violence,* London: United Nations Research Institute for Social Development.

Art, R. and Richardson, L. (2006) *Democracy and Terrorism: Lessons from the Past,* Washington, DC: United States Institute of Peace Press.

Arthur, P. (1997) '"Reading" Violence: Ireland'. In Apter, D. (ed.) *The Legitimization of Violence*, London: United Nations Research Institute for Social Development.

Asal, V., Fair, C. and Shellman, S. (2008) 'Consenting to a Child's Decision to Join *Jihad*: Insights from a survey of militant families in Pakistan', *Studies in Conflict and Terrorism*, 31(11): 1001–22.

Atran, S. (2004) 'Mishandling Suicide Terrorism', *The Washington Quarterly*, Summer.

Ayers, B. (2003) *Fugitive Days: A Memoir*, Harmondsworth, UK: Penguin.

Ayers, N. (2008) 'Ghost Martyrs in Iraq: An assessment of the applicability of rationalist models to explain suicide attacks in Iraq', *Studies in Conflict and Terrorism*, 31: 856–82.

Aydinli, E. (2008) 'Before Jihadists There Were Anarchists: A failed case of transnational violence', *Studies in Conflict and Terrorism*, 31(6): 903–23.

Bach Jensen, R. (2004) 'Daggers, Rifles and Dynamite: Anarchist Terrorism in Nineteenth Century Europe', *Terrorism and Political Violence*, 16(1): 116–53.

Bakker, E. (2006) *Jihadi terrorists in Europe, their characteristics and the circumstances in which they joined the jihad: An explanatory study*, Clingendael: Netherlands Institute of International Relations

Bandura, A. (1976) 'On Social Learning and Aggression'. In Hollander, E. and Hunt, R. (eds) *Current Perspectives in Social Psychology*, Oxford: Oxford University Press.

——(1998) 'Mechanisms of Moral Disengagement'. In Reich, W. (ed.) *Origins of Terrorism: Psychologies, Ideologues, Theologies, States of Mind*, Washington, DC: Woodrow Wilson Center Press.

——(1999) 'Moral Disengagement in the Perpetration of Inhumanities', *Personality and Social Psychology Review*, 3: 193–209.

——(2004) 'The Role of Selective Moral Disengagement in Terrorism and Counterterrorism'. In Moghaddam, F. and Marsella, A. (eds) *Understanding Terrorism: Psychosocial roots, consequences and interventions*. Washington, DC: American Psychological Association.

Barker, E. (1984) *The Making of a Moonie: Choice or Brainwashing?* Oxford: Basil Blackwell.

Barkun, M. (1997) *Religion and the Racist Right: The Origins of the Christian Identity Movement*, Chapel Hill: The University of North Carolina Press.

Barrett, R. and Bokhari, L. (2009) 'Deradicalization and Rehabilitation Programmes Targeting Religious Terrorists and Extremists in the Muslim World: An overview'. In Bjørgo, T. and Horgan, J. *Leaving Terrorism Behind: Individual and Collective Disengagement*, Abingdon: Routledge.

Baumann, B. (1981) *How It All Began: Personal Account of a West German Urban Guerilla*, London: Arsenal Pulp Press.

Beg, S. and Bokhari, L. (2009) 'Pakistan: In search of a disengagement strategy'. In Bjørgo, T. and Horgan, J. *Leaving Terrorism Behind: Individual and Collective Disengagement*, Abingdon: Routledge.

Benfold, R. (1993) Frame Disputes within the Nuclear Disarmament Movement, *Social Forces*, 71: 677–701.

Berlot, C. and Lyons, M. (2000) *Right-Wing Populism in America*, New York: The Guildford Press.

Bin Laden, O. (2002) 'A Message to the American People', *Jihad Unspun*, & October. Available at: www.jihadunspun.com/BinLadensnetwork/statements/amta. html.

Bishop, P. and Mallie, E. (1988) *The Provisional IRA*, London: Corgi.

Bjørgo, T. (ed.) (2005) *Root Causes of Terrorism: Myths, reality and ways forward*, Abingdon, UK: Routledge.

Bjørgo, T. (2009) 'Processes of Disengagement from Violent Groups of the Extreme Right'. In Bjørgo, T. and Horgan, J. (eds) *Leaving Terrorism Behind: Individual and collective disengagement,* Abingdon, UK: Routledge.

Bjørgo, T. and Horgan, J. (eds.) (2009) *Leaving Terrorism Behind: Individual and collective disengagement,* Abingdon, UK: Routledge.

Blanchard, D. and Prewitt, T. (1993) *Religious Violence and Abortion*, Gainesville, FL: University of Florida.

Blee, K. (2005) 'Women and Organized Racial Terrorism in the United States', *Studies in Conflict and Terrorism*, 28: 421–33.

Bloom, M. (2004) *Dying to Kill: The Global Phenomenon of Global Terror*, Columbia: Columbia University Press.

Blumer, H. (1939) 'Collective Behavior'. In Park, R. (ed.) *An Outline of the Principles of Sociology*, New York: Barnes and Noble.

Bogner, A. (1992) 'Ethnicity and the Monopolization of "Legitimate" Violence', Paper presented at the 7th EIDOS conference, Bielefeld, Germany, May.

Bonner, M. (2006) *Jihad in Islamic History*, Princeton: Princeton University Press.

Boucek, C. (2009) 'Extremist Re-education and Rehabilitation in Saudi Arabia'. In Bjorgo, T. and Horgan, J. *Leaving Terrorism Behind: Individual and Collective Disengagement,* Abingdon: Routledge.

Boudon, R. (2003) 'Beyond Rational Choice Theory', *Annual Review of Sociology*, 29: 1–21.

Bourdieu, P. (1977) *Outline of a Theory of Practice*, Cambridge: Cambridge University Press.

——(1984) *Distinction: A Social Critique of the Judgement of Taste*, Harvard: Harvard University Press.

——(1993) *Sociology in Question*, London: Sage.

——(1996) *The Rules of Art: Genesis and Structure of the Literary Field*, Cambridge: Polity Press.

——(2000) 'The Politics of Protest', (Interview), *Socialist Review* June: 18–20.

Bowers, W. (1984) *Legal Homicide*, Boston: Northeastern University Press.

Boyle, K. (2005) *Media and Violence*, London: Sage.

Brannan, D., Esler, P. and Stringberg, N. (2001) 'Talking to Terrorists': Towards an independent Analytical Framework for the Study of Violent Substate Activism, *Studies in Conflict and Terrorism* 24(1): 3–24.

Braungart, R. and Braungart, M. (1992) 'The Protest to Terrorism: The Case of SDS and the Weathermen', *International Social Movement Research*, 4(1): 45–78.

Brisard, J-C. and Martinez, D. (translator) (2005) *Zarqawi: The New face of al-Qaeda*, Cambridge, Polity Press.

Brocklehurst, H. (1999) *The Nationalisation and Militarisation of Children in Northern Ireland*, Unpublished Ph.D.: University of Wales.

Bruce, S. (1992) *The Red Hand: Protestant Paramilitaries in Northern Ireland*, Oxford: Oxford University Press.

Brunner, C. (2005) 'Female Suicide Bombers – Male suicide bombing? Looking for Gender in reporting the suicide bombings of the Israeli-Palestinian conflict', *Global Society*, 19(1): 29–48.

Bunt, G. (2003) *Islam in the Digital Age*, London: Pluto Press.

Burdman, D. (2003) 'Education, Indoctrination, and Incitement: Palestinian Children on their Way to Martyrdom', *Terrorism and Political Violence,* 15(1).

Burke, J. (2006) *On the Road to Kandahar: Travels though Conflict in the Islamic World,* London: Allen Lane.

Burleigh, M. (2008) *Blood and Rage: A Cultural History of Terrorism,* London: Harper Perennial.

Bushart, H., Craig, J. and Barnes, M. (1998) *Soldiers of God: White Supremacists and their Holy War for America,* New York: Pinnacle Books.

Castells, M. (1997) *The Power of Identity,* Oxford: Blackwell.

Clutterbuck, L. (2004) 'Progenitors of Terrorism: Russian Revolutionaries or Extreme Irish Republicans', *Terrorism and Political Violence,* 16(1).

Coleman, J. (1994) *Foundations of Social Theory,* Cambridge, MA: Belknap Press.

Collins, E. with McGovern, M. (1997) *Killing Rage,* London: Granta Books.

Collins, R. (2001) 'Social Movements and the Focus of Emotional Attention'. In Goodwin, J., Jasper, J. and Polletta, F. (eds), *Passionate Politics,* Chicago: University of Chicago Press.

Coogan, T.P. (1995) *The I.R.A.,* London: HarperCollins Publishers.

Copeland, L. (2002) 'Female Suicide Bombers: The new factor in Mideast's deadly equation', *New York Times,* 27 April.

Coulter, C. (1999) *Contemporary Northern Irish Society: An Introduction,* London: Pluto Press.

Crawford, C. (1999) *Defenders or Criminals? Loyalist Prisoners and Criminalisation,* Belfast: Blackstaff.

——(2003) *Inside the UDA: Volunteers and violence,* London: Pluto Press.

Crenshaw, M. (1981) 'The Causes of Terrorism', *Comparative Politics,* 13(4): 379–99.

——(1983) 'Introduction: Reflections on the effects of terrorism'. In Crenshaw, M. (ed.) *Terrorism, Legitimacy and Power: The consequences of political violence,* Middletown, CT: Wesleyan University Press.

——(1992) 'Decisions to Use Terrorism: Psychological Constraints on Instrumental Reasoning', *International Social Movement Research,* 4: 29–42.

——(1998) 'The Logic of Terrorism: Terrorist Behaviour as a Product of Strategic Choice.' In Reich, W. (ed.) *Origins of Terrorism: Psychologies, Ideologues, Theologies, States of Mind,* Washington, DC: Woodrow Wilson Center Press.

Croft, S. (2006) *Culture, Crisis and America's War on Terror,* Cambridge: Cambridge University Press.

Croissant, A. (2007) 'Muslim Insurgency, Political Violence, and Democracy in Thailand', *Terrorism and Political Violence,* 19(1): 1–18.

Cronin, A. K. (2009) 'How Terrorist Campaigns End'. In Bjørgo, T. and Horgan., J. *Leaving Terrorism Behind: Individual and Collective Disengagement,* Abingdon: Routledge.

Crossley, N. (2003) 'From Reproduction to Transformation: Social movement fields and the radical habitus', *Theory, Culture and Society,* 20(6): 43–68.

Crothers, L. (2002) 'The Cultural Foundations of the Modern Militia', *New Political Science,* 24 (2).

Cunningham, K. (2003) 'Cross-regional Trends in Female Terrorism', *Studies in Conflict and Terrorism,* 26: 171–95.

Davies, J. (1969) 'The J-Curve of Rising and Declining Satisfaction as a Cause of Some Great Revolutions and a Contained Rebellion'. In Graham, H. and Gurr, T., *Violence in America: Historical and Comparative Perspective.* New York: Praeger.

——(1971) *When Men Revolt and Why*, New York: Free Press.

Davis, J.M. (2003) *Martyrs: Innocence, Vengeance and Despair in the Middle East*, New York: Palgrave Macmillan.

Dawson, L. (2006) *Comprehending Cults: The Sociology of New Religious Movements*, Oxford: Oxford University Press.

——(2010) 'The Study of New Religious Movements and the Radicalization of Home-Grown Terrorists: Opening a Dialogue', *Terrorism and Political Violence*, 22 (1): 1–21.

Debray, R. (1967) *Revolution in the Revolution*, New York: MR Press.

Dees, M. (1996) *Gathering Storm: America's Militia Threat*, New York: HarperCollins.

De Graaf, B. and Malkki, L. (2010) 'Killing it Softly? Explaining the Early Demise of Left-Wing Terrorism in the Netherlands', *Terrorism and Political Violence*, 22(4): 623–40.

Degregori, C. (1997) 'The Maturation of a Cosmocrat and the Building of a Discourse Community: The case of the Shining Path'. In Apter, D. (ed.) *The Legitimization of Violence*, Basingstoke: Macmillan Press.

Della Porta, D. (1988) 'Recruitment Processes in Clandestine Political Organisations: Italian Left-Wing Terrorism'. In Klandermans, B., Kriesi, H. and Tarrow, S. (eds), *New Social Movements in Western Europe and the United States*. CT: JAI Press.

——(1992) 'Political Socialization in Left-Wing Underground Organizations: Biographies of Italian and German Militants', *International Social Movement Research*, Vol. 4.

——(1995) *Social Movements, Political Violence and the State: A Comparative Analysis of Italy and Germany*, Cambridge: Cambridge University Press.

——(2009) 'Leaving Underground Organizations: A Sociological Analysis of the Italian Case'. In Bjorgo, T. and Horgan, J. *Leaving Terrorism Behind: Individual and Collective Disengagement,* Abingdon: Routledge.

Della Porta, D. and Diani, M. (1999) *Social Movements: An Introduction*, Oxford: Blackwell Publishers Ltd.

Demant, F. and de Graaf, B. (2010) 'How to Counter Radical Narratives: Dutch Deradicalization Policy in the Case of Moluccan and Islamic Radicals', *Studies in Conflict and Terrorism*, 33(5): 408–28.

Devji, F. (2005) *Landscapes of the Jihad: Militancy, Morality, Modernity*, London, Hurst & Co.

Diani, M. (1995) *Green Networks: A Structural Analysis of the Italian Environmental Movement*, Edinburgh: Edinburgh University Press.

——(2007) 'Networks and Participation'. In Snow, D., Soule, S. and Kriesi, H. *The Blackwell Companion to Social Movements*, Malden, MA: Blackwell Publishing.

Dingley, J. and Mollica, M. (2007) 'The Human Body as a Terrorist Weapon: Hunger Strikes and Suicide Bombers', *Studies in Conflict and Terrorism*, 30: 459–92.

Dobratz, B. and Shanks-Meile, S. (2000) *The White Separatist Movement in the United States*, Baltimore: The Johns Hopkins University Press.

Dollard, J., Doob, L., Miller, N., Mowrer, O. and Sears, R. (1939) *Frustration and Aggression*, New Haven, CT: Yale University Press.

Drake, R. (1984), 'The Red and the Black: Terrorism in Contemporary Italy', *International Political Science Review* Vol. 5(3).

Durkheim, E. (1984) [1893] *The Division of Labour in Society*, London: Macmillan.

Duyvesteyn, I. (2004) 'How New Is the New Terrorism', *Studies in Conflict and Terrorism*, 27, 439–54.

Dworkin, A. (2002) 'The Women Suicide Bombers', *feminista!* 5(1) http://www.feminista. com/archives/v5n1/dworkin.html

Eickelman, D. and Piscatori, J. (1996) *Muslim Politics*, Princeton, NJ: Princeton University Press.

Einwohner, R. (2002) 'Bringing the Outsiders In: Opponents' Claims and the Construction of Animal Rights Activists' Identities', *Mobilization: An International Journal*, 7(3): 253–68.

Elias, N. (1991) *The Society of Individuals*, New York and London: Continuum.

——(1996) *The Germans*, Cambridge: Polity Press.

——(2000) [1939] *The Civilizing Process: Sociogenetic and Psychogenetic Investigations*, Oxford: Blackwell Publishers Ltd.

Elias, N. (2000) *The Court Society*, Mennell, S. (ed.), Dublin: University College Dublin Press.

Elias, N. (2010) *Humana Conditio*, Jephcott, E. (translated), Scott, A. and Scott, B. (eds) Dublin: University College Dublin Press.

Elias, N. and Scotson, J.L. (1965) *The Established and the Outsiders: A Sociological Enquiry into Community Problems*, London: Frank Cass Ltd.

Elias, N. and Scotson, J.L. (2008) *The Established and the Outsiders*, Wouters, C. (ed), Dublin: University College Dublin Press.

Enders, W. and Su, X. (2007) 'Rational Terrorists and Optimal Network Structure', *Journal of Conflict Resolution*, 51(1): 33–57.

English, R. (2003) *Armed Struggle: A History of the IRA*. London: Macmillan.

Epstein, S. (1994) 'Integration of the Cognitive and Psychodynamic Unconscious', *American Psychologist*, 49: 709–24.

Erickson, B. (1981) 'Secret Societies and Social Structure', *Social Forces*, 60(1): 188–210.

Eyerman, R. (2005) 'How Social Movements Move: Emotions and social movements'. In Flam, H. and King. D. (eds) *Emotions and Social Movements,* Abingdon: Routledge.

Fairweather, E., McDonough, R. and McFadyean, M. (1984) *Only the Rivers Run Free: Northern Ireland: The Women's War*, London: Pluto Press.

Fanon, F. (2007) 'Concerning Violence (The Wretched of the Earth)'. In Lawrence, B. and Karim, A. (eds) *On Violence*, Durham, NC: Duke University Press.

Farrell, W. (1990) *Blood and Rage: The Story of the Japanese Red Army.* Lexington Books: Lexington: Massachusetts.

Fausto-Sterling, A. (2000) *Sexing The Body: Gender Politics and the Construction of Sexuality*, New York: Basic Books.

Feith, D. (2008) *War and Decision: Inside the Pentagon at the Dawn of the War on Terror*, New York: HarperCollins Publishers.

Ferracuti, F. (1982) 'A Sociopsychiatric Interpretation of Terrorism', *Annals of the American Academy of Political and Social Science*, 463: 129–40.

Field, J. (2008) *Social Capital*, London: Routledge.

Fiorillo, E. (1979) 'Terrorism in Italy: Analysis of a problem', *Studies in Conflict and Terrorism*, 2(3–4): 261–70.

Fine, G. and Holyfield, L. (1996) 'Secrecy, Trust and Dangerous Leisure: Generating Group Cohesion in Voluntary Organisations', *Social Psychology Quarterly*, 59(1): 22–38.

Fireman, B., Gamson, W., Rytina, S. and Taylor, B. (1979) 'Encounters with unjust Authority'. In Kriesberg, L. (ed.) *Research in Social Movements, Conflicts and Change*, Volume 2, Greenwich, CT: JAI Press.

Fitzpatrick, D. (1992) 'Ireland since 1870'. In Foster, R.F. (ed) *The Oxford History of Ireland*, Oxford: Oxford University Press.

Flam, H. (1990) 'Emotional "Man": I. The Emotional Man and the Problem of Collective Action', *International Sociology,* 5: 39–56.

Flam, H. (2005) 'Emotions Map: A research map'. In Flam, H. and King. D. (eds) *Emotions and Social Movements,* Abingdon: Routledge.

Florez-Morris, M. (2007) 'Joining Guerrilla Groups in Colombia: Individual motivations and processes for entering a violent organisation', 30(7): 615–34.

Flynn, K. and Gerhardt, G. (1989) *The Silent Brotherhood: Inside America's Racist Underground*, New York: The Free Press.

Foran, J. (1997) 'The Comparative Historical Sociology of Third World Social Revolutions: Why a few succeed, why most fail'. In Foran, J. (ed.) *Theorizing Revolutions,* London: Routledge.

Foster, R.F. (1989) *Modern Ireland 1600–1972,* London: Penguin Books.

Foster, R.F. (1992) 'Ascendancy and Union'. In Foster, R.F. (ed.) *The Oxford History of Ireland*, Oxford: Oxford University Press.

Freilich, J and Pridemore, W. (2005) 'A Re-assessment of State-level Covariates of Militia Groups', *Behavioural Sciences and Law*, 23(4): 527–46.

Friedland. N. (1992) 'Becoming a Terrorist: Social and Individual Antecedents'. In Howard, L. (ed.) *Terrorism: Roots, Impact, Responses,* New York: Praeger.

Fuchs Ebaugh, H-R. (1988) *Becoming and Ex: The process of role exit*, Chicago: The University of Chicago Press.

Gallagher, A., Smith, A. and Montgomery, A. (2003) *Integrated Education in Northern Ireland: Participation, Profile and Performance*, Coleraine: UNESCO Centre, University of Ulster.

Gambetta, D. (2005) *Making Sense of Suicide Missions*, Oxford University Press.

Garfinkel, R. (2007) 'Personal Transformations: Moving from violence to peace', *United States Institute of Peace Special Report*, 186, April.

Garrison, A. (2004) 'Defining Terrorism: Philosophy of the Bomb, Propaganda by Deed and Change through Fear and Violence', *Criminal Justice Studies*, 17(3): 259–79.

Gentry, C. (2004) 'The Relationship between New Social Movement Theory and Terrorism Studies: The role of leadership, membership, ideology and gender', *Terrorism and Political Violence*, 16(2): 274–93.

Gerges, F. (2005) *The Far Enemy: Why Jihad went Global*, Cambridge: Cambridge University Press.

Gerges, F. (2006) *Journey of the Jihadist: Inside Muslim Militancy*, Orlando: Harcourt Inc.

Giddens, A. (1990) *The Consequences of Modernity*, Stanford: Stanford University Press.

Gilbert, P. (2002) 'Discourses of Female Violence and Societal Gender Stereotypes', *Violence against Women,* 8(11): 1271–1300.

Gilio, M. (1972) *The Tupamoros*, London: Secker and Warburg.

Gill, P. (2007) 'A Multi-Dimensional Approach to Suicide Bombing', *International Journal of Conflict and Violence*, 1(2): 142–59.

Glazer, M. and Glazer, P. (1999) 'On the Trail of Courageous Behavior', *Sociological Review*, 69(2): 276–95.

Glock, C. (1964) 'The Role of Deprivation in the Origin and Evolution of Religious Groups'. In Lee, R. and Marty, M. E. (eds) *Religion and Social Conflict*, New York: Oxford University Press.

Goldthorpe, J. (1991) 'The Uses of History in Sociology: Reflections on some Recent Tendencies', *The British Journal of Sociology*, 42(2): 211–30.

Goldthorpe, J. (1994) 'The uses of history in sociology: A reply', *The British Journal of Sociology*, 45(1): 55–77.

Goodwin, J., Jasper, J. and Polletta, F. (2001) 'Why Emotions Matter'. In Goodwin, J., Jasper, J. and Polletta, F. (eds) *Passionate Politics: Emotions and Social Movements*, Chicago: University of Chicago Press.

Goodwin, J., Jasper, J. and Polletta, F. (2007) 'Emotional Dimensions of Social Movements'. In Snow, D., Soule, S. and Kriesi, H., *The Blackwell Companion to Social Movements*, Malden, MA: Blackwell Publishing.

Gordon, C. and Arian. A. (2001) 'Threat and Decision Making', *Journal of Conflict Resolution*, 45(2): 196–215.

Goudsblom, J. (2001) 'The Paradox of Pacification' (translated Mennell, S.). Extract from Waar honger uit ontstond: Over evolutie en sociale processen (Amsterdam: Meulenhoff). Available from the Norbert Elias Foundation at http://www.norberte-liasfoundation.nl/network/essays.php

Graham, B. (2004) 'The Identity in the Present: The Shaping of Identity in Loyalist Ulster', *Terrorism and Political Violence*, 16(3): 483–500.

Grob-Fitzgibbon, B. (2004) 'From the Dagger to the Bomb: Karl Heinzen and the Evolution of Political Perror', *Terrorism and Political Violence*, 16 (1): 97–115.

Grossman, D. (1996) *On Killing: The Psychological Cost of Learning to Kill in War and Society*, Boston: Little, Brown and Co.

Gunaratna, R. (2003) *Inside Al Qaeda: Global Network of Terror*, Columbia: Columbia University Press.

Gunaratna, R. and bin Ali, M. (2009) 'De-radicalization Initiatives in Egypt: A Preliminary Insight', *Studies in Conflict and Terrorism*, 32: 277–91.

Gunawardena, A. (2006) 'Female Black Tigers: A Different Breed of Cat?' In Schweitzer, Y. (ed.) *Female Suicide Bombers*, Tel Aviv: Jaffee Center for Strategic Studies.

Gupta, D. (2008) *Understanding Terrorism and Political Violence: The Life Cycle of Birth, Growth, Transformation and Demise*, Abingdon: Routledge.

Gupta, D. and Mundra, K. (2005) *Suicide Bombing as a Strategic Weapon: An Empirical Investigation of Hamas and Islamic Jihad*, 17: 4.

Gurr, T. (1970) *Why Men Rebel*, Princeton: Princeton University Press.

Gurr, T. (1998) 'Terrorism in democracies: Its social and political bases'. In Reich, W. (ed.) *Origins of Terrorism: Psychologies, Ideologues, Theologies, States of Mind*, Washington DC: Woodrow Wilson Center Press.

Hafez, M. (2003) *Why Muslims Rebel: Repression and Resistance in the Islamic World*, Boulder, CO: Lynne Rienner Publishers.

Hafez, M. (2007) 'Martyrdom Mythology in Iraq: How Jihadists Frame Suicide Terrorism in Videos and Biographies', *Terrorism and Political Violence*, 19(1): 95–115.

Hall, S. (1985) 'Signification, Representation, Ideology: Althusser and the Post-structuralist Debates', *Critical Studies in Mass Communications*, 2(1): 91–114.

Halliday, F. (1998) 'Irish Nationalism in Perspective', *Democratic Dialogue – Special Reports*, available at http://www.democraticdialogue.org/working/irish-nationalism.htm

Hamm, M. (2007) *Terrorism as Crime: From Oklahoma to Al-Qaeda and Beyond*, New York: New York University Press.

Hardin, R. (2006) *Trust*, Cambridge: Polity Press.

Hayes, B. and McAllister, I. (2005) 'Public Support for Political Violence and Para-militarism in Northern Ireland and the Republic of Ireland', *Terrorism and Political Violence*, 17(4): 599–617.

Heck, P. (2004) 'Jihad Revisited', *Journal of Religious Ethics*, 32(1): 95–128.

Hegghammer, T. (2006) 'Terrorist Recruitment and Radicalization in Saudi Arabia', *Middle East Policy*, XIII(4).

Hegghammer, T. (2009) 'Jihad, Yes, But Not Revolution: Explaining the Extraversion of Islamist Violence in Saudi Arabia', *British Journal of Middle Eastern Studies*, 36 (3): 395–416.

Heinzen, K. (2004) [1849] 'Murder'. In Laqueur, W. (ed.) *Voices of Terror*, New York: Reed Press.

Heitmeyer, W. (2005) 'Right-wing Terrorism'. In Bjørgo, T. (ed.), *Root Causes of Terrorism: Myths, reality and ways forward,* Abingdon, UK: Routledge.

Hewitt, C. (2003) *Understanding Terrorism in America: From the Klan to Al Qaeda*, London: Routledge.

Hodgson, M.G.S. (1974) *The Venture of Islam: Conscience and History in a World Civilization*. Volumes 1–3, Chicago: The University of Chicago Press.

Hoffman, B. (2006) *Inside Terrorism*, Colombia: Colombia University Press.

Hogg, M. and Vaughan, G. (2005) *Social Psychology*, London: Pearson Prentice Hall.

Holsti, O. (1972) 'Crisis, Stress and Decision Making'. In *Crisis, Escalation, War,* Montreal: McGill-Queen's University Press.

Horgan, J. (2005) *The Psychology of Terrorism*, London: Routledge.

Horgan, J. (2009a) 'Individual Disengagement: A Psychological Analysis'. In Bjørgo, T. and Horgan, J. *Leaving Terrorism Behind: Individual and Collective Disengagement,* Abingdon: Routledge.

Horgan, J. (2009b) *Walking Away from Terrorism: Accounts of disengagement from radical and extremist movements*, Abingdon: Routledge.

Horgan, J. and Braddock, K. (2010) 'Rehabilitating the Terrorists? Challenges in Assessing the Effectiveness of De-radicalization Programs', *Terrorism and Political Violence*, 22(2): 267–91.

Hothschild, A. (1979) 'Emotion Work, Feelings Rules and Social Structures', *American Journal of Sociology*, 85: 551–75.

Hothschild, A. (1983) *The Managed Heart*, Berkeley, CA: University of California Press.

House of Commons, (2006) *Report of the Official Account of the Bombings in London on 7 July 2005*, London: The Stationery Office.

Iannacone, L. (2004) 'The Market for Martyrs', *Working Paper 36*, Mercatus Center, George Mason University.

ICG (International Crisis Group) (2007) '"Deradicalization" and Indonesian Prisons', *Asia Report No 142*, 19 November.

Irvine, M. (1991) *Northern Ireland: Faith and Faction*, London: Routledge.

Ismael, N. (2006) 'The Role of Kinship in Indonesia's Jemaah Islamiya', *Terrorism Monitor* IV(11).

Issacharoff, A. (2005) 'The Palestinian and Israeli Media on Female Suicide Terror-ists'. In Schweitzer, Y. (ed) *Female Suicide Bombers: Dying for Equality*? Tel Aviv: Institute for National Security Studies. Available at: http://www.isn.ethz.ch/isn/Digital-Library/Publications/Detail/?lng=en&id=91112

Jacobs, R. (1997) *The Way the Wind Blew: A History of the Weather Underground*, London: Verso.

Jacoby, T. (2008) *Understanding Conflict and Violence: Theoretical and inter-disciplinary approaches*, London: Routledge.

Jacques, K. and Taylor, P. (2008) 'Male and Female Suicide Bombers: Different sexes, different reasons?' *Studies in Conflict and Terrorism*, 31(4): 304–26.

Jamieson, A. (1989) *The Heart Attacked: Terrorism and Conflict in the Italian State*, London: Marion Boyars.

Jarman, N. (1997) *Material Conflicts: Parades and Visual Display in Northern Ireland*, Oxford: Berg.

Jasper, J. (1997) *The Art of Moral Protests*, Chicago, IL: University of Chicago Press.

Jasper, J. (1998) 'The Emotions of Protest: affective and reactive emotions in and around social movements', *Sociological Forum,* 13 (3): 397–424.

Jenkins, B. (1985) 'Future Trends in International Terrorism', RAND Corporation Available at http://www.rand.org/pubs/papers/2006/P7176.pdf

Jenkins, B. (1987) 'The Future Course of International Terrorism', *The Futurist*. Available at www.wfs.org/jenkins.htm

Jenkins, R. (2002) *Pierre Bourdieu*, London: Routledge.

Jenkins, R. (2004) *Social Identity*, London: Routledge.

Jessee, D. (2006) 'Tactical Means, Strategic Ends: Al Qaeda's use of denial and deception', *Terrorism and Political Violence*, 18: 367–88.

Johnson, V. and Frombgen, E. (2009) 'Racial Contestation and the Emergence of Populist Nationalism in the United States', *Social Identities*, 15(5): 631–58.

Johnston, H. (2008) 'Ritual, Strategy and Deep Culture in the Chechen National Movement', *Critical Studies on Terrorism*, 1(3): 321–42.

Jones, S. and Libicki, M. (2008) *How Terrorist Groups End: Lessons for countering al Qa'ida*, Santa Monica: RAND Corporation.

Juergensmeyer, M. (2003) *Terror in the Mind of God*, London: University of California Press.

Kaplan, J. (2007) 'The Fifth Wave: The new tribalism', *Terrorism and Political Violence,* 19: 545–70.

Karl. J. (1995) *The Right to Bear Arms: The Rise of America's New Militias*, New York: Harper Paperbacks.

Kassel, W. (2009) 'Terrorism and the International Anarchist Movement of the Late Nineteenth and Early Twentieth Centuries', *Studies in Conflict and Terrorism*, 32(3): 237–52.

Kee, R. (1995) *Ireland: A history*, London: Abacus.

Keitner, C. (2002) 'Victim or Vamp? Images of violent women in the Criminal Justice System', *Columbia Journal of Law and Gender*, 11(1): 38–87.

Kelly, L. (1991) 'Unspeakable Acts', *Trouble and Strife*, 21: 13–20.

Kepel, G. (2004a) *Jihad: The Trail of Political Islam*, London: I.B. Tauris.

Kepel, G. (2004b) *The War for Muslim Minds*, Cambridge, MA: Harvard University Press.

Kerr, A. (1996) *Perceptions: Cultures in Conflict*, Derry: Guildhall Press.

Khalilov, R. (2003) 'Moral Justifications of Secession: The case of Chechnya', *Central Asian Survey*, 22(4): 405–20.

Khatib, L. (2003) 'Communicating Islamic Fundamentalism as Global Citizenship', *Journal of Communication Inquiry,* 27(4): 389–409.

Khosrokhavar, F. (2005) *Suicide Bombers: Allah's New Martyrs*, London: Pluto Press.

Kiberd, D. (1992) 'Irish Literature and Irish History'. In Foster, R.F. (ed.) *The Oxford History of Ireland*, Oxford: Oxford University Press.

Kim, H. and Bearman, P. (1997) 'The Structure and Dynamics of Movement Participation', *American Sociological Review*, 62(1): 70–93.

Kimhi, S. and Even, S. (2004) 'Who are the Palestinian Suicide Bombers?' *Terrorism and Political Violence*, 16(4): 815–40.

Klandermans, B. (1994) 'Transient Identities? Membership Patterns in the Dutch Peace Movement'. In Larana, E., Johnston, H. and Gusfield, J. (eds) *New Social Movements: From Ideology to Identity*, Philadelphia, PA: Temple University Press.

Klandermans, B. (2003) *A Social Psychology of Disengagement*. Working Paper, Free University, Amsterdam.

Klandermans, B. (2007) 'The Demand and Supply of Participation: Social-Psychological correlates of participation in social movements'. In Snow, D., Soule, S. and Kriesi, H. *The Blackwell Companion to Social Movements*, Malden, MA: Blackwell Publishing.

Koopmans, R. (1993) 'The Dynamics of Protest Waves: West Germany, 1965 to 1989', *American Sociological Review*, 58(5): 637–58.

Kornhauser, A. (1959) *The Politics of Mass Society*, Glencoe, IL: Free Press.

Krueger, A. and Malecková, J. (2003) 'Education, poverty and terrorism: Is there a causal connection', *Journal of Economic Perspectives* 17(4): 119–44.

Lachkar, J. (2002) 'The Psychological Make-up of a Suicide Bomber', *Journal of Psychohistory*, 29: 349–67.

Lane, R. (1997) *Murder in America: A History*, Columbus, OH: Ohio State University Press.

Lapidus, I. (2002) *A History of Islamic Societies* (Second Edition), Cambridge: Cambridge University Press.

Laqueur, W. (1977) Terrorism, Boston: Little Brown.

Laqueur, W. (2001) *The New Terrorism: Fanaticism and the arms of mass destruction*, London: Phoenix Press.

Law, R. (2009) *Terrorism: A History*, Cambridge: Polity.

Leiken, R. (2004) *Bearers of global Jihad? Immigration and national security after '9/11'*, Nixon Center.

Lentini, P. and Bakashmar, M. (2007) 'Jihadist Bheading: A Convergence of Technology, Theology and Teleology', *Studies in Conflict and Terrorism*, 30(4): 303–25.

Levenson, D. (2003) 'The Life that Makes Us Die/The Death that Makes Us Live'. In Van Gosse (ed.) *Radical History Review: Terror and History*, Durham, NC: Duke University Press.

Levi, P. (1987) *The Drowned and the Saved*, New York: Summit Books.

Levitas, D. (2002) *The Terrorist Next Door: The Militia Movement and the Radical Right*, New York: Thomas Dunne Books.

Lewis, J. (2007) 'Precision Terror: Suicide Bombing as Control Technology', *Terrorism and Political Violence*, 19(2): 223–45.

Liston, R. (1977) *Terrorism*, New York: Thomas Nelson Inc.

Lofland, J. and Stark, R. (1965) 'Becoming a World-Saver: A theory of conversion to a deviant perspective', *American Sociological Review*, 30(6): 862–75.

Long, D. (1990) *The Anatomy of Terrorism*, New York: The Free Press.

Lumley, R. (1990) *States of Emergency: Cultures of Revolt in Italy from 1968 to 1978*, London: Verso.

Lutz, J. and Lutz, B. (2005) *Terrorism: Origins and Evolution*, New York: Palgrave MacMillan.

MacDonald, E. (1991) *Shoot the Women First*, London: First Estate.

MacGinty, R. (2010) 'Social Network Analysis and Counterinsurgency: A Counter-productive Strategy', *Critical Studies on Terrorism*, 3(2): 209–26.

Magouirk, J. (2008) 'Connecting a Thousand Points of Hatred', *Studies in Conflict & Terrorism*, 31(4): 327–49.

Maikovich, A.K. (2005) 'A New Understanding of Terrorism using Cognitive Dissonance Principles', *Journal for the Theory of Social Behaviour*, 35(4): 373–97.

Malešević, S. (2010) 'How Pacifist were the Founding Fathers: War and violence in classical sociology', *European Journal of Social Theory*, 13(2): 193–212.

Mann, M. (1994) 'In praise of macro sociology: a reply to Goldthorpe', *The British Journal of Sociology*, 45(1): 37–54.

Marwell, G. and Ames, R. (1979) 'Experiments on the Provision of Public Goods. I. Resources, Interest, Group Size, and the Free Rider Problem', *American Journal of Sociology*, 84(6): 1335–60.

Marwell, G. and Oliver, P. (1993) *The Critical Mass in Collective Action*, Cambridge: Cambridge University Press.

McAdam, D. (1986) 'Recruitment to High-Risk Activism: The case of Summer Freedom', *The American Journal of Sociology*, 92(1): 64–90.

McAdam, D., Tarrow, S. and Tilly, C. (2001) *Dynamics of Contention*, New York: Cambridge University Press.

McCauley, C. (2002) 'Psychological issues in understanding terrorism and the response to terrorism'. In Stout, C. (ed.) *The Psychology of Terrorism: Theoretical understandings and perspectives*, Westport, CT: Praeger.

McCauley, C. and Segal, M. (1988) 'Social Psychology of Terrorist Groups'. In Hendrick, C. *Review of Personality and Social Psychology*, Vol. 9, Beverly Hills, CA: Sage Publications.

McDonald, H. and Cusack, J. (2005) *UDA: Inside the Heart of Loyalist Terror*, Dublin: Penguin.

McGarry, F. (2010) *The Rising: Ireland, Easter 1916* Oxford: Oxford University Press.

McKay, S. (2005) 'Girls as "weapons of terror" in Northern Uganda and Sierra Leonean rebel fighting forces', *Studies in Conflict and Terrorism*, 28(5): 385–97.

Melucci, A. (1989) *Nomads of the Present*, London: Hutchinson's Radius.

Melucci, A. (1990) 'Challenging Codes: Framing and Ambivalence'. Paper presented at the workshop *Social Movements: Framing Processes and Opportunity Structure*. Held in Berlin 5–7 July.

Melzer, P. (2009) 'Death in the Shape of a Young Girl: Feminist responses to media representations of women terrorists during the "German Autumn" of 1977', *International Feminist Journal of Politics*, 11(1): 35–62.

Menkhaus, R. (2003) 'State collapse in Somalia: Second thoughts', *Review of African Political Economy*, 30: 97.

Menkhaus, R. (2004) 'Vicious circles and the security development nexus in Somalia', *Conflict, Security and Development*, 4(2).

Mennell, S. (1994) 'The Formation of We-images: A Process Theory'. In Calhoun, C. (ed.) *Social Theory and the Politics of Identity*, Oxford: Blackwell.

Mennell, S. (2007) *The American Civilizing Process*, Cambridge: Polity Press.

Merari, A. (2005) 'Social, organisational and psychological factors in suicide bombing'. In Bjørgo, T. (ed.) (2005), *Root Causes of Terrorism: Myths, reality and ways forward*, Abingdon, UK: Routledge.

Merkl, P. (1986) 'Conclusion: Collective purposes and individual motives'. In Merkl, P. (ed.) *Political Violence and Terror: Motifs and Motivations*, Berkeley: University of California Press.

Michel, L. and Herbeck, D. (2001) *American Terrorist: Timothy McVeigh and the Oklahoma City Bombing*, New York: Regan Books.

Miller, D. (1978) *Queen's Rebels. Ulster Loyalism in Historical Perspective*, Dublin: Gill and Macmillan.

Mills, C. Wright (1940) 'Situated actions and vocabularies of motive', *American Sociological Review*, 5: 404–13.

Milton-Edwards, B. (2006) *Islam and Violence in the Modern Era*, Basingstoke: Palgrave Macmillan.

Misztal, B. (2010) 'Collective Memory in a Global Age', *Current Sociology* 58(1): 24–44.

Møller, B. (2009) *The Somali Conflict: The role of external actors*, Copenhagen: Danish Institute for International Studies, www.diis.dk

Moghaddam, F. (2004) 'Cultural Preconditions for Potential Terrorist Groups: Terrorism and societal change'. In Moghaddam, F. and Marsella, A. (eds) *Understanding Terrorism: Psychosocial roots, consequences and interventions*, Washington, DC: American Psychological Association.

Moore, B., Jr. (1966) *Social Origins of Dictatorship and Democracy*, Harmondsworth: Penguin.

Moore, B., Jr. (1978) *Injustice: the social bases of obedience and revolt*, White Plains, NY: M.E. Sharpe.

Morgan, R. (2001) *The Demon Lover: The Roots of Terrorism*, London: Piatkus Publishers.

Morrow, D. (1995) 'Church and Religion in the Ulster Crisis'. In Dunn, S. (ed.), *Facets of the Conflict in Northern Ireland*, Basingstoke: MacMillan Press.

Moss, D. (1997) 'Politics, Violence, Writing: The Rituals of "Armed Struggle" in Italy'. In Apter, D. (ed.) *The Legitimization of Violence*, London: United Nations Research Institute for Social Development.

Mulaj, K. (2010) 'Introduction: Violent Non-State Actors: Exploring their State Relations, Legitimation, and Operationality'. In Mulaj, K. (ed.) *Violent Non-State Actors in World Politics*, London: Hurst & Company.

Nacos, B. (2005) 'The Portrayal of Female Terrorists in the Media: Similar framing patterns in the news coverage of women in politics and terrorism', *Studies in Conflict and Terrorism*, 28(5): 435–51.

Neidhardt, F. (1992) 'Left-wing and Right-wing Terrorist Groups: A Comparison for the German Case', *International Social Movement Research*, 4: 215–35.

Nelson, S. (1982) 'From Soldiers to Politicians – And Back: Political Violence and the Protestant Para-Militaries of Northern Ireland'. In *Collected Seminar Papers No. 30*, London: University of London, Institute of Commonwealth Studies.

Ness, C. (2005) 'In the Name of the Cause: Women's work in secular and religious terrorism', *Studies in Conflict and Terrorism*, 28(5): 353–73.

Neuberger, L. and Valentini, T. (1996) *Women and Terrorism*, Basingtoke: Macmillan Press Ltd.

Neumann, P. (2005) 'The Bullet and the Ballot Box: The Case of the IRA', *The Journal of Strategic Studies*, 28(6): 941–75.

Neumann, P. (2009) *Old and New Terrorism*, Cambridge: Polity Press.

Newman, G. and Lynch, M. (1987) 'From Feuding to Terrorism: The Ideology of Vengeance', *Contemporary Crises*, 11: 223–42.

Niblock, T. (2006) *Saudi Arabia: Power, legitimacy and survival*, Abingdon: Routledge.

Nisbett, R. and Cohen, D. (1996) *Culture of Honor: The psychology of violence in the South*, Boulder, CO: Westview.

Novaro, C. (1991) 'Social Networks and Terrorism: The Case of Prima Linea'. In Catanzaro, R. (ed.) *The Red Brigades and Left-wing Terrorism in Italy*, London: Pinter Publishers.

Oberschall, A. (1993) *Social Movement: Ideologies, interests and identities*, New Brunswick, NJ: Transaction.

Oliver, A-M. and Steinberg, P. (2005) *The Road to Martyrs Square*, Oxford: Oxford University Press.

Oliver, P. (1984) 'If you don't do it, Nobody Else Will: Active and Token Contributors to Collective Action', *American Sociological Review*, 49: 601–10.

Oliverio, A-M. (1998) *The State of Terror*, Albany: State University of New York Press.

Oliverio, A-M. and Lauderdale, P. (eds) (2005) *Terrorism: a New Testament*, Whitby, Ontario: de Sitter Publications.

Olson, M. (1963) *The Logics of Collective Action*, Cambridge, MA: Harvard University Press.

Omi, M. and Winant, H. (1994) *Racial Formation in the United States*, New York: Routledge.

Opps, K-D. (1989) *The Rationality of Political Protest,* Boulder, CO: Westview.

Pape, R. (2005) *Dying to Win*, New York: Random House.

Patkin, T. (2004) 'Explosive Baggage: Female Palestinian Suicide Bombers and the Rhetoric of Emotion', *Women and Language*, 27(2): 79–89.

Paz, R. (2002) 'Qa'idat al-Jihad', *International Institute for Counter-terrorism, http://www.ict.org.il/articles/articledet.cfm?articleid=436*

Pearlstein, R. (1991) *The Mind of the Political Terrorist*, Wilmington, DE: Scholarly Resources.

Pedahzur, A. (ed.) (2006) *Root Causes of Suicide Terrorism: The Globalization of Martyrdom*, London: Routledge.

Piazaa, J. (2006) 'Rooted in Poverty? Terrorism, Poor Economic Development and Social Cleavages', *Terrorism and Political Violence*, 18: 159–77.

Pisano, V. (1979) 'A Survey of Terrorism of the Left in Italy: 1970–78'. In Alexander, Y. (ed.) *Terrorism: An international journal (special issue)*, New York: Crane Russak.

Pisano, V. (1987) *The Dynamics of Subversion and Violence in Contemporary Italy*, Stanford, CA: Hoover Institution Press.

Piven, J. (2002) 'On the psychosis (religion) of terrorists'. In Stout, C. (ed.) *The Psychology of Terrorism: Theoretical understandings and perspectives*, Westport, CT: Praeger.

Poole, D. and Rénique, G. (2003) 'Terror and the Privatized State: A Peruvian Parable'. In Van Gosse (ed.) *Radical History Review: Terror and History*, Durham, NC: Duke University Press.

Porch, D. and Rasmussen, M. (2008) 'Demobilization of Paramilitaries in Colombia: Transformation or Transition?' *Studies in Conflict and Terrorism*, 31(6): 520–40.

Post, J. (2005) 'The New Face of Terrorism: Socio-Cultural Foundations of Contemporary Terrorism', *Behavioural Sciences and the Law*, 23: 451–65.

Post, J. Ruby, K. and Shaw, E. (2002) 'The Radical Group in Context: 1. An integrated framework for the analysis of group risk for terrorism', *Studies in Conflict and Terrorism*, 25(1): 73–100.

Post, J., Sprinzak, E. and Denny, L. (2003) 'The Terrorists in their Own Words: Interviews with 35 Incarcerated Middle Eastern Terrorists', *Terrorism and Political Violence*, 15(1).

Potok, M. (2010) 'Rage on the Right', *Southern Poverty Law Center, Intelligence Report*, Spring, No. 127.

Pratap, A. (2001) *Island of Blood*, London: Penguin.

Price, L. (2005) *Feminist Frameworks: Building Theory on Violence Against Women*, Black Point, NS: Fernwood Publishing.

Putnam,R. (2000) *Bowling Alone: The Collapse and Renewal of American Community*, New York: Simon and Schuster.

Ranstorp, M. (2003) 'Terrorism in the Name of Religion'. In Howard, R. and Sawyer, R. (eds) *Terrorism and Counterterrorism: Understanding the new security environment*, Guildford, CT: McGraw-Hill.

Rapoport, D. (1989) 'Introduction'. In Rapoport, D. and Alexander, Y. (eds) *The Morality of Terrorism: Religious and Secular Justifications*, New York: Columbia University Press.

Rapoport, D. (2003) 'The Four Waves of Rebel Terror and September 11'. In Kegley, C.W. (ed.) *The New Global Terrorism: Characteristics, Causes & Controls*, Englewood Cliffs, NJ: Prentice Hall.

Rashid, A. (2002) *Jihad: The Rise of Militant Islam in Central Asia*, New Haven, CT: Yale University Press.

Rashwan, D. (2009) 'The Renunciation of Violence by Egyptian Jihadi Organizations'. In Bjørgo, T. and Horgan, J. (eds) *Leaving Terrorism Behind: Individual and collective disengagement*, Abingdon, UK: Routledge.

Raufer, X. (2005) 'Foreword: Terrorism, scientific methods and the fog of media warfare'. In Horgan, J. *The Psychology of Terrorism*, London: Routledge.

Reader, I. (2000) *Religious Violence in Contemporary Japan: The Case of Aum Shinrikyō*, Curzon Press: Richmond, Surrey.

Reich, W. (ed) (1998) *Origins of Terrorism: Psychologies, Ideologues, Theologies, States of Mind*, Washington, DC: Woodrow Wilson Center Press.

Reinares, F. (2004) 'Who Are the Terrorists? Analysing changes in the sociological profile among members of ETA', *Studies of Conflict and Terrorism*, 27(6): 465–88.

Reuter, C. (2004) *My Life is a Weapon*, Princeton: Princeton University Press.

Richani, N. (2010) 'Fragmentation of Sovereignty and Violent Non-State Actors in Colombia'. In Mulaj, K. (ed.) *Violent Non-State Actors in World Politics*, London: Hurst & Company.

Richardson, J., van der Lans, J. and Derks, F. (1986) 'Leaving and Labelling: Voluntary and Coerced Disaffiliation from Religious Social Movements', *Research in Social Movements*, 9: 97–126.

Ristock, J. (2002) *No More Secrets: Violence in Lesbian Relationships*, London: Routledge.

Robbins, T. (1988) *Cults, Converts and Charisma: The Sociology of New Religious Movements*, London: Sage.

Robertson, R. (1978) *Meaning and Change*, Oxford: Basil Blackwell.

Rosenberger, J. (2003) 'Discerning the Behaviour of the Suicide Bomber', *Journal of Religion and Health* 42(1): 13–20.

Ross, J. (1999) 'Beyond the Conceptualisation of Terrorism: A psychological-structural model of the causes of this activity'. In Summers, C. and Markusen, E. (eds)

*Collective Violence: Harmful behaviour in groups and governments*, Lanham, Maryland: Rowman & Littlefield Publishers.

Roth, S. (2003) *Building Movement Bridges: The coalition of labor union movement*, Westport, CT: Praeger.

Roy, O. (2004) *Globalised Islam: The Search for a New Ummah*, London: Hurst & Co.

Rudolph, E. (2005) 'Allocution', (Birmingham Court) 18 July 2005 http://www.armyofgod.com/EricRudolphAllocutionRelease.html

Sageman, M. (2004) *Understanding Terror Networks*, Philadelphia: University of Pennsylvania Press.

Sageman, M. (2008) *Understanding Terror Networks*, Philadelphia: University of Pennsylvania Press.

Salib, E. (2003) 'Suicide Terrorism: a case of *folie à plusieurs?*' *British Journal of Psychiatry* 182: 475–76.

Sánchez-Cuenca, I. (2010) 'The Persistence of Nationalist Terrorism: The Case of ETA'. In Mulaj, K. (ed.) *Violent Non-State Actors in World Politics*, London: Hurst & Company.

Savigear, P. (1982) 'Clan Violence and Political Violence in Nineteenth and Twentieth Century Corsica'. In *Collected Seminar Papers No 30*, London: University of London, Institute of Commonwealth Studies.

Schmid, A. (1984) *Political Terrorism: A Research Guide*, New Brunswick, NJ: Transaction Books.

Schweitzer, Y. (ed.) (2006) *Female Suicide Bombers*, Tel Aviv: Jaffee Center for Strategic Studies.

Sedgwick, M. (2007) 'Inspiration and the Origins of Global Waves of Terrorism', *Studies in Conflict and Terrorism*, 30(2): 97–112.

Silj, A. (1979) *Never Again Without a Rifle: The Origins of Italian Terrorism*, New York: Karz Publishers.

Silke, A. (2003) (ed.) *Terrorists, Victims and Society: Psychological Perspectives on Terrorism and its Consequences*, Chichester, UK: John Wiley and Sons Ltd.

Silke, A. (2006) 'The Role of Suicide in Politics, Conflict and Terrorism', *Terrorism and Political Violence*, 18(1): 35–46.

Silke, A. (2008) 'Holy Warriors: Exploring the Psychological Processes of Jihadi Radicalization', *European Journal of Criminology*, 5(1): 99–123.

Simmel, G. (1906) 'The Sociology of Secrecy and of Secret Societies', *The American Journal of Sociology*, XI(4): 441–98.

Simmel, G. (1950) *The Sociology of Georg Simmel*, Translated and edited by Kurt Wolff, Glencoe, IL: Free Press.

Simmel, G. (1965a) 'Submission'. In Spykman, N. *The Social Theory of Georg Simmel*, New York: Atherton Press.

Simmel, G. (1965b) 'The Individual and the Group'. In Spykman, N. *The Social Theory of Georg Simmel*, New York: Atherton Press.

Simmel, G. (1999) *Soziologie. Untersuchungen über die Formen der Vergesellschaftung*, Vol. II, edited by O.Rammstedt, Frankfurt: Suhrkamp.

Sinclair, A. (2003) *An Anatomy of Terror: A History of Terrorism*, London: Macmillan.

Singular, S. (2001) *The Uncivil War: The Rise of Hate, Violence, and Terrorism in America*, Beverly Hills, CA: New Millennium Press.

Sjoberg, L. and Gentry, C. (2007) *Mothers, Monsters, Whores: Women's violence in global politics*, London: Zed Books.

Sjoberg, L. and Gentry, C. (2008) 'Reduced to Bad Sex: Narratives of violent women from the bible to the War on Terror', *International Relations*, 22(1): 5–23.

Skaine, R. (2006) *Female Suicide Bombers*, Jefferson, NC: McFarland & Company.

Skeggs, B. (1997) *Formations of Class and Gender*, London: Sage.

Skeggs, B. (2004) *Class, Self, Culture*, London: Routledge.

Skocpol, T. (1979) *States and Social Revolutions: A Comparative Analysis of France, Russia and China*, Cambridge: Cambridge University Press.

Skocpol, T. (1984) *Vision and Method in Historical Sociology*, Cambridge: Cambridge University Press.

Slotkin, R. (1973) *Regeneration Through Violence: The Mythology of the American Frontier, 1600–1860*, New York: Atheneum.

Smelser, N. (2007) *The Faces of Terrorism: Social and Psychological Dimensions*, Princeton, NJ: Princeton University Press.

Snow, D., Zurcher, L. and Ekland-Olson, S. (1980) 'Social Networks and Social Movements: A microstructural approach differential recruitment', *American Sociological Review*, 45: 787–801.

Sonder, B. (2000) *The Militia Movement*, Franklin Watts: New York.

Speckhard, A. (2008) 'The Emergence of Female Suicide Terrorists', *Studies in Conflict and Terrorism*, 31(6): 1023–51.

Speckhard, A. and Akhmedova, K. (2006) 'The Making of a Martyr: Chechen suicide terrorism', *Journal of Studies in Conflict and Terrorism*, 29(5): 429–92.

Speitel, V. (1980) 'Wir Wollten Alles und Gleichzeitig Nights', *Der Spiegel*, No. 31.

Spierenburg, P. (2006) 'Democracy Came Too Early: A tentative explanation for the problem of American homicide', *American Historical Review*, 111(1): 104–14.

Stark, R. and Bainbridge, W. (1980) 'Networks of Faith: Interpersonal Bonds and Recruitment to Cults and Sects', *American Journal of Sociology*, 85(6).

Steinberg, G. (2006) 'Saudi Arabia'. In Faath, S. (ed.), *Anti-Americanism in the Islamic World*, London: C. Hurst & Co.

Stemmann, J. (2006) 'Middle East Salafism's Influence and the Radicalization of Muslim Communities in Europe', *MERIA*, 10(3).

Stenersen, A. (2008) 'The Internet: A virtual training camp?' *Terrorism and Political Violence*, 20(2): 215–33.

Stern, J. (2003) *Terror in the Name of God*, New York: Ecco.

Stout, M. (2009) 'In Search of Salafi Jihadi Strategic Thought: Mining the words of the terrorists', *Studies in Conflict and Terrorism*, 32(10): 876–92.

Sutton, P. and Vertigans, S. (2005) *Resurgent Islam: A Sociological Approach*, Cambridge: Polity Press.

Tamimi, A. (2007) *Hamas: Unwritten Chapters*, London: Hurst & Co.

Tapia, A. (2000) *Structural Response to Y2K*, Unpublished Ph.D. Dissertation, Graduate School of the University of New Mexico.

Tarrow, S. (1989) *Democracy and Disorder: Protest and Politics in Italy 1965 – 1975*, Oxford: Clarendon Press.

Tarrow, S. (1996) 'States and Opportunities: The political structuring of social movements'. In McAdam, D. *et al.* (eds) *Perspectives on Social Movements: Political opportunities, mobilizing structures and cultural framings*, Cambridge: Cambridge University Press.

Taylor, C. (2000) '"And Don't Forget to Clean the Fridge': Women in the secret sphere of terrorism". In DeGroot, G. and Bird-Peniston, C. (eds) *A Soldier and a Woman: Sexual integration in the military*, Harlow: Pearson Education.

Taylor, M. and Horgan, J. (2006) 'Conceptual Framework for Addressing Psychological Process in The Development of The Terrorist', *Terrorism and Political Violence*, 18(3): 585–601.

Taylor, M. and Quayle, E. (1994) *Terrorist Lives*, London: Brassey's Defence Publishers.

Taylor, P. (1998) *Provos: the IRA and Sinn Fein*, London: Bloomsbury Publishing.

Taylor, P. (2000) *Loyalists*, London: Bloomsbury Publishing.

Thomas, W.I. (1928) *The Child in America*, New York: Alfred A. Knopf.

Tilly, C. (1978) *From Mobilization to Revolution*, Reading, MA: Addison Wesley.

Toolis, K. (1995) *Rebel Hearts*, London: Picador.

Townshend, C. (2002) *Terrorism: A very short introduction*, New York: Oxford Press.

Trautmann, F. (1980) *The Voice of Terror: A Biography of Johann Most*, Westport, CT: Greenwood Press.

Trujillo, H., Jordán, J., Gutiérrez, J. and González-Cabrera, J. (2009) 'Radicalisation in Prisons? Field research in 25 Spanish prisons', *Terrorism and Political Violence*, 21(4): 558–79.

Turner, B.S. (1993) *Max Weber: From History to Modernity*, London: Routledge.

Van Dyke, N. and Soule, S. (2002) 'Structural Social Change and the Mobilizing Effect of Threat: Explaining Levels of Patriot and Militia Organizing in the United States', *Social Problems*, 49(4): 497–520.

Van Krieken, R. (1998) *Norbert Elias*, London: Routledge.

Varon, J. (2004) *Bringing the War Home*, Berkeley and Los Angeles: University of California Press.

Vertigans, S. (2008) *Terrorism and Societies*, Aldershot: Ashgate.

Vertigans, S. (2009) *Militant Islam: A Sociology of Characteristics, Causes and Characteristics*, Abingdon: Routledge.

Vertigans, S. (2010a) 'Somalia's insecurity and the normalisation of violence'. In Hoffman, E. (ed.) *Somalia: Economic, Political and Social Issues*, New York: Nova Publishers.

Vertigans, S. (2010b) 'British Muslims and the UK Government's "war on terror" within: Evidence of a clash of civilizations or emergent de-civilizing processes', *The British Journal of Sociology*, 61(1): 26–44.

Victor, B. (2004) *Army of Roses*, London: Constable & Robinson.

Victoroff, J. (2005) 'The Mind of the Terrorist: A review and critique of psychological approaches', *Journal of Conflict Resolution*, 49(1): 3–42.

Vinci, P. (1979) 'Some Considerations on Contemporayr Terrorism'. In Alexander, Y. (ed.) *Terrorism: An international journal (special issue)*, New York: Crane Russak.

Vinitzky-Seroussi, V. (2002) 'Commemorating a Difficult Past: Yitzhak Rabin's Memorials', *American Sociological Review*, 67(1): 30–51.

Volkan, V. (2001) 'September 11 and Societal Regression', *Mind and Human Interaction*, 12(3): 196–216.

Von Hippel, K. (2002) 'The Roots of Terrorism: Probing the Myths'. In *The Political Quarterly Publishing Co. Ltd.*

Von Knop, K. (2007) 'The Female Jihad: Al Qaeda's Women', *Studies in Conflict and Terrorism*, 30: 397–414.

Wacquant, L. (2004) 'Decivilizing and Demonizing: The remaking of the black American ghetto'. In Loyal, S. and Quilley, S. (eds) *The Sociology of Norbert Elias*. Cambridge: Cambridge University Press.

Waldmann, P. (2007) 'Is there a Culture of Violence in Colombia', *Terrorism and Political Violence*, 19(4): 593–609.

Wallerstein, I. (1974) *The Modern World-System: Capitalist Agriculture and the Origins of the European World-Economy in the Sixteenth Century*, New York: Academic Press.

Wallerstein, I. (1980) *The Modern World – System II: Mercantilism and the Consolidation of the European World-Economy, 1600–1750*, New York: Academic Press.

Wallerstein, I. (1989) *The Modern World – System III: The Second Era of Great Expansion of the Capitalist World-Economy, 1730–1840s*, San Diego, CA: Academic Press.

Wallis, R. (1977) *The Road to Total Freedom: A Sociological Analysis of Scientology*, New York: Columbia.

Wallis, R. (1984) *The Elementary Forms of New Religious Life*, London: Routledge and Kegan Paul.

Weaver, B. (1997) 'Violence as Memory and Desire: Neo-Nazism in contemporary Germany'. In Apter, D. (ed.) *The Legitimization of Violence*, Basingstoke: Macmillan Press.

Webb, J. and Cutter, S. (2009) 'The Geography of U.S. Terrorist Incidents, 1970–2004', *Terrorism and Political Violence*, 21(3): 428–49.

Weber, M. (1949) '"Objectivity" in Social Science and Social Policy'. In Shils, E. and Finch, H. (eds) *The Methodology of the Social Sciences*, New York: Free Press.

Weber, M (1966[1922]) *The Sociology of Religion*, London: Methuen & Co Ltd.

Weber, M. (1978) *Economy and Society, Vols I & II*. Edited by Roth, G. and C. Wittich, Berkeley and Los Angeles: University of California Press.

Weimann, G. (2006) 'Virtual Training Camps: Terrorists' use of the Internet'. In Forest, J. (ed.) *Teaching Terror: Strategic and Tactical Learning in the Terrorist World*, Lanham, MD: Rowman and Littlefield.

Weinberg, L. (1979) 'Patterns of Neo-Fascist Violence in Italian Politics'. In Alexander, Y. (ed.) *Terrorism: An international journal (special issue)*, New York: Crane Russak.

Weinberg, L. (1986) 'The Violent Life: An Analysis of Left- and Right-Wing Terrorism in Italy'. In Merkl, P. (ed.) *Political Violence and Terror: Motifs and Motivations*, Berkeley: University of California Press.

Weinberg, L. and Eubank, W.L. (1987) *The Rise and Fall of Italian Terrorism*, Boulder and London: Westview Press.

Whaley-Eager, P. (2008) *From Freedom Fighters to Terrorists: Women and Political Violence*, Aldershot: Ashgate.

Wieviorka, M. (1997) 'ETA and Basque Political Violence'. In Apter, D. (ed.) *The Legitimization of Violence*, London: United Nations Research Institute for Social Development.

Wilkinson, P. (1974) *Political Terrorism*, London: Macmillan.

Wilkinson, P. (1981) *The New Fascists*, London: Wiley-Blackwell.

Wilkinson, P. (2003) 'Why Modern Terrorism? Differentiating Types and Distinguishing Ideological Motivations'. In Kegley, C.W. (ed.) *The New Global Terrorism: Characteristics, Causes & Controls*, Englewood Cliffs, NJ: Prentice Hall.

Woodcock, G. (2004) *Anarchism: A history of libertarian ideas and movements*, Toronto: Broadview Press, Ltd.

Wouters, C. (1977) 'Informalization and the Civilizing Process'. In Gleichmann, P.R., Goudsbloam. J. and Korte, H. (eds) *Human Figurations: Essays for Norbert Elias*, Amsterdam: Amsterdams Sociologisch Tijdschrift.

Wouters, C. (1986) 'Formalization and Informalization: Changing Tension and Balances in Civilizing Processes', *Theory, Culture and Society*, 3(1): 1–19.

Wouters, C. (2004) *Sex and Manners. Female Emancipation in the West since 1890*, London: Sage.

Wouters, C. (2007) *Informalization: Manners and emotions since 1980*, London: Sage.

Wright, S. (1991) 'Reconceptualizing Cult Coercion and Withdrawal: A comparative analysis of divorce and apostasy', *Social Forces*, 70(1): 125–45.

Wyatt-Brown, B. (1982) *Honour: Ethics and Behaviour in the Old South*, Oxford: Oxford University Press.

Zahab, M. (2008) 'I Shall be Waiting for You at the Door of Paradise': The Pakistani martyrs of the Lashkar-E Taiba (Army of the Pure). In Rao, A., Böck, M. and Bollig, M. (eds) *The Practice of War: The Production, Reproduction and Communication of Armed Violence*, Oxford/New York: Berghahn.

Zárate, V. (2003) 'Terrorism and Political Violence during the Pinochet Years: Chile, 1973–89'. In Van Gosse (ed.) *Radical History Review: Terror and History*, Durham, NC: Duke University Press.

Zaroulis, N. and Sullivan, G. (1984) *Who Spoke Up? American protest against the war in Vietnam*, Garden City, NY: Doublesday.

Zimring, F. (2003) *The Contradictions of American Capital Punishment*, Oxford: Oxford University Press.

Zubaida, S. (2000) 'Trajectories of Political Islam: Egypt, Iran and Turkey'. In D. Marquand and R. Nettler (eds) *Religion and Democracy*, Oxford: Blackwell Publishers.

# Index

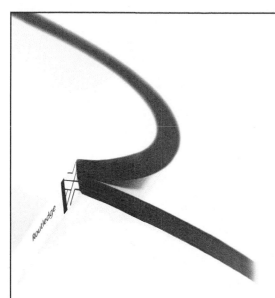